AMERICA'S STORY

THE COMPLETE EDITION

By VIVIAN BERNSTEIN

Reviewers

John Alexander
Social Studies Consultant
Jefferson Parish Schools
Harvey, LA

Dr. John L. Esposito
Georgetown University
Washington, D.C.

Eric R. Godoy
Teacher of Second Language Learners
West Chicago Elementary School District
West Chicago, IL

Harcourt Achieve

Rigby • Saxon • Steck-Vaughn

www.HarcourtAchieve.com
1.800.531.5015

About the Author

Vivian Bernstein is the author of *America's History: Land of Liberty, World History and You, World Geography and You, American Government,* and *Decisions for Health.* She received her Master of Arts degree from New York University. Bernstein is active with professional organizations in social studies, education, and reading. She gives presentations to school faculties and professional groups about social studies instruction and improving content area reading. Bernstein was a teacher in the New York City Public School System for a number of years.

Staff Credits

Executive Editor: Tina Posner
Supervising Editor: Donna Townsend
Editor: Linda Doehne

Design Staff: Stephanie Arsenault, Donna Cunningham, Joan Cunnignham, Deborah Diver, John-Paxton Gremillion, Scott Huber, Heather Jernt, Alan Klemp, Joyce Spicer

Acknowledgments

Text Credits: p. 259 Dear Mrs. Parks: A Dialogue with Today's Youth. Text copyright © 1996 by Rosa L. Parks. Permission arranged with Lee & Low Books, Inc., New York, NY 10016. p. 230 Reproduced with permission of Curtis Brown Ltd, London on behalf of The Estate of Sir Winston S. Churchill. Copyright Winston S. Churchill. p. 236 Reprinted by permission of Louisiana State University Press from Voices of D-Day: The Story of the Allied Invasion Told by Those Who Were There edited by Ronald J. Drez. Copyright © 1994 by Louisiana State University Press.

Cartography: MapQuest.com, Inc., Ortelius Design, Inc.
Information for page 219 map provided courtesy Jesse Davidson Aviation Archives.

Photo Credits: Photo Credits: Cover: (bkgd) Donnovan Reese/Getty Images; (a) ©The Granger Collection, New York; (c) ©Corbis; (d) ©Dennis Macdonald/PhotoEdit; (e) ©Corbis

Additional Photography by Comstock Royalty Free and Getty Images Royalty Free.
i ©Donovan Reese/Getty Images; x (a) ©Associated Press, AP; (b) ©Stone/Getty Images; xi (a) ©Jeff Greenbert/Index Stock Imagery; (b) ©SuperStock/PictureQuest; (c) ©Brand X Pictures/PicturQuest; 4–6, 9 ©The Granger Collection; 10 (a, b) ©The Granger Collection (c) ©North Wind Picture Archives;14 ©The Granger Collection; 15 (a) ©Bettmann/CORBIS; (b) ©North Wind Picture Archives; 16 ©North Wind Picture Archives; 17 ©Eric Neurath/Stock Boston; 20–22 ©The Granger Collection; 23 ©North Wind Picture Archives; 24 ©Photodisc/Getty Royalty Free/HA Collection; 25–26 ©The Granger Collection; 27 (a, b) ©The Granger Collection; (c) ©Bettmann/Corbis; 28 ©Courtesy of APVA Preservation Virginia; 31 ©The Granger Collection; 32 (a) ©Bettmann/Corbis; (b, c) ©The Granger Collection; 33 ©The Granger Collection; 34 ©North Wind Picture Archives; 38–41 (a) ©The Granger Collection; (b) ©North Wind Picture Archives; 42 ©The Granger Collection; 43 ©Bettmann/Corbis; 46 ©Bettmann/Corbis; 47 (a) ©The Granger Collection; (b) ©Reagan Bradshaw/HA Collection; (c) ©The Granger Collection; 48 (a) ©The Valentine Richmond History Center; (b, c) ©The Granger Collection; 49 (a) ©The Granger Collection; (b) ©Bettmann/Corbis; 50 ©Faustinus Dareat/HA Collection; 53 ©Bettmann/Corbis; 54 ©The Granger Collection; 55 (a, b) ©The Granger Collection; 58 ©Archivo Iconografico, S.A./Corbis; 59 (a) ©The Granger Collection; (b) Walter Bibikow/Taxi/Getty Images; 60–61 (a) ©The Granger Collection; (b) ©North Wind Picture Archives; 62 Stone/Getty images; 65 ©The Granger Collection; 66 (a) ©Reagan Bradshaw /HA Collection; (b) Pan America/Picturequest; 67 (a) ©Reagan Bradshaw/HA Collection; (b) ©Photos.com; (c) ©Pan America/Picturequest; 68 (a) AFP/Getty Images; (b) ©Bob Daemmrich; 72–74 ©The Granger Collection; 75 (a) ©Bettmann/Corbis; (b) ©North Wind Picture Archives; (c) ©The Granger Collection; 76 ©courtesy Missouri Historical Society, St. Louis; 77, 80–81 (a, b) ©The Granger Collection; (c) ©Stock Montage; 82 (b) ©North Wind Picture Archives; (c) ©The Granger Collection; 83, 87 ©The Granger Collection; 88 (a) ©Hulton Archive/Getty Images; (b) ©North Wind Picture Archives; (c) ©Kevin Fleming /Corbis; 89 ©The Granger Collection; 90, 93–94 ©The Granger Collection; 95 ©The New York Public Library/Art Resource, NY; 96 ©North Wind Picture Archives; 97, 101 ©The Granger Collection; 102 (a) ©Brown Brothers; (b) ©Mount Holyoke College Art Museum, South Hadley, MA; (c) ©The Granger Collection; 103 (a) ©Corbis; (b) ©Bettmann/Corbis; 104 (a) ©Bettmann/Corbis; (b) ©The Granger Collection; 108–109 ©courtesy The Bucks County Historical Society, Doylestown, PA; 110 ©North Wind Picture Archives; 111(a) ©North Wind Picture Archives; (b, c) ©Courtesy University of Texas; 112 (a) ©courtesy The Institute for Texan Cultures; (b) ©courtesy The Barker Texas History Center, University of Texas, Austin; (c) ©courtesy The Institute for Texan Cultures; (d) ©The Granger Collection; 113 (a) ©courtesy of the State Preservation Board, Austin, Texas. CHA 1989.46, Photographer Unknown, pre 1991, pre conservation; (b) ©courtesy The Institute for Texan Cultures; (c) ©Quinn Stewart; 116 Texas State Library and Archive Commission; 117 (a) ©The Bettmann Archive/Corbis; (b) ©The Granger Collection; 119, 122 ©North Wind Picture Archives; 124–125 ©The Granger Collection;126 ©Brown Brothers; 130–132 ©The Granger Collection; 133 (a) ©The Bettmann Archive/Corbis; (b) ©The Granger Collection; (c) ©Corbis; 134, 138 ©The Granger Collection; 139 (a) ©Quinn Stewart; (b) ©The Granger Collection; *continued on p.390*

continued on p.390

Contents

To the Reader   ix

The Five Themes of Geography   x

UNIT 1   THE SETTLERS OF AMERICA   2

Chapter 1   The First Americans   4

Think and Apply: Fact or Opinion   7

Skill Builder: Understanding Continents   8

Chapter 2   Christopher Columbus   9

Using Graphic Organizers: Main Idea and Supporting Details . .   12

Skill Builder: Using Map Directions   13

Chapter 3   The Spanish Explore America   14

Using Geography Themes – Place: Santa Fe, New Mexico   17

Think and Apply: Categories   18

Skill Builder: Using a Map Key   19

Chapter 4   The Pilgrims' Thanksgiving   20

Think and Apply: Cause and Effect   23

Skill Builder: Reading a Flow Chart   24

Chapter 5   The English Settle America   25

Using Primary Sources: Objects from Jamestown   28

Using Graphic Organizers: Sequencing Events   29

Skill Builder: Reading a Historical Map   30

Chapter 6   The French Come to America   31

Think and Apply: Fact or Opinion   35

Skill Builder: Using Map Directions   36

Unit One Review   37

UNIT 2   BUILDING A NEW COUNTRY   38

Chapter 7   Americans Fight for Freedom   40

Think and Apply: Understanding Different Points of View   44

Skill Builder: Reading a Time Line   45

Chapter 8   A New Country Is Born   46

Using Primary Sources: Diary of a Valley Forge Surgeon   50

Think and Apply: Drawing Conclusions   52

Chapter 9 Benjamin Franklin 53
Using Graphic Organizers: Cause and Effect 56
Skill Builder: Reading a Bar Graph 57

Chapter 10 George Washington 58
Using Geography Themes — Location: Washington, D.C. 62
Think and Apply: Sequencing Events 64

Chapter 11 The Constitution 65
Using Graphic Organizers: Main Idea and
    Supporting Details 69
Skill Builder: Reading a Diagram 70

Unit Two Review 71

UNIT 3 THE UNITED STATES GROWS **72**

Chapter 12 The United States Doubles in Size 74
Skill Builder: Reviewing Map Directions 78
Think and Apply: Categories 79

Chapter 13 The War of 1812 80
Using Primary Sources: Chief Tecumseh's Speech, 1810 84
Think and Apply: Drawing Conclusions 86

Chapter 14 The Industrial Revolution 87
Using Graphic Organizers: Cause and Effect 91
Skill Builder: Reading a Line Graph 92

Chapter 15 Andrew Jackson 93
Using Geography Themes — Movement: The Trail of Tears 97
Think and Apply: Fact or Opinion 100

Chapter 16 Americans Work for Reform 101
Think and Apply: Finding the Main Idea 105
Skill Builder: Reading a Chart 106

Unit Three Review 107

UNIT 4 THE NATION GROWS AND DIVIDES **108**

Chapter 17 Independence for Texas 110
Using Primary Sources: Letters from William Barrett Travis 114
Think and Apply: Understanding Different Points of View 115

Chapter 18 The United States Grows Larger 116
Skill Builder: Reviewing Map Directions 120
Using Graphic Organizers: Cause and Effect 121

Chapter 19 On to Oregon and California 122
   Using Geography Themes – Human/Environment
      Interaction: The Gold Rush. 126
   Think and Apply: Categories. 128
   Skill Builder: Reading a Historical Map. 129

Chapter 20 The Southern States Leave 130
   Using Geography Themes – Region: The South in 1861 134
   Think and Apply: Fact or Opinion 136
   Skill Builder: Reading a Bar Graph 137

Chapter 21 The Civil War 138
   Think and Apply: Sequencing Events; Drawing Conclusions 143
   Skill Builder: Reading a Table 144

Unit Four Review 145

UNIT 5 AFTER THE CIVIL WAR **146**

Chapter 22 Reconstruction 148
   Using Primary Sources: Up from Slavery. 151
   Using Graphic Organizers: Main Idea and Supporting Details . . 152

Chapter 23 Americans Move West 153
   Using Geography Themes – Region: The Great Plains 157
   Think and Apply: Cause and Effect 159
   Skill Builder: Reading a Flow Chart 160

Chapter 24 The United States Gets More Land 161
   Think and Apply: Fact or Opinion; Sequencing Events 165
   Skill Builder: Using Map Directions 166

Chapter 25 New Inventions Change the United States 167
   Using Graphic Organizers: Sequencing Events. 171
   Skill Builder: Reading a Chart. 172

Unit Five Review 173

UNIT 6 THE UNITED STATES BECOMES A MODERN NATION **174**

Chapter 26 Starting a New Life in America 176
   Using Geography Themes – Place: New York City, New York. . . 180
   Using Graphic Organizers: Concept Web. 181
   Skill Builder: Reading a Bar Graph 182

Chapter 27 Big Business Grows Bigger 183
  Using Graphic Organizers: Cause and Effect 186
  Skill Builder: Using a Map Key to Read a Resource Map 187

Chapter 28 Unions Help the Working People 188
  Think and Apply: Drawing Conclusions 192
  Skill Builder: Reading a Line Graph 193

Chapter 29 Women Work for a Better America 194
  Using Primary Sources: Twenty Years at Hull House 197
  Think and Apply: Fact or Opinion 198

Chapter 30 Working for Reform After 1900 199
  Think and Apply: Categories 203
  Skill Builder: Reading a Circle Graph 204

Unit Six Review 205

UNIT 7 PROBLEMS AT HOME AND ACROSS THE SEA **206**

Chapter 31 World War I 208
  Using Graphic Organizers: Main Idea and Supporting Details . . 212
  Skill Builder: Reading a Historical Map 213

Chapter 32 The 1920s Bring Change 214
  Using Geography Themes — Movement: Airmail Across
    the United States 218
  Think and Apply: Fact or Opinion 220
  Skill Builder: Reading a Time Line 221

Chapter 33 The Great Depression 222
  Using Graphic Organizers: Cause and Effect 226
  Skill Builder: Using a Map Key 227

Chapter 34 World War II Begins 228
  Using Primary Sources: A World War II Political Cartoon 232
  Think and Apply: Understanding Different Points of View 233
  Skill Builder: Reading a Chart 234

Chapter 35 The End of World War II 235
  Think and Apply: Drawing Conclusions 239
  Skill Builder: Reading a Historical Map 240

Unit Seven Review 241

UNIT 8 OUR CHANGING NATION **242**

Chapter 36 The Cold War 244
Think and Apply: Understanding Different Points of View 248
Skill Builder: Reading a Historical Map 249

Chapter 37 America During the 1950s 250
Think and Apply: Fact or Opinion 253
Skill Builder: Comparing Circle Graphs 254

Chapter 38 Martin Luther King, Jr. 255
Using Primary Sources: Dear Mrs. Parks 259
Using Graphic Organizers: Main Idea and Supporting Details . . 260

Chapter 39 Americans Travel in Space 261
Using Geography Themes – Location: John F. Kennedy
    Space Center 264
Think and Apply: Categories 266
Skill Builder: Reading a Line Graph 267

Chapter 40 César Chávez and the Farm Workers 268
Think and Apply: Sequencing Events 271
Skill Builder: Using a Map Key to Read a Product Map 272

Chapter 41 War in Vietnam 273
Think and Apply: Cause and Effect 277
Skill Builder: Reading a Bar Graph 278

Unit Eight Review 279

UNIT 9 CHALLENGES IN TODAY'S WORLD **280**

Chapter 42 The United States and Its Neighbors 282
Using Geography Themes – Human/Environment
    Interaction: Acid Rain 286
Using Graphic Organizers: Main Idea and Supporting Details . . 288
Skill Builder: Reading a Double Line Graph 289

Chapter 43 The United States As a World Leader 290
Think and Apply: Cause and Effect 294
Skill Builder: Reading a Double Bar Graph 295

Chapter 44 A Changing Nation 296
Think and Apply: Categories 300
Skill Builder: Writing an Outline 301

Chapter 45 America Since the Year 2000 302
   Think and Apply: Sequencing Events 307
   Skill Builder: Reading a Newspaper. 308

Chapter 46 Working for a Better Tomorrow 309
   Using Primary Sources: The Debate for President on
      October 12, 2004 313
   Think and Apply: Categories. 314

Unit Nine Review 315

Map of the United States 316

Map of the United States: Landforms. 317

Map of the World: Countries. 318

Map of the World: Landforms. 320

Declaration of Independence. 322

United States Constitution 327

The Fifty States. 355

Territories and Possessions of the United States. 363

Presidents of the United States. 364

Glossary. 367

Index. 382

To the Reader

America's Story tells the story of our country, the United States of America. This book tells how our country changed from a small nation to a very large one.

Our country's story began with the Native Americans. Later, people from Europe began to settle in America. Great Britain ruled 13 American colonies. Time passed, and people in the 13 colonies fought and won a war against the British. After the war the colonies became a free country called the United States of America. American leaders wrote laws that protected the freedom of the people.

The United States had only 13 states. Slowly the nation grew larger. More and more states became part of the United States.

As the nation grew, problems between the northern states and the southern states also grew. People in the North and South did not agree about slavery. Some southern states left the United States and started a new nation. This led to a long, hard war. After the war, the United States became one nation again.

The nation changed as millions of people from other nations came to live in America. American cities grew larger. Many Americans settled in the West. Americans fought in two world wars. Since these wars, the United States has been a world leader.

While you read *America's Story*, follow these steps to become a better student. Start by learning the New Words for each chapter. Study the maps and pictures in each chapter. Then read the chapter carefully. Finally, think carefully as you write your answers for the "Using What You've Learned" pages.

As you read *America's Story*, learn how Americans have worked to make our country a land of freedom for more than 225 years.

The Five Themes of Geography

Geography is the study of Earth and the people, plants, and animals that live on it. Geographers divide geography into five **themes**, or main ideas. When you know the five themes, you can begin to think like a geographer.

Movement

How do people, ideas, and goods move? People travel on the Acela train at speeds of up to 150 miles an hour.

Place

What makes a place special? The city of San Francisco is built on steep hills.

Location

Where is a place located? Pittsburgh, Pennsylvania, is found where the Allegheny River and the Monongahela River join to form the Ohio River.

Human-Environment Interaction

How do people change the place they live? People built the Hoover Dam to control the Colorado River. Now the river stores water for cities and farms and makes electric power.

Region

How is one area different from another? The Midwest is a part of the United States where fields of corn and wheat stretch for miles.

Christopher Columbus reaches America.
1492

1400   1500

The Settlers of America

What do you think it was like to go across an ocean hundreds of years ago? You would not see land for many days. No one would come to help you if you lost your way. You might get sick. Rats might eat the food on your ship. Yet hundreds of years ago, brave people took this dangerous trip to come to America.

About 500 years ago, people from Europe started coming to America. People came for different reasons. Some came to explore. Others came to find gold. Still others came because they wanted more freedom. Many people from Europe settled in America. The Pilgrims were one group. But the people from Europe were not the first to live here. Native Americans had been living in America for thousands of years. American Indians helped the Pilgrims and some other groups of settlers live in America.

Read to Learn

- How did Native Americans live their lives?
- Who were the people from Europe who explored and settled in America?
- Why did different groups of people make the dangerous trip to America?

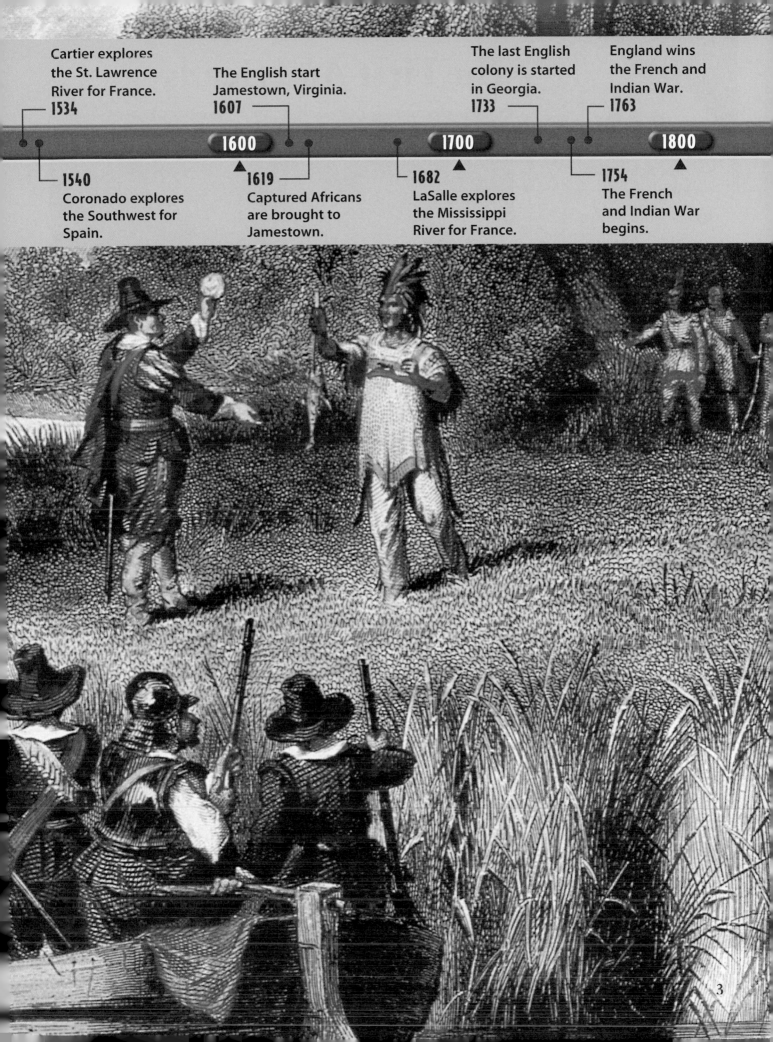

Cartier explores the St. Lawrence River for France.
1534

The English start Jamestown, Virginia.
1607

The last English colony is started in Georgia.
1733

England wins the French and Indian War.
1763

1600

1700

1800

1540
Coronado explores the Southwest for Spain.

1619
Captured Africans are brought to Jamestown.

1682
LaSalle explores the Mississippi River for France.

1754
The French and Indian War begins.

3

CHAPTER 1

Find Out

❶ How did Native Americans live long ago?

❷ Why did Native Americans live differently in different parts of the United States?

❸ What have other people learned from Native Americans?

NEW WORDS

religions
cotton
buffalo

PEOPLE & PLACES

American Indians
America
Asia
Alaska
Native Americans
United States
  of America
Americans
Northwest
Southwest
Midwest
Great Plains
East

The First Americans

➤ **Learning from Pictures How did Native Americans of the Northwest get food?**

Native Americans were the first people to live in America. Long ago they lived in Asia. It is believed that land once connected Asia and America. People moved across this land to a part of America called Alaska. Over time they settled in many parts of America. Native Americans are sometimes called American Indians.

Thousands of years later, people from other lands began coming to America. About 230 years ago, the name of our country became the United States of America. Native Americans lived in our country long before it was called the United States. Native Americans were the first Americans.

Native Americans in different parts of the United States spoke different languages. They also lived in different kinds of houses. They wore different kinds of clothes. They ate different kinds of foods. They believed in different **religions**.

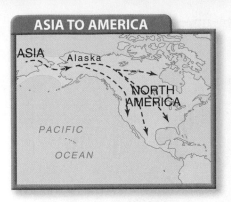

Long ago people walked across land from Asia into America.

UNITED STATES REGIONS

Areas of the United States where different groups of Native Americans lived

Native Americans who lived on the Great Plains hunted buffalo.

Many Native Americans lived in the Northwest of the United States. In the Northwest, there were thick forests. There were many fish in the ocean and rivers. Native Americans of the Northwest went fishing to get food. They ate fish every day. They traveled in long canoes made from trees in the forest. They also built houses from trees.

Other groups of Native Americans lived in the Southwest. In the Southwest, there was little rain. There were few trees. There were very few fish and animals to eat. Native Americans of the Southwest became farmers. They used river water to grow food. They grew corn and beans for food. They also grew **cotton**. They made their clothes from cotton.

In the Midwest of the United States, the land is very flat. We call this flat land the Great Plains. Millions of **buffalo** lived on the Great Plains. Many Native Americans lived on the Great Plains. They became buffalo hunters. They used every part of the buffalo that they killed. They ate buffalo meat. They made needles from buffalo bones. They made clothes and tents out of buffalo skins.

In the East of the United States, there were many forests. Animals lived in the forests. Many groups of Native Americans lived in these forests. They became hunters. They killed deer and turkeys for food. They also became farmers. They grew corn, pumpkins, and beans for their families.

▲ **Native Americans who lived on the Great Plains made tents out of buffalo skins.**

There were some ways that all Native Americans were alike. They loved plants and animals. They took good care of their land. They enjoyed games and telling stories.

All Native Americans made their own tools. They needed tools for hunting, farming, and fishing. Native Americans made their tools out of stones and animal bones. They made knives out of stones. Some groups of Native Americans made metal tools. Many Native Americans hunted with bows and arrows. They did not have guns.

When people later came to America, Native Americans taught them many things. They taught them how to plant foods such as corn, tomatoes, and potatoes. They also taught people how to use plants to make medicines.

There are many Native Americans in the United States today. They enjoy old and modern ways of life. Many now work at different kinds of jobs. They also still enjoy songs, dances, games, and stories that people enjoyed long ago. Many people like to buy beautiful Native American art. Native Americans today are proud that they were the first people to build our country. They are proud that they were the first Americans.

Using What You've Learned

Read and Remember

Choose a Word Choose a word in blue print to finish each sentence. Write the correct answers on your paper.

Americans   fishing   medicines
corn   buffalo   hunters

1. Native Americans were the first _____ .

2. Native Americans who lived in the Northwest went _____ for their food.

3. Native American farmers of the Southwest grew beans and _____ .

4. Animals that lived on the Great Plains were the _____ .

5. Native Americans who lived on the Great Plains became _____ .

6. Native Americans used special plants to make _____ .

Think and Apply

Fact or Opinion A **fact** is a true statement. An **opinion** is a statement that tells what a person thinks.

Fact   The land is very flat in the Midwest.

Opinion   The Midwest is the best place to live.

Write F on your paper for each fact below. Write O for each opinion. You should find two sentences that are opinions.

1. Native Americans spoke different languages.

2. Millions of buffalo lived on the Great Plains.

3. It was easy to live on the Great Plains.

4. Native Americans made tools from stones and bones.

5. The best tools were made from stones.

6. Today many people buy Native American art.

Skill Builder

Understanding Continents We live on the planet Earth. Earth has large bodies of land called **continents**. There are seven continents. Most continents have many countries. We live on the continent of North America. Our country, the United States, is in North America.

Here is a list of the continents in order of their size. The largest continent is first on the list.

1. Asia
2. Africa
3. North America
4. South America
5. Antarctica
6. Europe
7. Australia

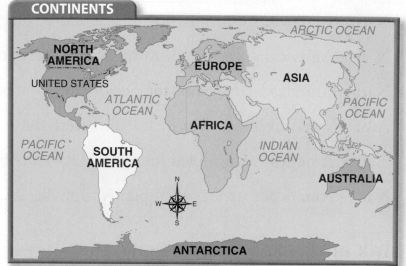

Look at the map above. On your paper, write a sentence to answer each question.

1. What are the seven continents?
2. Which continent has the United States?
3. Which is the largest continent?
4. Which ocean separates North America from Africa and Europe?
5. Which ocean is near Africa, Asia, and Australia?
6. Which continent is connected to North America by land?

Journal Writing

Think about the different groups of Native Americans. Choose two groups. Write about where they lived. Then tell how they got food. Write four to six sentences in your journal.

Christopher Columbus

Find Out

❶ Which people knew about America before Columbus took his trip?

❷ Where did Columbus want to go?

❸ Why did Queen Isabella help Columbus?

NEW WORDS

spices
claimed
New World

PEOPLE & PLACES

Christopher
   Columbus
Italy
Atlantic Ocean
Europe
India
China
Queen Isabella
Spain
Bahamas

➤ **Learning from Pictures How did these explorers feel when they reached land?**

Christopher Columbus lived long ago. Columbus was born around 1451 in Italy. He became a sailor. He also made maps.

In the 1400s, people knew less about the world than we know today. No one knew how large the Atlantic Ocean really was. Some people believed the world was flat. No one in Europe knew there was the land we now call America. Only Native Americans knew about their land.

At that time, people from Europe went to India and China to get jewels, silks, and **spices**. India and China are on the continent of Asia. People traveled thousands of miles to the east to reach India and China. Their route was long and dangerous.

Queen Isabella gave Christopher Columbus three ships.

Columbus sailed with three ships—the _Niña_, the _Pinta_, and the _Santa María_. ➤

Christopher Columbus wanted to find an easier way to travel to Asia. Columbus thought the world was round. He believed he could go to India by sailing west across the Atlantic Ocean.

Columbus needed ships and sailors to sail across the Atlantic Ocean. Columbus went to see Isabella, the queen of Spain. Queen Isabella thought about Columbus's plan for seven years. She thought that Columbus might reach India by sailing across the Atlantic Ocean. She wanted Columbus to find gold for Spain. So Queen Isabella decided to help him.

Queen Isabella gave Columbus three small ships. The names of the ships were the _Niña_, the _Pinta_, and the _Santa María_.

Columbus wanted to become rich from his trip. He wanted gold. Queen Isabella said Columbus could keep some of the gold he might find.

Columbus and the sailors sailed west across the Atlantic Ocean for more than a month. They did not see

land for many days. The sailors were afraid. They wanted to turn back for Spain. But Columbus was brave. He said to sail until October 12. Then they would turn back if they did not see land.

On October 12, 1492, the sailors saw land. On that day the three ships reached a small island.

Columbus thought he was in India. But he was not in India. He was on a small island in the Americas. The island was part of a group of islands. Today these islands are a country called the Bahamas.

People already lived on the island where Christopher Columbus landed. Columbus called these people Indians because he thought he was in India. Now they are known as Native Americans.

Columbus **claimed** America for Spain. For the people of Europe, America was a **New World**. Of course, it was not a new world to the Native Americans who lived there. Soon after Columbus's trip, more people from Europe began to come to America.

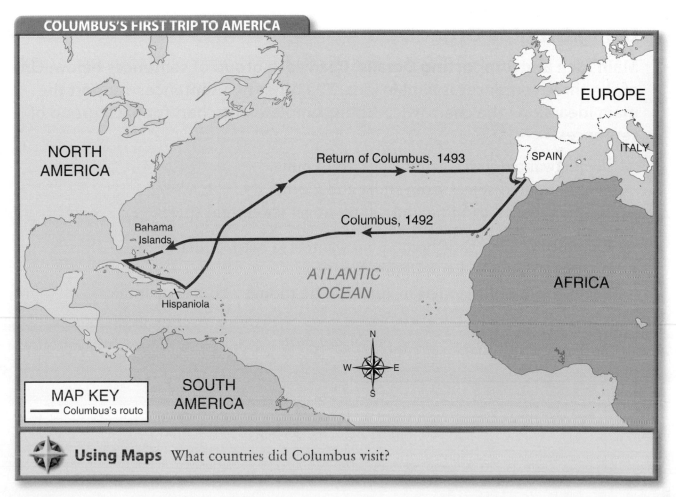

COLUMBUS'S FIRST TRIP TO AMERICA

NORTH AMERICA

EUROPE

SPAIN

ITALY

Return of Columbus, 1493

Columbus, 1492

Bahama Islands

Hispaniola

ATLANTIC OCEAN

AFRICA

SOUTH AMERICA

MAP KEY
—— Columbus's route

N
W E
S

Using Maps What countries did Columbus visit?

Using What You've Learned

Read and Remember

Choose the Answer Write the correct answers on your paper.

1 Why did people from Europe want to go to India and China?
    to travel   to get jewels, silks, and spices   to see buffalo

2 Where did Columbus want to go?
    America   India   Europe

3 What did Queen Isabella give to Columbus?
    jewels   ships   spices

4 What ocean did Columbus sail across?
    Pacific Ocean   Indian Ocean   Atlantic Ocean

5 When did Columbus reach America?
    1412   1451   1492

Using Graphic Organizers

Main Idea and Supporting Details Read each group of sentences below. One of the three sentences is a main idea. The other two sentences support the main idea. Copy the chart twice. Then complete one chart for each group of sentences.

1 People wanted jewels from India and China.
People wanted spices from India and China.
People traveled to India and China to get jewels and spices.

2 Columbus sailed west because he wanted to reach India.
No one in Europe knew about America.
When Columbus landed in America, he thought he was in India.

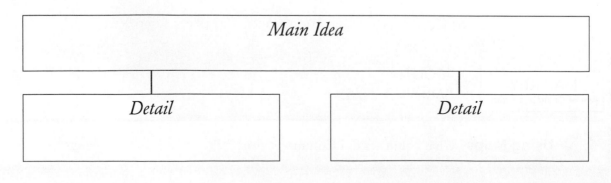

Skill Builder

Using Map Directions The four main directions are **north**, **south**, **east**, and **west**. On maps, these directions are shown by a **compass rose**. You can also use the letters, **N**, **S**, **E**, and **W** to show directions on a compass rose.

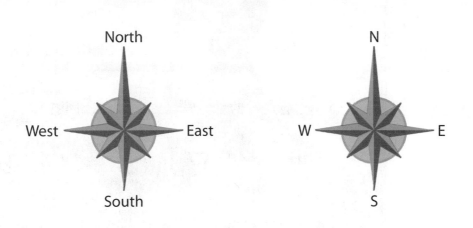

Look back at the map on page 11. Then finish each sentence with the word **north**, **south**, **east**, or **west**. Write the correct answers on your paper.

1. Europe is _____ of the Atlantic Ocean.

2. North America is _____ of the Atlantic Ocean.

3. South America is _____ of North America.

4. Europe is _____ of Africa.

5. Africa is _____ of South America and North America.

6. The Bahama Islands are _____ of Africa.

The Spanish Explore America

Find Out

❶ Why did the Spanish explore America?

❷ What did Native Americans and the Spanish learn from one another?

❸ Why did the Spanish build missions?

NEW WORDS

slavery
missions
priests

PEOPLE & PLACES

Mexico
South America
Spanish
Estevanico
African
Francisco Coronado
Hernando de Soto
Florida
Mississippi River
Southeast
Africa
Catholics
Texas
California
New Mexico
Santa Fe

➤ **Learning from Pictures How can you tell that this explorer is in a desert?**

Christopher Columbus claimed America for Spain in 1492. Soon people from Spain began to travel across the Atlantic Ocean. They settled in Mexico and South America.

The Spanish heard stories about seven cities that were made of gold. The Spanish wanted to find the cities. They began to explore the land north of Mexico. Today this area is part of the Southwest of the United States.

One of the first people to explore the Southwest for Spain was Estevanico. He was an African. In 1539 Estevanico searched the Southwest for the seven cities of gold. He never found gold. Some think he was killed by Native Americans.

Francisco Coronado

Hernando de Soto

Francisco Coronado also wanted to find the cities of gold. In 1540 he and 300 Spanish soldiers went to the Southwest. Coronado searched for two years. He found Native American farmers and villages in the Southwest. But he never found the seven cities of gold. In 1542 Coronado went home to Mexico. The king of Spain said the Southwest belonged to Spain.

Hernando de Soto also wanted to find the seven cities of gold for Spain. De Soto started in Florida with more than 700 people in 1539. While he was looking for gold, he came to a very wide river. It was the Mississippi River. He was the first person from Europe to see this river. De Soto never found the seven cities of gold. The Spanish king said that the Southeast area De Soto explored belonged to Spain, too.

Native Americans and the Spanish learned from one another. Native Americans taught the Spanish to grow beans, tomatoes, corn, pumpkins, and cotton. The Spanish brought animals from Europe. They brought

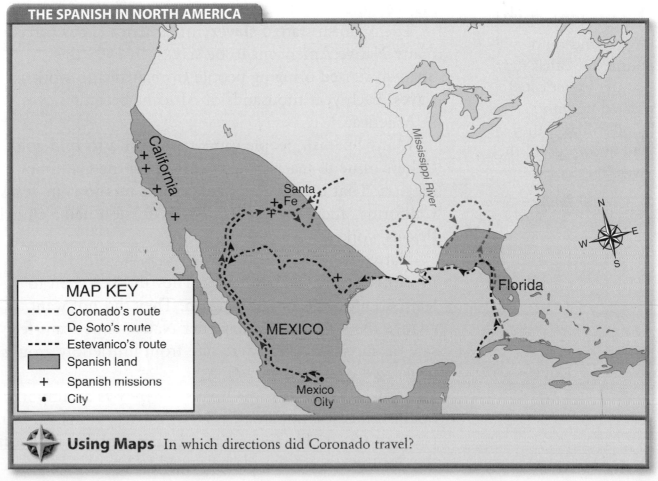

THE SPANISH IN NORTH AMERICA

MAP KEY
- - - - Coronado's route
- - - - De Soto's route
- - - - Estevanico's route
Spanish land
+ Spanish missions
• City

California
Santa Fe
Mississippi River
Florida
MEXICO
Mexico City

Using Maps In which directions did Coronado travel?

The Spanish built many missions in North America to teach Native Americans the Catholic religion. ➤

pigs, cows, sheep, and horses. The Spanish taught the Native Americans to grow oranges and wheat.

The Spanish started **slavery** in America. They forced many Native Americans to be slaves. In 1503 the Spanish started bringing people from Africa to work as slaves. Each year thousands of Africans became slaves in America.

Many Spanish people came to America to find gold. Others came to teach Native Americans the Catholic religion. That is why the Spanish built **missions** in Texas, California, and New Mexico. Every mission had a church. **Priests** worked in the missions.

Native Americans had to work very hard at the missions. Many were unhappy. They did not want to learn about the Catholic religion. They did not want to change the way they lived. Other Native Americans felt safe on missions. They were safe from unfriendly groups who lived outside the missions.

Some missions became towns. There was an important Spanish mission in Santa Fe, New Mexico. It helped bring people to Santa Fe. Today Santa Fe is a city. For 300 years the Southwest and Florida belonged to Spain.

Using Geography Themes

Place: Santa Fe, New Mexico

Geographers use five **themes**, or main ideas, to learn about different areas and people on Earth. The theme of **place** tells what makes an area different from other areas in the world. Place tells about an area's land, plants, and weather. It also tells about an area's people and what they built there.

Read the paragraphs about Santa Fe. Study the photo and the map.

Santa Fe is the **capital** of New Mexico. It is in the Southwest of the United States. The Spanish built it around 1610. Santa Fe is in high hills near the Sangre de Cristo Mountains. It is the highest and oldest capital in the nation. It has many buildings made from bricks of dried mud.

Many Pueblo Indians live in villages around Santa Fe. Pueblo Indians lived in the Santa Fe area long before the Spanish came. In 1610 the Spanish built a mission in Santa Fe for Native Americans. Today it is called the San Miguel Mission.

On your paper, write the answer to each question.

1. In what area of the United States is Santa Fe, New Mexico?
2. What mountains are near Santa Fe?
3. What are many buildings in Santa Fe made of?
4. Who live in the villages around Santa Fe?
5. Look at the map. What river goes through Santa Fe?
6. What are two buildings that people built in Santa Fe?

17

Using What You've Learned

Read and Remember

Finish the Sentence On your paper, write the word or words that finish each sentence.

1. One of the first people to explore the Southwest for Spain was _____ .
   Estevanico   Columbus   De Soto

2. Coronado explored the _____ of the United States.
   Northwest   Southwest   Southeast

3. De Soto looked for gold in _____ .
   Florida   New Mexico   California

4. De Soto was the first person from Europe to see the _____ .
   Atlantic Ocean   Northeast   Mississippi River

5. Estevanico, Coronado, and De Soto tried to find the _____ cities of gold.
   five   six   seven

6. The Spanish built _____ for the Native Americans.
   farms   stores   missions

7. The Southwest and Florida belonged to Spain for _____ years.
   50   300   thousands of

Think and Apply

Categories Read the words in each group. Decide how they are alike. Choose the best title in blue print for each group. Write the title on your paper.

Hernando de Soto   **King of Spain**
Francisco Coronado   **Explorers**

1. looked for seven cities of gold
   explored the Southwest
   found Native American villages

2. said the Southwest belonged to Spain
   said the Southeast belonged to Spain
   ruler of Spain

③ Estevanico
Francisco Coronado
Hernando de Soto

④ looked for seven cities of gold
explored Florida
saw the Mississippi River

Skill Builder

Using a Map Key Maps often show many things. Sometimes a map uses little drawings to show what something on the map means. A **map key** tells what those drawings mean. Look at the map key below. On your paper, write what each drawing means.

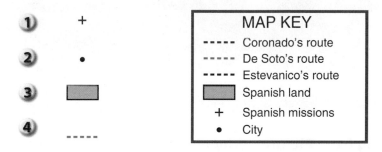

①   +

②   •

③   ▬

④   -----

```
MAP KEY
- - - - -   Coronado's route
- - - - -   De Soto's route
- - - - -   Estevanico's route
▬           Spanish land
   +        Spanish missions
   •        City
```

Use the map and map key on page 15 to finish these sentences. On your paper, write the number or word that finishes each sentence.

① There are _____ missions on this map.
  20   10   7

② There were _____ missions in California.
  4   10   15

③ The _____ River is on the map.
  Mississippi   Florida   Santa Fe

④ De Soto's route began in the _____ .
  east   north   west

⑤ Coronado's route began in the _____ .
  north   south   east

The Pilgrims' Thanksgiving

Find Out

❶ Why did the Pilgrims want to go to America?

❷ What happened to the Pilgrims during their first winter in America?

❸ How did Native Americans help the Pilgrims?

NEW WORDS

Church of England
freedom of religion
Mayflower Compact
governor
colony
peace treaty

PEOPLE & PLACES

Pilgrims
England
Holland
Dutch
English
Massachusetts
Plymouth
Wampanoag
Massasoit
Squanto

➤ **Learning from Pictures** Why did the Pilgrims bring their families with them?

A long time ago, the Pilgrims lived in England. All the people in England had to pray in the king's church. This church was called the **Church of England**. The Pilgrims did not like the Church of England. They wanted to pray in their own church.

The Pilgrims left England and went to a small country called Holland. There was **freedom of religion** in Holland. The Pilgrims prayed in their own church in Holland.

The people of Holland are called the Dutch. They speak the Dutch language. The Pilgrims did not like living in Holland. They wanted to keep their English ways. They decided to go to America. In America they could live as they wanted and have freedom of religion.

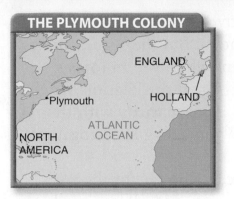

The Pilgrims traveled across the Atlantic Ocean.

The *Mayflower*

➤ **Learning from Pictures What did Squanto use to help make corn grow?** ➤

In 1620 the Pilgrims left Holland for America. They had a ship. Their ship was the *Mayflower*. The trip took 66 days. The weather was rainy and cold. Many Pilgrims became sick during the long, cold trip.

At last the *Mayflower* reached America. It landed in Massachusetts. Before leaving their ship, the Pilgrims made a plan for a government. That plan was the **Mayflower Compact**. The plan said the Pilgrims would work together to make laws. The laws would be fair to all. The Pilgrims would not have a king in America. They would choose a **governor** and rule themselves. The Mayflower Compact was the first government in America that allowed people from Europe to rule themselves.

The Pilgrims landed in November. They started a **colony** called Plymouth. Plymouth was the second English colony in America. In Chapter 5, you will read about the first English colony in America.

The first winter in Plymouth was very cold. There was little food. Many Pilgrims became sick and died.

There were no groups of Native Americans in Plymouth when the Pilgrims landed. But the Wampanoag were a group of Native Americans who lived in forests near Plymouth. They came and helped the Pilgrims. Their leader was Massasoit. He signed a **peace treaty** with the Pilgrims. The Pilgrims and the Wampanoag lived together in peace.

Squanto was a Native American who taught the Pilgrims how to plant corn. He showed the Pilgrims where to find many fish. He taught the Pilgrims to hunt for deer and turkeys in the forests.

The Pilgrims worked hard in Plymouth. They planted seeds to grow food. They built a church. They built houses. By November 1621 the Pilgrims had a lot of food.

The Pilgrims had a Thanksgiving party in November 1621. They invited their Wampanoag friends. The Wampanoag brought deer. The Pilgrims brought turkeys. This Thanksgiving lasted three days. The Pilgrims gave thanks to God for helping them. They said "thank you" to the Wampanoag for helping them. This was the Pilgrims' first Thanksgiving in America.

▲ **The Pilgrims and the Wampanoag enjoyed a Thanksgiving party in 1621.**

Using What You've Learned

Read and Remember

Choose the Answer Write the correct answers on your paper.

1. Where did the Pilgrims first live?
   Holland   England   America

2. Why did the Pilgrims come to America?
   to farm   to have freedom of religion   to meet Native Americans

3. What was the name of the Pilgrims' ship?
   Niña   Mayflower   Pinta

4. What town in America did the Pilgrims start?
   Massachusetts   Plymouth   Santa Fe

Think and Apply

Cause and Effect A **cause** is something that makes something else happen. What happens is called the **effect**.

> **Cause**   The Pilgrims wanted fair laws
>
> **Effect**   so they wrote the Mayflower Compact.

Match each cause on the left with an effect on the right. On your paper, write the letter of the effect.

Cause

1. The Pilgrims did not want to pray in the Church of England, so _____

2. The Pilgrims could not keep their English ways in Holland, so _____

3. The Pilgrims had little food for their first winter, so _____

4. The Wampanoag wanted peace, so _____

5. The Pilgrims had a lot of food for their second winter, so _____

Effect

a. many Pilgrims died.

b. Massasoit signed a peace treaty with the Pilgrims.

c. they had a Thanksgiving party to thank God and the Wampanoag.

d. they went to Holland.

e. they went to America.

23

Skill Builder

Reading a Flow Chart A **flow chart** is a chart that shows you facts in their correct order. The flow chart on this page shows how the Wampanoag grew corn in fields in the 1600s. Whole kernels are the seeds of the corn plant. A hoe is a tool for digging in soil.

Read the flow chart. On your paper, write the word or words that finish each sentence below.

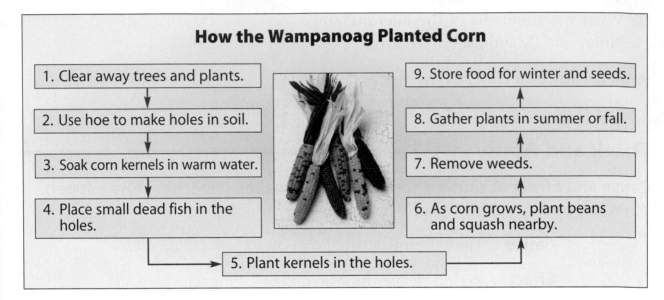

How the Wampanoag Planted Corn

1. Clear away trees and plants.
2. Use hoe to make holes in soil.
3. Soak corn kernels in warm water.
4. Place small dead fish in the holes.
5. Plant kernels in the holes.
6. As corn grows, plant beans and squash nearby.
7. Remove weeds.
8. Gather plants in summer or fall.
9. Store food for winter and seeds.

1 The first step is to _____ trees.
    shake   clear away   plant

2 The Wampanoag placed _____ with the kernels in the holes.
    fish   worms   weeds

3 In Step 6 beans and _____ are planted nearby.
    squash   tomatoes   orange trees

4 The last step is to _____ some food.
    store   grow   burn

Journal Writing

Write a paragraph in your journal that tells why the Pilgrims gave thanks. Give at least three reasons why they might have been thankful.

The English Settle America

Find Out

❶ Why was the first winter in Jamestown very hard?

❷ Which people came to America for freedom of religion?

❸ Why did Roger Williams start Providence?

NEW WORDS

settlers
tobacco
religious
in debt

PEOPLE & PLACES

Jamestown
Virginia
Puritans
Roger Williams
Providence
Rhode Island
Anne Hutchinson
Maryland
New York
Quakers
William Penn
Pennsylvania
James Oglethorpe
Georgia

Learning from Pictures What did the English do to start a colony in Jamestown?

The Pilgrims were not the first group of English people to live in America. The first group of English people came to America in 1585, but their colony failed.

Before long more English people moved to America. They came for three reasons. Many people came to get rich. Some people came for freedom of religion. Others came because they thought they could have a better life.

In 1607 the English started another colony in America. It was called Jamestown. It was in Virginia. At first the Jamestown **settlers** did not want to grow food or build houses. They did not want to plant seed to grow food. They only wanted to look for gold. The settlers were very hungry during the first winter. Many settlers died. More people came to live in Jamestown. Then the settlers began to work harder. They built farms and houses.

In 1619 the Jamestown settlers made Africans help them grow tobacco. ➤

Jamestown

Providence

The settlers began to grow **tobacco**. People smoked tobacco in pipes. The settlers sold their tobacco to England for a lot of money. In 1619 Dutch traders brought captured Africans to Jamestown. The settlers made the Africans help them grow tobacco. After some years, the Africans were freed. Later large numbers of Africans were forced to work as slaves. They were never freed.

The Puritans were a group of people who did not want to pray in the Church of England. In 1628 a group of Puritans came to Massachusetts for freedom of religion. The Puritans started the first schools in America. Everyone in Massachusetts had to pray in Puritan churches. The Puritans did not let other people have freedom of religion.

Roger Williams lived with the Puritans. He told them that everyone should have freedom of religion. He left Massachusetts and traveled through the forests. Roger Williams met Native Americans who helped him. He bought land from them. Roger Williams started the city of Providence on that land in 1636. Later, the land became the colony of Rhode Island. Providence was the first city in America where there was freedom of religion for all.

Anne Hutchinson was a woman who lived in Massachusetts. Her **religious** ideas were different from the Puritan ideas. Hutchinson also left Massachusetts. She went to Rhode Island in 1638 and started a new town.

William Penn brought settlers to Pennsylvania.

James Oglethorpe helped people move to Georgia.

Anne Hutchinson's ideas were different from the ideas of other Puritans. >

More English people came to America for freedom of religion. Catholics were sent to jail if they prayed in Catholic churches in England. So 92 Catholics came to America in 1634. They started a colony called Maryland.

People from Holland had started a colony near the Atlantic Ocean in 1624. Then in 1664 England took control of the Dutch colony. It became an English colony. It was called New York.

The Quakers were another group of people who would not pray in the Church of England. William Penn was a Quaker. In 1681 the English king gave Penn some land in America. Penn started the Pennsylvania colony on that land. Penn also bought the land from Native Americans who lived there. The Native Americans liked Penn. People had freedom of religion in Pennsylvania.

In England there were some people who did not have any money. People who were **in debt** were put into jail. These people could not work or help their families. James Oglethorpe started the Georgia colony to help these people. In 1733 Oglethorpe went to Georgia with 120 of these people. Poor people from many countries in Europe also moved to the Georgia colony.

Each year more people came to live in the English colonies. By 1753 there were 13 English colonies along the Atlantic Ocean.

Using Primary Sources

Objects from Jamestown

Primary sources are the words and objects of people who have lived at different times. Some primary sources are journals, newspapers, and tools. These words and objects help us learn about people's lives and about history.

We know what life was like in Jamestown from objects that were found there. Parts of beds, curtains, and cooking pots teach us how the settlers lived. Helmets give us clues about how the settlers protected themselves. People have found knives for cutting in Jamestown. They also have found tools for building houses.

The objects on this page were found in the earth at Jamestown. They are from the 1600s. These objects help us understand how Jamestown settlers lived almost 400 years ago.

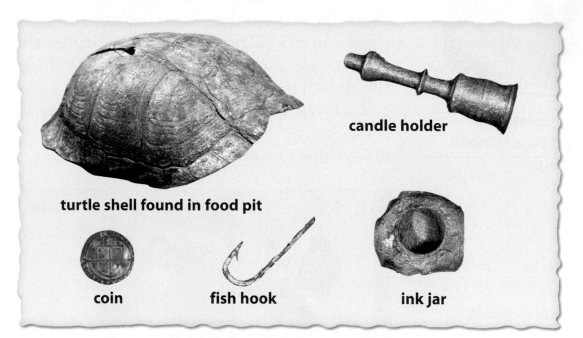

candle holder

turtle shell found in food pit

coin   fish hook   ink jar

On your paper, write the answer to each question.

1. How do we know the Jamestown settlers used money?
2. What object shows that some settlers could read and write?
3. What do you think the settlers did with candles?
4. What are two foods that the settlers probably ate?
5. **Think and Write** How do the objects from Jamestown compare with similar objects today? How have they changed?

Using What You've Learned

Read and Remember

Write the Answer On your paper, write a sentence to answer each question.

1. What were three reasons English people came to America?

2. What did captured Africans do in Jamestown?

3. Why did the Puritans come to America?

4. Which group of English people started the first schools in America?

5. Which was the first city in America to allow freedom of religion for all?

6. Who did James Oglethorpe bring to Georgia?

Using Graphic Organizers

Sequencing Events Read each of the sentences below. Copy and then complete the graphic organizer by listing the events in the correct order.

The English started Jamestown, one of the first colonies in America.

Roger Williams and Anne Hutchinson left Massachusetts to have freedom of religion.

In 1681 William Penn started the peaceful colony of Pennsylvania.

The Puritans started a colony in Massachusetts in 1628.

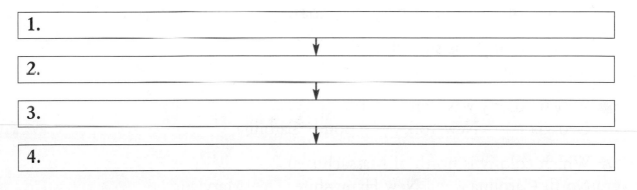

1.

2.

3.

4.

Journal Writing

Which colony would you want to live in if you had moved to America in 1755? Write a paragraph in your journal that tells which colony you would choose. Explain your reasons.

Skill Builder

Reading a Historical Map A **historical map** shows how an area used to look. The historical map on this page shows the 13 English colonies in the year 1753. The 13 colonies are numbered on the map in the order that people from Europe first settled there. Study the map.

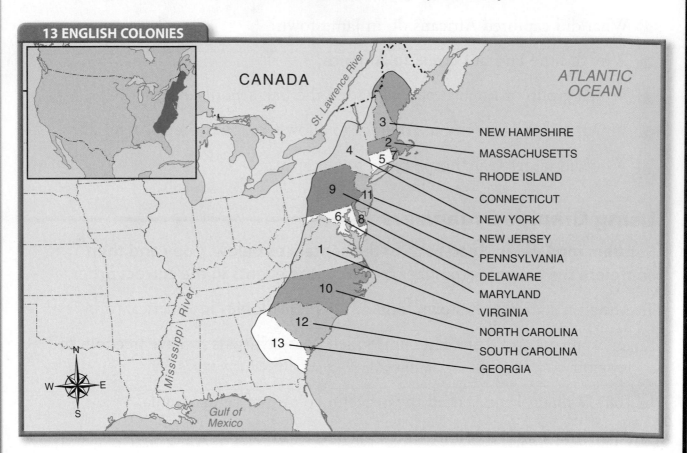

13 ENGLISH COLONIES

Write the correct answers on your paper.

1 Which colony was started first?
Rhode Island   Virginia   Delaware

2 Which colony was started last?
Georgia   New York   South Carolina

3 Which colony is north of Massachusetts?
North Carolina   New Hampshire   Maryland

4 Which colony is west of New Jersey?
Connecticut   Massachusetts   Pennsylvania

NEW WORDS

shortcut
body of water
snowshoes

PEOPLE & PLACES

France
French
King Louis
Jacques Cartier
Canada
St. Lawrence River
New France
René Robert Sieur de la Salle
Gulf of Mexico
Louisiana
St. Louis
New Orleans
George Washington
North America

The French Come to America

➤ **Learning from Pictures Who greeted these French explorers as they traveled along the St. Lawrence River?**

Many English people came to America for freedom of religion. Many poor people came to America to earn money. We learned that many Spanish people came to America to find gold. People from France also came to America. People from France are called the French.

King Francis I of France wanted to find a **shortcut** to Asia. In 1534 the king sent Jacques Cartier to America. Cartier wanted to find a river in America that he could follow west all the way to Asia. Cartier sailed to Canada. He could not find a river that went to Asia. He explored the St. Lawrence River. Look at the map on page 33. Find the St. Lawrence River. Cartier said that all the land around the St. Lawrence River belonged to France. French land in America was called New France.

La Salle called the land around the Mississippi River "Louisiana."

René Robert Sieur de la Salle

Jacques Cartier

René Robert Sieur de la Salle also explored America for France. In 1682 La Salle traveled from the St. Lawrence River to the Mississippi River. Then he paddled a canoe down the Mississippi River to the south. In the south there is a **body of water** called the Gulf of Mexico. La Salle was the first person we know of who traveled all the way down the Mississippi River to the Gulf of Mexico.

René Robert Sieur de la Salle called the land near the Mississippi River "Louisiana." He put a big cross and a French flag on the land of Louisiana. La Salle said that Louisiana belonged to King Louis of France. The land around the Mississippi River and the land around the St. Lawrence River were part of New France.

The French started two cities on the Mississippi River. These two French cities were St. Louis and New Orleans. New Orleans was near the Gulf of Mexico.

Some French people moved to America. They came for two reasons. One reason was to get furs. Native Americans hunted animals for their furs. The French traded with the Native Americans for these furs. In France they sold these furs for a lot of money. The second reason the French came to America was to teach Native Americans how to be Catholics.

French fur trapper wearing snowshoes

The French owned much more land in America than the English owned. But there were many more English settlers than French settlers. Few French people wanted to live in America. The French did not allow freedom of religion. Only Catholics could live in New France. So the French colony grew very slowly.

Native Americans helped the French in many ways. They taught the French how to trap animals for furs. They taught the French how to use canoes to travel on rivers. They also showed the French how to make **snowshoes**. Many parts of New France had lots of snow in the winter. When the French wore snowshoes, they could walk on very deep snow.

Native Americans had fewer fights with the French than with the Spanish or the English. The Spanish had forced Native Americans to work as slaves. The French never treated them as slaves. The English took land away from Native Americans in order to build farms and towns. The French did not take Native American lands.

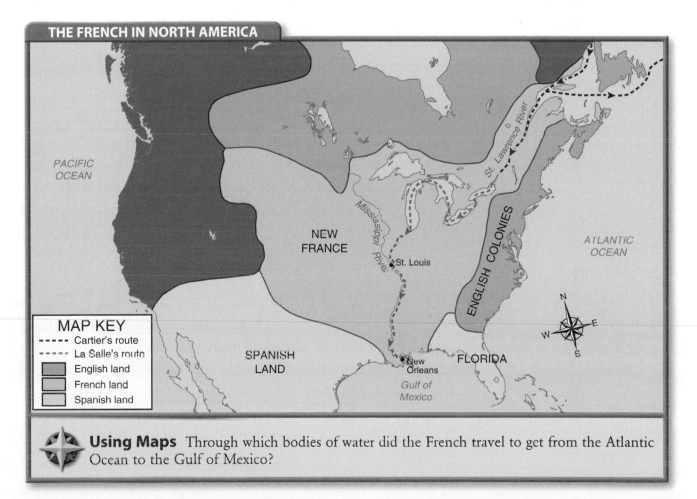

THE FRENCH IN NORTH AMERICA

PACIFIC OCEAN

St. Lawrence River

NEW FRANCE

Mississippi River

St. Louis

ENGLISH COLONIES

ATLANTIC OCEAN

SPANISH LAND

New Orleans

FLORIDA

Gulf of Mexico

MAP KEY
- - - - Cartier's route
- - - - La Salle's route
English land
French land
Spanish land

N E S W

Using Maps Through which bodies of water did the French travel to get from the Atlantic Ocean to the Gulf of Mexico?

In 1763 France lost most of its land in America when England won the French and Indian War.

England did not want France to own land in America. Many English people in the 13 colonies wanted to move west to Louisiana. France did not want English people to live in Louisiana. England and France had been enemies in Europe for many years. They became enemies in America. By 1754 England and France were fighting a war in America. This war was called the French and Indian War. Some Native Americans fought for the French, and some fought for the English. George Washington lived in the Virginia colony. He helped the English soldiers fight.

The French and the English also fought in Europe. In 1756 they began fighting in Europe. England won this war in 1763.

England also won the French and Indian War. This war ended in 1763. After the war, England owned Canada. England owned all the land that was east of the Mississippi River. Spain owned the land that was west of the Mississippi River. St. Louis and New Orleans belonged to Spain. France lost most of its land in North America. France kept two small islands in Canada and the Caribbean. In 1763 England and Spain owned most of the land in North America.

Using What You've Learned

Read and Remember

Finish the Story Use the words in blue print to finish the story. On your paper, write the words you choose.

furs　　Louisiana　　Mississippi　　canoes　　Catholic　　French

The French explorer La Salle traveled down the __(1)__ River. He paddled all the way to the Gulf of Mexico. La Salle called all the land around the Mississippi River " __(2)__ ." This land became part of the large French colony called New France. Some French people came to America to get __(3)__ . Others came to teach the __(4)__ religion to Native Americans. Some Native Americans taught the French how to use __(5)__ and snowshoes. In 1763 the __(6)__ lost the French and Indian War to the English.

Think and Apply

Fact or Opinion Write **F** on your paper for each fact below. Write **O** for each opinion. You should find four sentences that are opinions.

1. The French king wanted to find a shortcut to Asia.

2. Jacques Cartier explored the St. Lawrence River.

3. La Salle was a smarter explorer than Cartier.

4. The land around the Mississippi and St. Lawrence rivers was part of New France.

5. Before 1754 France owned more land in America than England did.

6. Only Catholics could live in New France.

7. Wearing snowshoes is the best way to walk on deep snow.

8. New France was a better place to live than in the English colonies.

9. The French were stronger soldiers than the English soldiers.

10. The French and the English fought in Europe and in America.

Skill Builder

Using Map Directions In Chapter 2 you learned that there are four main directions on a map. They are north, south, east, and west. A compass rose also shows four in-between directions. They are **northeast**, **southeast**, **northwest**, and **southwest**. Southeast is between south and east. Southwest is between south and west. Sometimes the in-between directions are shortened to **NE**, **SE**, **NW**, and **SW**.

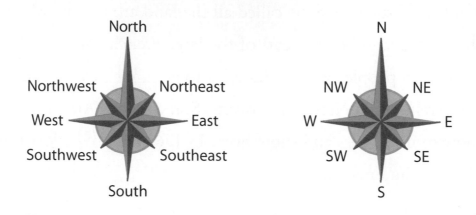

Look at the map on page 33. On your paper, write the word that finishes each sentence.

1. The St. Lawrence River is in the _____ .
   northeast   northwest   southwest

2. The English colonies were in the _____ .
   northwest   southwest   east

3. The Mississippi River was _____ of the English colonies.
   south   west   east

4. Florida is in the _____ .
   southeast   northeast   northwest

5. The Atlantic Ocean was to the _____ of the English colonies.
   north   west   east

6. New Orleans is in the _____ .
   northwest   northeast   south

Review

The historical map on this page shows the Spanish, French, and English colonies in North America in 1754. Study the map. Then use the words in blue print to finish the story. On your paper, write the words you choose.

Atlantic Ocean	Gulf of Mexico	New Orleans	Florida
Southwest	St. Lawrence	Jamestown	New France

Spain had land in the Southeast called __(1)__ . Spain also had land in the __(2)__ . Then in 1607 the English started __(3)__ in Virginia. All of the 13 English colonies were near the __(4)__ .

In 1534 Cartier explored a river in Canada called the __(5)__ River. La Salle traveled south on the Mississippi River to the __(6)__ . The French built the city of __(7)__ near the Gulf of Mexico. The French called their colony in America __(8)__ .

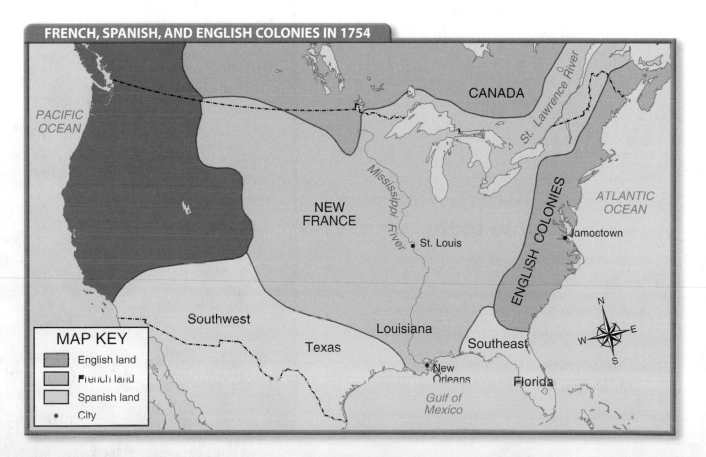

FRENCH, SPANISH, AND ENGLISH COLONIES IN 1754

MAP KEY
- English land
- French land
- Spanish land
- • City

Building a New Country

Imagine what it was like to live in America in 1776. Many Americans were angry at the British leaders who ruled over them. They were angry about unfair laws that the British leaders wrote for the colonies. Americans became so angry about these laws that they decided to fight for their freedom.

Americans in the 13 colonies were not ready to fight. They did not have enough guns, money, or soldiers. The British army was much stronger. How could the Americans win? It would take the help of many different people, including George Washington.

Americans throw tea into the Atlantic Ocean at the Boston Tea Party.
1773

1760		1770

1765
The British write the Stamp Act.

Read to Learn

- What would you have done if you had lived in 1776?
- Would you have joined the fight to make the 13 colonies a free country?
- How did Americans build a new country, the United States of America?

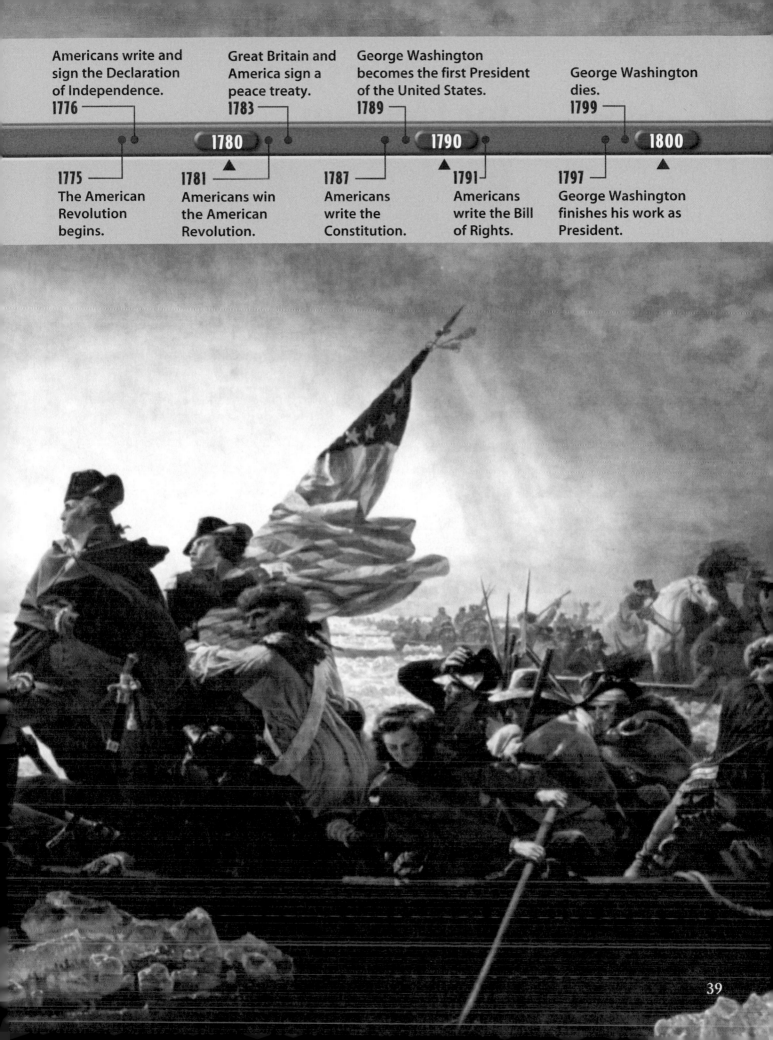

Americans write and sign the Declaration of Independence.
1776

Great Britain and America sign a peace treaty.
1783

George Washington becomes the first President of the United States.
1789

George Washington dies.
1799

1780

1790

1800

1775
The American Revolution begins.

1781
Americans win the American Revolution.

1787
Americans write the Constitution.

1791
Americans write the Bill of Rights.

1797
George Washington finishes his work as President.

Americans Fight for Freedom

Find Out

❶ Why did Americans think that the new laws from Great Britain were unfair?

❷ What happened during the Boston Tea Party?

❸ Why did Americans start to fight against the British in 1775?

NEW WORDS

nation
tax
Stamp Act
Parliament
port
Boston Tea Party
American Revolution

PEOPLE & PLACES

Great Britain
British
King George III
Boston

British leaders who made laws were called Parliament.

Many people from England came to live in America. They came to live in the 13 colonies. The people who lived in the colonies were called Americans. Many people came to America because they wanted more freedom.

In 1707 England and three small countries became part of a larger **nation**. The larger nation was called Great Britain. People who lived in Great Britain were called the British. Great Britain ruled the 13 American colonies. The king of Great Britain was the king of the American colonies. From 1760 to 1820, King George III was the king of Great Britain.

In 1763 the English, or British, won the French and Indian War. The war helped the American colonies. Americans felt safer because France no longer ruled Canada. Great Britain ruled Canada after this war. The British had spent a lot of

King George III

money to fight the French. The British wanted the colonies to help pay for the French and Indian War.

The British made new laws. The laws said that Americans had to send some of their money to Great Britain. The money that Americans had to send was called **tax** money. This tax money would help Great Britain get back the money it had spent on the war.

In 1765 the British made a new tax law for the colonies. It was called the **Stamp Act**. The Stamp Act said that Americans had to pay a tax on things made from paper, such as newspapers. A special stamp was placed on the newspapers to show that the tax was paid.

Americans did not like the Stamp Act. They said this tax law was unfair. It was unfair because Americans did not help make the tax law. Some Americans decided not to pay the new taxes. Some Americans burned stamps to show they were angry about the new law.

Americans wanted the same freedom to make laws that the British had. In Great Britain the British helped make their own laws. They did this by voting for leaders who would make laws for them. The British leaders who worked together to make laws for Great Britain were called **Parliament**. Americans wanted to send their own leaders to Great Britain. They wanted these leaders to be in Parliament and make laws. The British would not let Americans make laws in Parliament.

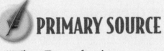

PRIMARY SOURCE

"The Revolution was in the minds and hearts of the people. This . . . change in . . . the people was the real American Revolution"

—*John Adams*

Americans burned stamps to show they did not like the Stamp Act.

Boston

Learning from Pictures
At the Boston Tea Party, Americans threw British tea into the ocean. Why do you think people took off their hats and cheered?

Parliament wrote more tax laws for the 13 colonies. The British leaders did not let Americans help write any of these laws. Americans did not like the new laws.

In 1773 the British made another law. This law said that Americans must pay a tea tax. This meant that Americans had to pay a tax when they paid for their tea. Americans had to send the tax money to Great Britain. Americans were very angry because they did not help write the tea tax law.

Boston was a large **port** city in Massachusetts near the Atlantic Ocean. Three ships with boxes of tea came to Boston. The Americans did not want to pay a tea tax. They did not want the tea. They wanted to send the tea ships back to Great Britain. The British said that Americans had to pay for the tea.

Some Americans decided to throw the boxes of tea into the ocean. One night in 1773, they dressed up as a group of Native Americans. They went on the tea ships. The Americans threw every box of tea into the Atlantic Ocean. This is known as the **Boston Tea Party**. The Boston Tea Party made King George very angry.

▲ **The first battle of the American Revolution was in Massachusetts.**

King George punished the people of Boston. He closed Boston's port. Ships could not come to or go from the port. King George said the port would be closed until Americans paid for all the tea. The king sent many British soldiers to Massachusetts.

The British had made another law that Americans did not like. This law said that Americans must give British soldiers food and a place to sleep. The soldiers paid Americans when they ate and slept in their homes. But Americans did not like the British soldiers. They did not want the soldiers in their homes. King George sent more soldiers to Massachusetts. Americans became angrier and angrier.

The angry Americans formed an army. In 1775 America began to fight Great Britain for freedom. The fighting began in Massachusetts. The British won the first battles. But the Americans would not stop fighting. They were fighting for the same freedom that people had in Great Britain. They wanted the freedom to write their own laws. A war had started in 1775 between Great Britain and America. Americans called this war the **American Revolution**.

Using What You've Learned

Read and Remember

Match Up Finish each sentence in Group A with words from Group B. On your paper, write the letter of each correct answer.

Group A

1. Great Britain wants the colonies to help pay for the _____

2. The new tax laws were not fair to Americans because _____

3. During the Boston Tea Party Americans went on three British ships and _____

4. After the Boston Tea Party, King George punished Americans by _____

5. In 1775 America began fighting a war with Great Britain that the Americans _____

Group B

a. closing the port of Boston.

b. called the American Revolution.

c. French and Indian War.

d. threw all the tea in the ocean.

e. Americans did not help write the laws in Parliament.

Think and Apply

Using Different Points of View People can look in different ways at something that happens. Look at these two points of view.

Americans should give British soldiers food.

British soldiers should get their own food.

In 1775 the Americans and the British had different points of view about how to rule the 13 colonies. Read each sentence. On your paper, write **American** for each sentence that shows the American point of view. Write **British** for each sentence that shows the British point of view.

1. Only people in Great Britain should write laws in Parliament.

2. Americans should help write their own laws in Parliament.

3. Americans should not pay a tea tax if they did not help write the tax law.

4. Americans should pay for all the tea they threw in the ocean.

5. Americans have enough freedom.

6. Americans should fight the British for more freedom.

Skill Builder

Reading a Time Line A **time line** is a drawing that shows years on a line. Look at this time line. Read the time line from left to right.

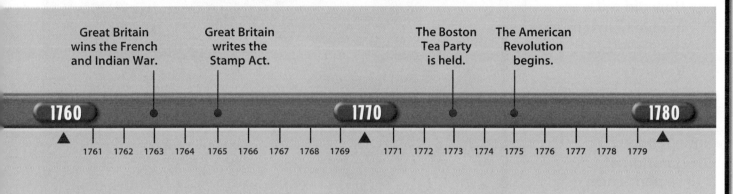

The year 1765 comes before 1766, and 1767 comes after 1766. On your paper, write the answer to each question.

1. What year comes before 1775?

2. What year comes after 1775?

Events are sometimes placed on time lines. Read the events on the time line. On your paper, write the answer to each question.

3. When did Great Britain win the French and Indian War?

4. When did Great Britain write the Stamp Act?

5. When was the Boston Tea Party?

Journal Writing

What would you do if you were an American living in the 13 colonies in 1775? Would you help the Americans or the British? Write a paragraph in your journal that tells what you would do and why.

A New Country Is Born

Find Out

❶ Why did Americans write the Declaration of Independence?

❷ Why was George Washington a great army leader?

❸ How did different people help win the American Revolution?

NEW WORDS

independent
Declaration of Independence
equal
Loyalists
general

PEOPLE & PLACES

Thomas Jefferson
Philadelphia
Friedrich von Steuben
Germany
Thaddeus Kosciusko
Poland
Bernardo de Gálvez
African Americans
James Armistead
Deborah Sampson
Molly Pitcher
Haym Salomon
Jewish American

In 1776 Thomas Jefferson and other leaders wrote the Declaration of Independence.

The American Revolution began in the year 1775. At first Americans were fighting the British because they wanted more freedom. American leaders wrote to King George. They asked him to let Americans write their own laws in Parliament. But King George would not give Americans more freedom. So in 1776 many Americans decided that they wanted the colonies to become **independent**. Independent means "free."

Americans decided to tell the world that the colonies no longer belonged to Great Britain. In 1776 Thomas Jefferson and four other leaders were asked to write the **Declaration of Independence**. The Declaration of Independence was an important paper. It said, "All men are created **equal**." This means that all people are just as

Thomas Jefferson was one of the writers of the Declaration of Independence.

Learning from Pictures General Washington was the leader of the American army. How were the soldiers trying to stay warm during the cold winter?

important as a king. The Declaration said all people should have freedom. It also said that the 13 colonies were an independent nation.

The leaders of the 13 colonies met in Philadelphia in the Pennsylvania colony. On July 4, 1776, the leaders agreed to the ideas of the Declaration of Independence.

Some Americans in the colonies did not want the colonies to be free. These people were called **Loyalists**. The Loyalists fought for Great Britain during the American Revolution.

The American Revolution lasted six years. During that time George Washington was the leader of the American army. The soldiers called him **General** Washington. George Washington was a great leader. He tried to be fair to the soldiers, and he was a good fighter. The American army lost many battles, or fights. The soldiers were often hungry and cold during the winters. But General Washington did not give up. The Americans continued to fight for independence.

Many people tried to help the Americans win the war. France and Great Britain were enemies. French soldiers came to America and fought against the British.

James Armistead

Deborah Sampson

People from other nations also helped Americans fight. Friedrich von Steuben came from Germany to help. He taught Americans how to be better soldiers. Thaddcus Kosciusko came from Poland to help Americans fight. Bernardo de Gálvez was the Spanish governor of Louisiana. He led his soldiers against the British.

All kinds of Americans fought together in the war. Farmers, sailors, business owners, and teachers all became soldiers.

About five thousand African Americans fought against the British. They fought in every important battle. James Armistead was a brave African American soldier. He was a spy for the Americans.

Women also helped win the war. They did the farm work when the men were fighting. They grew food for the soldiers. They made clothes for the army. Women also cared for soldiers who were hurt during the war. Deborah Sampson and a few other women dressed like soldiers and fought in the war.

One woman, Molly Pitcher, brought water to American soldiers when they were fighting. Molly's husband, John, was a soldier. One day John was hurt during a battle. He could not fight. Molly took John's place in the battle against the British soldiers.

Learning from Pictures How did Molly Pitcher help fight in the American Revolution?

Americans cheered for Washington and his soldiers when they won the American Revolution.

Haym Salomon

Haym Salomon was a Jewish American who helped the Americans win. He had left Poland to come to America for freedom of religion. Haym Salomon worked hard and became rich. He knew the American army had little money. The soldiers did not have enough food, clothes, or guns. Some soldiers did not even have shoes. Haym Salomon gave most of his money to the American army. The soldiers bought food, guns, shoes, and clothes with this money.

The American Revolution ended in 1781. The Americans had won. Great Britain and the colonies signed a peace treaty in 1783. People in other countries learned how the Americans won their fight for freedom. Soon people in other countries wanted more freedom, too.

After the war was over, the 13 colonies were independent. The 13 colonies became 13 states. The Americans called their new country the United States of America.

During the war, American leaders had written laws for the United States. But there were problems with those laws. In 1787 American leaders decided to write new laws for their country. In Chapter 11 you will learn how those new laws helped the nation grow.

49

Using Primary Sources

Diary of a Valley Forge Surgeon

Winters were very hard during the American Revolution. In the winter of 1777, George Washington and his army were at Valley Forge, Pennsylvania. The weather was snowy and very cold. There was very little food. Many of the soldiers did not even have shoes. Albigence Waldo was a surgeon, or a kind of doctor, at Valley Forge. He wrote about that hard winter. Here is part of his diary.

troops
soldiers

lame
hurt

recovered
got better

assured
made sure

December 12
. . . We were order'd to march over the River—It snows—I'm Sick—eat nothing. . . . Cold and uncomfortable.

December 14
*. . . The Army . . . now begins to grow sickly. . . . Yet they still show a spirit . . . not to be expected from so young **Troops**. I am Sick. . . . Poor food . . . Cold Weather. . . . There comes a bowl of beef soup—full of burnt leaves and dirt. . . . There comes a Soldier, his bare feet are seen thro' his worn out Shoes . . . his Shirt hanging in Strings. . . . I am Sick, my feet **lame**, my legs are sore. . . .*

December 18
*I have pretty well **recovered**. How much better should I feel, were I **assured** my family were in health.*

On your paper, write the answer to each question.

1. What was the army ordered to do on December 12?

2. What was wrong with the soup the soldiers had on December 14?

3. Waldo wrote about a soldier on December 14. What was wrong with the soldier's clothes?

4. On what day did Waldo write that he felt better?

5. **Think and Write** Think about Waldo's diary. Why was winter at Valley Forge so hard for the soldiers?

Using What You've Learned

Read and Remember

Finish the Sentence On your paper, write the date, word, or words that finish each sentence.

1. Americans in the 13 colonies told the world they were independent in _____ .

   1765   1776   1783

2. Americans agreed to the Declaration of Independence in _____ .
   Boston   Philadelphia   Jamestown

3. _____ taught Americans how to be better soldiers.
   King George   Friedrich von Steuben   Molly Pitcher

4. _____ was a brave African American soldier.
   Haym Salomon   James Armistead   Thomas Jefferson

5. The American Revolution ended in _____ .
   1765   1776   1781

True or False On your paper, write **T** for each sentence that is true. Write **F** for each sentence that is false.

1. Thomas Jefferson helped write the Declaration of Independence.

2. Some Americans who fought for Great Britain during the American Revolution were called Loyalists.

3. France sent French soldiers to help the British fight.

4. Bernardo de Gálvez fought against the British.

5. Americans called their new country the United Colonies of America.

Journal Writing

Suppose that you worked for a newspaper in 1776. In your journal, write a short news story about the Declaration of Independence. Tell why Americans wrote the Declaration, and write some of the things it said.

Think and Apply

Drawing Conclusions Read the first two sentences below. Then read the third sentence. It has an idea that follows from the first two sentences. It is called a **conclusion.**

American farmers and business owners helped win the war.

Women and African Americans helped win the war.

CONCLUSION Many different Americans were important in the war.

Read each pair of sentences. Then look in the box for the conclusion you can make. On your paper, write the letter of the conclusion.

1. American colonists wanted more freedom.

   King George would not give Americans more freedom.

2. Americans called Loyalists fought for Great Britain during the American Revolution.

   The Loyalists liked King George.

3. George Washington was fair to the soldiers.

   George Washington lost many battles but never gave up.

4. Many women grew food and made clothes for the army.

   Women took care of soldiers who were hurt.

5. Haym Salomon was a rich man.

   He knew the American army needed a lot of money.

Conclusions

a. George Washington was a great army leader.

b. Haym Salomon gave money to the American army.

c. Some Americans did not want the colonies to become independent.

d. Americans decided the colonies should be independent.

e. American women helped in many ways during the war.

Benjamin Franklin

Find Out

❶ What kinds of work did Benjamin Franklin do in Boston and Philadelphia?

❷ How did Benjamin Franklin help the city of Philadelphia?

❸ How did Benjamin Franklin help the American colonies become independent?

NEW WORDS

printing shop
printer
published
electric sparks
Constitution

PEOPLE & PLACES

Benjamin Franklin

Learning from Pictures When Benjamin Franklin was a young man, he worked in his brother's printing shop. What do you think they printed?

Benjamin Franklin was born in Boston, Massachusetts, in 1706. He had 16 brothers and sisters. In those days, people used candles to light their homes. Franklin's father earned money by making soap and candles.

Ben Franklin was a smart boy. He loved to read books. He went to school until he was ten years old. Then Franklin made soap and candles with his father.

Franklin had an older brother who owned a **printing shop**. When Ben Franklin was 12 years old, he went to work for his brother. Ben Franklin became a **printer**. Franklin and his brother **published** a newspaper together. Ben Franklin enjoyed his work, but he did not like working with his brother. He decided to run away from Boston.

53

PENNSYLVANIA

Philadelphia

Ben Franklin went to Philadelphia, Pennsylvania. He worked in a printing shop in Philadelphia. When Franklin was 24 years old, he published his own newspaper. People read Benjamin Franklin's newspaper in all 13 American colonies.

Ben Franklin wanted Philadelphia to be a better city. Franklin started the city's first hospital. He started a fire department. He started a school in Philadelphia. Franklin started Philadelphia's first public library.

Franklin knew there was something called electricity. He wanted to learn more about electricity. One night there were rain and lightning outside. Franklin tied a key to the end of a kite string. He flew the kite outside. Lightning hit the kite. **Electric sparks** jumped off the key. Then Ben Franklin knew that lightning is a kind of electricity. People all over America and Europe read about Ben Franklin's work with electricity. He became famous.

Benjamin Franklin used a kite and a key to show that lightning is a kind of electricity. ➤

Benjamin Franklin

In 1765 Benjamin Franklin and many other Americans became angry about the Stamp Act. Franklin traveled to Great Britain. He spoke to Parliament about the Stamp Act. He told the British why the tax law was not fair. Soon after that, the Stamp Act ended.

Franklin thought the American colonies should be an independent country. He helped Thomas Jefferson write the Declaration of Independence in 1776. He was one of the men who signed the Declaration. Franklin wanted to help his country win the American Revolution. He was then seventy years old. Franklin went to France. He asked the French people to help the Americans fight. France sent soldiers and ships to the American colonies. France helped the Americans win the war.

In 1787 Ben Franklin was 81 years old. He helped write new laws for his country. The new laws were called the **Constitution**. Franklin and the other leaders spent four months writing the Constitution in Philadelphia.

Benjamin Franklin died in Philadelphia when he was 84 years old. He helped Philadelphia become a great city. He helped the United States become a free country.

Benjamin Franklin went to France to get help for the American soldiers. ▶

Using What You've Learned

Read and Remember

Find the Answers Find the sentences below that tell how Benjamin Franklin helped Philadelphia and America. On your paper, write the sentences you find. You should find four sentences.

1. Benjamin Franklin was born in Boston in 1706.

2. Franklin started a hospital and a public library in Philadelphia.

3. Franklin started a fire department in Philadelphia.

4. Franklin helped Thomas Jefferson write the Declaration of Independence.

5. Franklin was about seventy years old during the American Revolution.

6. Franklin helped write the Constitution in 1787.

Using Graphic Organizers

Cause and Effect Read each of the sentences under *Cause* below. Then read each of the sentences under *Effect*. Copy and then complete the graphic organizer to match each cause on the left with an effect on the right.

Cause

1. Franklin learned how to be a printer in Boston, so _____

2. Lightning hit Franklin's kite and sparks flew off the key, so _____

3. Franklin wanted the American colonies to become independent, so _____

Effect

a. he signed the Declaration of Independence.

b. Franklin learned that lightning is a kind of electricity.

c. he found a job as a printer in Philadelphia.

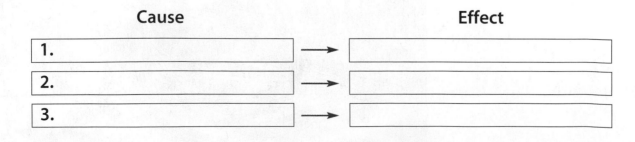

Cause		Effect
1.	→	
2.	→	
3.	→	

Skill Builder

Reading a Bar Graph **Graphs** are drawings that help you compare facts. The graph on this page is a **bar graph**. It uses bars of different lengths to show facts. The bar graph below shows the **population** of America's three largest cities in 1776. The number of people in a city is its population.

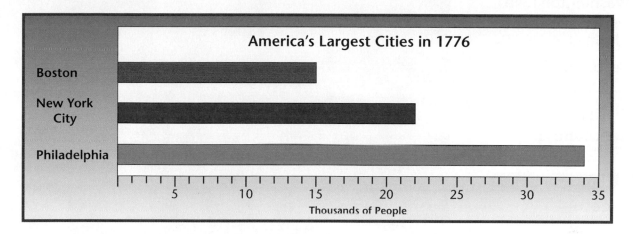

America's Largest Cities in 1776

Thousands of People

Use the bar graph to answer each question. Write the correct answers on your paper.

1 How many people lived in Boston in 1776?
    15,000   22,000   34,000

2 How many people lived in Philadelphia in 1776?
    15,000   22,000   34,000

3 What was the population of New York City in 1776?
    5,000   10,000   22,000

4 Which city had the largest population in 1776?
    Boston   New York City   Philadelphia

5 Which of these three cities had the smallest population in 1776?
    Boston   New York City   Philadelphia

Journal Writing

In your journal, write a paragraph telling why Benjamin Franklin was so important in American history.

George Washington

Find Out

❶ How did George Washington help win the American Revolution?

❷ How did George Washington help the United States after the American Revolution?

❸ How did Martha Washington help her country?

NEW WORDS

manage
commander in chief
surrendered
Constitutional
  Convention
First Lady
boundaries

PEOPLE & PLACES

Martha Washington
Mount Vernon
New York City
Trenton, New Jersey
Yorktown
Pierre L'Enfant
Benjamin Banneker
Washington, D.C.

Many Americans call George Washington the "Father of Our Country."

George Washington was born in the Virginia colony on February 22, 1732. His parents owned a large house with a lot of farmland. George Washington was a quiet, shy boy. His father died when he was 11 years old. Washington then helped his mother **manage** the family farm. He learned how to be a good farmer.

George Washington was a soldier in Virginia. He was tall and strong. In 1754 Great Britain and France began fighting the French and Indian War. Washington became a leader of the Virginia army. He was 22 years old. Washington and the Americans helped the British win the war.

Martha Washington

George and Martha Washington lived at Mount Vernon in Virginia. ➤

In 1759 George Washington married a wealthy woman named Martha. They lived in a large, beautiful house in Virginia. They called their home Mount Vernon. There were large farms at Mount Vernon. Washington loved to manage his farms.

In 1775 the American Revolution began. George Washington wanted the American colonies to become independent. He became the **commander in chief** of the American army. This means that he was the leader of all the American soldiers. The soldiers called him General Washington.

General Washington lost a battle in New York City, New York. But he did not give up. He took his army south to Pennsylvania. On Christmas 1776 Washington took his army to Trenton, New Jersey. Find Trenton on the map on page 60. Washington knew that the British army there would be having Christmas parties. They would not be ready to fight. Washington's army surprised the British army. The British army **surrendered**. General Washington won the Battle of Trenton, but the war was not over.

The British and the Americans continued to fight. The American army did not have enough food, clothes, or guns. Many soldiers became sick during the cold winters. Most soldiers liked George Washington. They stayed with him and helped him fight for American freedom.

New York City
Trenton
Yorktown

KEY
* Battle site

Important battles

In 1781 British soldiers surrendered to General Washington in Yorktown, Virginia.

Martha Washington helped the American army during the war. Martha stayed with George during the six cold winters of the American Revolution. She sewed clothes for the soldiers. She fixed their torn shirts and pants. Martha took care of soldiers who became sick or hurt.

In 1781 the Americans won an important battle at Yorktown, Virginia. There the British army surrendered to George Washington. The American Revolution was over. In 1783 Great Britain and the colonies signed a peace treaty. Then General Washington said goodbye to the army. He was ready to go home to Mount Vernon.

Soon the American people needed George Washington again. They wanted him to help write the Constitution. In 1787 American leaders met in Philadelphia to write new laws for the United States. These meetings were called the **Constitutional Convention**. Washington became president of the Constitutional Convention. He helped the leaders work together to write laws. After that he wanted to return to Mount Vernon. But Americans voted for George Washington to be the new country's first President.

Learning from Pictures In 1789 George Washington became the first President of the United States. What do you think he is doing in this picture?

Benjamin Banneker

George Washington became our President in 1789. Martha Washington became the **First Lady**. The government of the United States was in New York City. So George and Martha Washington left Mount Vernon. They traveled to New York City. Washington was America's hero. As he traveled, crowds everywhere cheered for him.

American leaders wanted the United States to have a new capital city. Washington found a beautiful place for the capital between Maryland and Virginia. He asked a Frenchman named Pierre L'Enfant to plan the new city.

Benjamin Banneker, a free African American, helped L'Enfant plan the new city. Banneker knew a lot about math and science. He used math and science to help plan the **boundaries** of the new capital. Banneker also wrote to American leaders about ending slavery in the new country. In 1800 the government moved to the new capital. The capital is now called Washington, D.C.

George Washington was President for eight years. As President, George Washington helped the United States become a stronger nation. In 1797 Washington returned to Mount Vernon. He died at his home in 1799.

George Washington was one of our greatest American leaders. He led our country in war and in peace. Many people call him the "Father of Our Country."

61

Using Geography Themes

Location: Washington, D.C.

The theme of **location** tells where a place is found. Sometimes people use directions to tell where a place is. People also can say what the place is near or what is around it.

Read the paragraphs about Washington, D.C. Study the photo below and the map on page 63.

After the American Revolution, American leaders decided the United States needed a capital city. The leaders of the United States government would work in the new capital.

In 1790 the leaders decided the capital would be in a southern area of the United States. They wanted the new city to be on the Potomac River. This river flows between Maryland and Virginia. Ships could sail from the Atlantic Ocean into Chesapeake Bay. From the bay, ships could sail on the Potomac River to the new capital. President George Washington picked the area on the Potomac River for the capital city.

Washington, D.C., is not part of any state. It is on land between Maryland and Virginia. The land belongs to the United States government. After George Washington died, the capital was named Washington, D.C. It has been the capital of the United States since 1800.

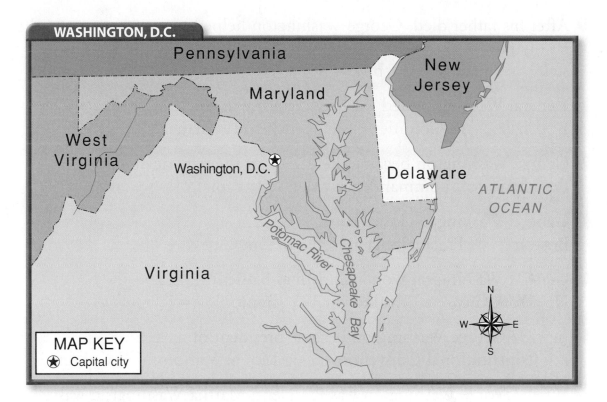

WASHINGTON, D.C.

MAP KEY
★ Capital city

On your paper, write the answer to each question.

1. Look at the map. Between what two states is Washington, D.C., the nation's capital?
2. Along what river is Washington, D.C.?
3. What state is just to the north of Washington, D.C.?
4. What bay leads to the Potomac River?
5. Do you travel north or south to get from Pennsylvania to Washington, D.C.?
6. What are three ways to describe where Washington, D.C., is located?

Using What You've Learned

Read and Remember

Finish the Sentence On your paper, write the word or words that finish each sentence.

1. After his father died, George Washington helped his mother _____ the family farm.
   sell   manage   buy

2. General Washington led the Virginia army in the _____ War.
   British   13 Colonies'   French and Indian

3. George Washington became the _____ of the American army.
   President   commander in chief   captain

4. General Washington lost a battle in _____ .
   Boston   Philadelphia   New York City

5. General Washington won a Christmas battle in _____ .
   New York City   Yorktown   Trenton

6. In 1787 George Washington became president of _____ .
   the Constitutional Convention   Mount Vernon   Georgia

7. When George Washington was President, Martha Washington was _____ .
   general   First Lady   commander in chief

8. Pierre L'Enfant and _____ planned the capital city of Washington, D.C.
   Benjamin Franklin   James Armistead   Benjamin Banneker

Think and Apply

Sequencing Events Number your paper from 1 to 5. Write the sentences to show the correct order.

George Washington became the first President of the United States.

Washington helped the British win the French and Indian War.

The British army surrendered to George Washington in Yorktown.

George Washington helped write the Constitution.

General Washington led the American army during the American Revolution.

The Constitution

Find Out

❶ Why did the United States need a good constitution after the American Revolution?

❷ How do Americans write their own laws?

❸ How does the Bill of Rights protect your freedom?

NEW WORDS

Congress
Senate
House of
    Representatives
senators
representatives
Supreme Court
justices
branches of
    government
freedom of the press
amendments
Bill of Rights

PEOPLE & PLACES

Capitol
White House

➔ **Learning from Pictures Many leaders met together to write the United States Constitution. What do you think their meetings were like?**

The American Revolution was won in 1781. The United States was an independent country with 13 states. American leaders had written laws for the country. But there were problems with these first laws. The leaders decided to write a new constitution. In 1787 leaders from 12 of the states went to Philadelphia. There they wrote the United States Constitution at the Constitutional Convention.

Before the American Revolution, Great Britain made laws for the 13 colonies. Americans liked the way the British voted for leaders to write laws in Parliament. The United States leaders planned the Constitution so that Americans could help write their own laws. How do Americans do this?

The United States Constitution in 1787

The Constitution says that Americans should choose, or vote for, people to work for them in their government. Our country's laws are made by men and women in **Congress**. In some ways our Congress is like Great Britain's Parliament. Americans vote for people who will make laws for them in Congress. There are two houses, or parts, of Congress. The **Senate** and the **House of Representatives** are the two houses of Congress.

Men and women who write laws are called **senators** and **representatives**. Every state sends two senators to work in the Senate. States with many people send many representatives to work in the House of Representatives. States with fewer people send fewer representatives to work in the House of Representatives. The senators and representatives meet in a building called the Capitol. The Constitution says that Americans should vote for people to be their senators and representatives. Americans help write their own laws by voting for their senators and representatives.

▲ **Congress writes laws in the Capitol building in Washington, D.C. The two houses of Congress are the Senate and the House of Representatives.**

Bill of Rights in 1791

The White House

The Constitution says the President should carry out the country's laws. Americans vote for a President every four years. The President also helps make our laws. The White House is where the President lives and works.

The Constitution also gives the United States its **Supreme Court**. Nine **justices**, or judges, work in the Supreme Court. The Supreme Court justices decide whether our laws agree with the Constitution.

The White House, the Capitol, and the Supreme Court buildings are in the city of Washington, D.C. Important government leaders live and work in the capital city.

Together Congress, the President, and the Supreme Court make up the three **branches of government**. The Constitution gives our country these three branches. Each branch has separate powers. Congress is the branch with the power to write laws. The President leads the branch that has the power to carry out the laws. The Supreme Court is the branch that decides whether the laws agree with the Constitution.

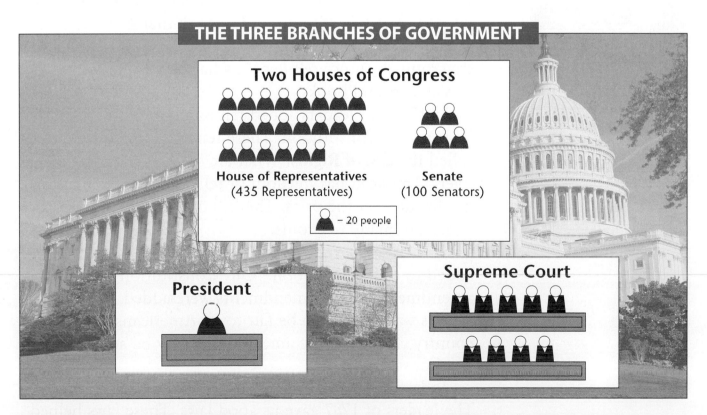

THE THREE BRANCHES OF GOVERNMENT

Two Houses of Congress

House of Representatives
(435 Representatives)

Senate
(100 Senators)

– 20 people

President

Supreme Court

Congress, the President, and the Supreme Court work together in the government.

The President sometimes meets with all the senators and representatives of Congress in the Capitol building.

An American voting

Some of our leaders were not happy with the Constitution when it was written in 1787. The Constitution did not say that Americans had freedom of religion. The Constitution did not say that Americans had **freedom of the press**. "Freedom of the press" means the government cannot tell people what they can say in newspapers and books.

In 1791 our leaders added ten **amendments**, or new laws, to the Constitution. These ten amendments are called the **Bill of Rights**. What are some of these rights? Every American has freedom of religion. Every American has freedom of the press. The Bill of Rights gives every American many freedoms.

Since 1791, seventeen more amendments have been added to the Constitution. Our Constitution now has 27 amendments. These amendments were added because our leaders wanted laws to be fair to all Americans. As our country changes, more amendments may be added to the Constitution.

Today our Constitution is more than 200 years old. The leaders of 1787 gave us good laws. These laws helped the United States become a great country.

Using What You've Learned

Read and Remember

Write the Answer On your paper, write one or more sentences to answer each question.

1. Where did American leaders write the Constitution?

2. What do senators and representatives do in Congress?

3. How many senators does each state have in the United States Senate?

4. What does the President do?

5. In what city are the White House, Capitol, and Supreme Court buildings?

6. Why did the leaders add the Bill of Rights to the Constitution?

7. What are some of the rights that the Bill of Rights added to the Constitution?

8. How many amendments does our Constitution now have?

Using Graphic Organizers

Main Idea and Supporting Details Read each group of sentences below. One of the three sentences is a main idea. The other two sentences support the main idea. Copy the chart on page 70 three times. Then complete one chart for each group of sentences.

1. Before the American Revolution, Great Britain made laws for the colonies.
   Americans made a constitution that said they could help write their own laws.
   Americans wanted to help write their own laws.

2. The Constitution says Americans can choose people to work in their government.
   Americans vote for their senators and representatives.
   Americans vote for their President every four years.

3. The President and the Supreme Court are two branches of the United States government.
   The Senate and the House of Representatives make up one branch of the United States government.
   The United States government has three branches.

69

Main Idea

Detail	Detail

Skill Builder

Reading a Diagram A **diagram** is a picture that helps you understand information. The diagram on page 67 helps you understand our government. Look back at the diagram. Use the words and numbers to finish the sentences. On your paper, write the words or numbers you choose.

President	nine	435
senators	three	100

1 The United States government has _____ branches.

2 The government has one _____ .

3 The government has _____ Supreme Court justices.

4 There are fewer _____ than representatives.

5 There are _____ members of the House of Representatives.

6 There are _____ members of the Senate.

Journal Writing

After the American Revolution, Americans wanted their new Constitution to say that people could help write their own laws. Write a paragraph in your journal that explains how early American leaders set up our government so that Americans could help write laws.

Review

The historical map on this page shows the United States in 1800. Study the map. Then use the words in blue print to finish the story. On your paper, write the words you choose.

Yorktown   **Philadelphia**   **Boston**
New York City   **Washington, D.C.**   **Trenton**

Americans were angry when the British said they had to pay a tax on tea. So Americans in ___(1)___ threw tea into the Atlantic Ocean. In 1776 Americans signed the Declaration of Independence in ___(2)___ .

During the American Revolution, George Washington won a Christmas battle at ___(3)___ . In 1781 the British army surrendered to Washington at ___(4)___ . In 1789 Washington went to ___(5)___ to become the first President. As President he planned the country's new capital. The name of the capital is ___(6)___ . American leaders live and work in the capital city.

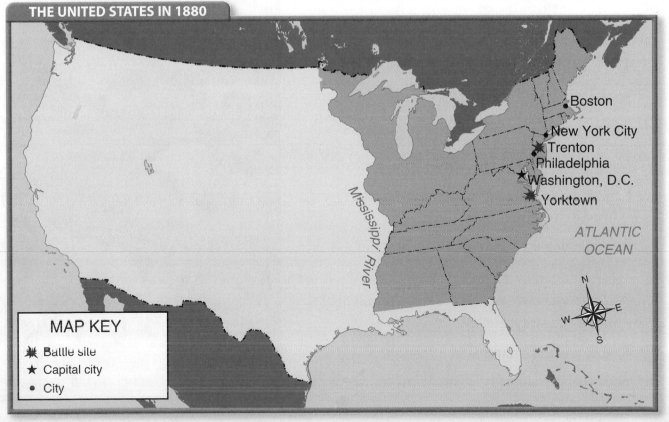

THE UNITED STATES IN 1880

Boston
New York City
Trenton
Philadelphia
Washington, D.C.
Yorktown

ATLANTIC OCEAN

Mississippi River

MAP KEY
✳ Battle site
★ Capital city
• City

The United States Grows

Suppose you were an explorer in the year 1803. The United States had bought a large piece of land west of the Mississippi River. President Thomas Jefferson had decided to send people to explore it. Your trip would be long and slow. You would cross mountains and rivers. You would meet many groups of Native Americans.

There were many changes in the United States in the early 1800s. The country became much larger. From 1812 to 1814, the United States fought a second war against Great Britain. Americans started working in factories. American cities grew larger. Many people worked to make the United States a better place to live.

Read to Learn

- What would you have done if you had lived in the early 1800s?

- Would you have explored new lands in the West?

- Would you have worked to solve problems in the growing country?

- How has the United States changed?

Thomas Jefferson becomes the third President. **1801**

Lewis and Clark explore Louisiana. **1804**

1800

1810

1803 —
The United States buys New Orleans and Louisiana.

The War of 1812 begins.
1812

Sequoyah makes the first Native American alphabet.
1821

Andrew Jackson becomes President.
1829

Elizabeth Cady Stanton holds a meeting for women's rights.
1848

1820

1830

1840

1850

1814
Great Britain and the United States sign a peace treaty to end the war.

1825
The Erie Canal is completed.

1837
Mount Holyoke Female Seminary opens.

1838
The Cherokee are forced to move west.

Find Out

❶ Why was New Orleans important to the United States?

❷ How did the United States double in size in 1803?

❸ How did Lewis and Clark help Thomas Jefferson?

NEW WORDS

crops
Louisiana Purchase
doubled

PEOPLE & PLACES

West
Napoleon Bonaparte
Meriwether Lewis
William Clark
York
Rocky Mountains
Pacific Ocean
Sacagawea

The United States Doubles in Size

> **Learning from Pictures** A Shoshone Indian woman named Sacagawea helped Lewis and Clark travel to the Pacific Ocean. Why do you think Lewis and Clark needed Sacagawea's help?

The man who wrote most of the Declaration of Independence became President of the United States in 1801. Americans voted for Thomas Jefferson to be their third President.

The American Revolution was over. The United States owned all the land east of the Mississippi River except Florida. At first, most Americans lived in the 13 states near the Atlantic Ocean. But every year more Americans moved to the West. By 1800 almost one million Americans lived on the land between the 13 states and the Mississippi River. They built homes and farms. They started new states for the United States. In 1803 the United States had 17 states.

Thomas Jefferson

Napoleon Bonaparte

The United States bought New Orleans from France as part of the Louisiana Purchase in 1803.

Sometimes Americans moved to land that was being used by Native Americans. There were fights between Indian nations and settlers about who would use the land. Many Native Americans were forced off their land.

New Orleans was an important port city near the Gulf of Mexico and the Mississippi River. Many American farmers lived near the Mississippi River. They sent their farm **crops** in boats down the Mississippi River to New Orleans. American farmers sold their farm crops in New Orleans. Ships from New Orleans carried the crops to port cities on the Atlantic Ocean.

Spain owned Louisiana and the city of New Orleans. You read about Louisiana in Chapter 6. Spain allowed American ships to use the port of New Orleans. In 1800 Spain gave New Orleans and Louisiana back to France. New Orleans was a French city again. President Jefferson was worried. Perhaps France would not allow Americans to use the port.

President Jefferson knew that American farmers needed the port of New Orleans. He wanted the United States to own New Orleans. Thomas Jefferson decided to offer to buy the city from France.

Napoleon Bonaparte was the ruler of France. France was fighting many wars in Europe. Napoleon needed

UNDER MY WINGS EVERY THING PROSPERS

Clark's journal

money for the French wars. Jefferson asked Napoleon to sell New Orleans to the United States. Napoleon said he would sell New Orleans and all of Louisiana to the United States. In 1803 the United States paid $15 million for Louisiana. Look at the map of the **Louisiana Purchase** on this page. The United States now owned New Orleans and much land to the west of the Mississippi River. The United States **doubled** in size in 1803.

President Jefferson wanted to learn about the land, plants, and animals of Louisiana. He wanted to know about the many Indian nations who lived on this land. Jefferson asked Meriwether Lewis to explore Louisiana. Lewis asked William Clark to explore the new land with him. They formed a group with about 42 men.

Lewis and Clark started their trip across Louisiana in 1804. During the trip Lewis and Clark kept journals. They wrote about the people, plants, animals, and mountains.

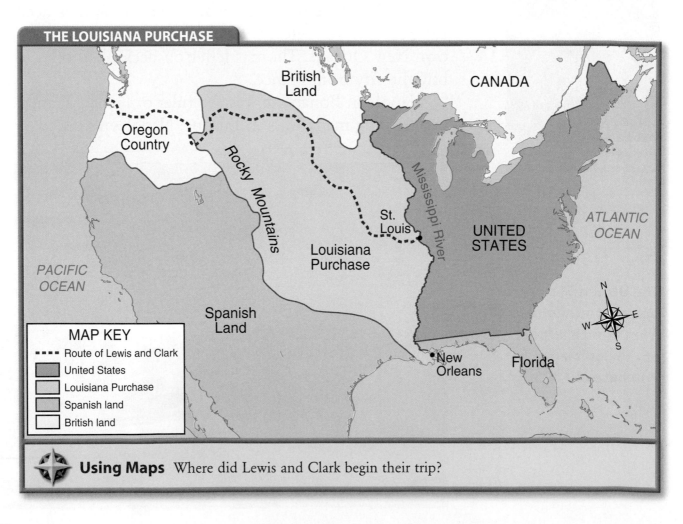

THE LOUISIANA PURCHASE

British Land

CANADA

Oregon Country

Rocky Mountains

Mississippi River

St. Louis

Louisiana Purchase

UNITED STATES

ATLANTIC OCEAN

PACIFIC OCEAN

Spanish Land

New Orleans

Florida

MAP KEY
- - - - Route of Lewis and Clark
United States
Louisiana Purchase
Spanish land
British land

Using Maps Where did Lewis and Clark begin their trip?

Sacagawea and York helped Lewis and Clark get along with Native Americans.

An African American named York traveled with Lewis and Clark. York was Clark's slave. He was a good hunter. York helped Lewis and Clark explore the west. Sometime after the trip ended, Clark gave York his freedom.

During their trip Lewis and Clark reached the tall Rocky Mountains. They wanted to cross these mountains and go to the Pacific Ocean. A Shoshone Indian woman told Lewis and Clark that she could help them cross the Rocky Mountains. Her name was Sacagawea. She was about 17 years old. Sacagawea said Lewis and Clark needed horses to cross the mountains. She helped them trade with the Shoshone for horses.

Sacagawea and her husband led the group across the Rocky Mountains. Sacagawea had a baby boy. She carried the baby on her back. She helped the men find food. The trip across the mountains was slow and dangerous. After many months, the group traveled west to the Pacific Ocean. The map on page 76 shows their route. In 1806 Lewis, Clark, and Sacagawea returned to their homes. They had explored 8,000 miles of land in the West.

Lewis and Clark told Thomas Jefferson about the land they had explored. They made new maps of the West. Thomas Jefferson helped the United States double in size. York, Sacagawea, Lewis, and Clark helped Americans learn about the land in the West.

Using What You've Learned

Read and Remember

True or False On your paper, write **T** for each sentence that is true. Write **F** for each sentence that is false.

1. After the American Revolution, the United States owned all the land east of the Mississippi River.

2. Few Americans moved west to the land between the first 13 states and the Mississippi River.

3. New Orleans was an important port for American farmers.

4. Spain gave Louisiana back to France in 1800.

5. Napoleon Bonaparte did not want to sell Louisiana to the United States.

6. The United States paid $15 million for Louisiana and New Orleans.

7. York and Sacagawea helped Lewis and Clark explore the West.

Skill Builder

Reviewing Map Directions Study the map on page 76. Choose a word in blue print to finish each sentence. Write the correct answers on your paper.

east	south	northwest
west	north	southeast

1. The Pacific Ocean is _____ of the Rocky Mountains.

2. Canada is _____ of the United States.

3. Before the Louisiana Purchase, most Americans lived _____ of the Mississippi River.

4. New Orleans was _____ of the United States.

5. Oregon Country was in the _____ .

6. Florida was _____ of Oregon Country.

Think and Apply

Categories Read the words in each group. Decide how they are alike. Find the best title in blue print for each group. Write the title on your paper.

Lewis and Clark	**Napoleon Bonaparte**	**York**
Jefferson	**Sacagawea**	**Louisiana**

1. wrote most of the Declaration of Independence
   third President of the United States
   wanted the United States to buy Louisiana from France

2. ruler of France
   wanted to sell Louisiana
   needed money for wars in Europe

3. west of the Mississippi River
   had the port city of New Orleans
   doubled the size of the United States

4. explored Louisiana
   kept journals
   made maps of the West

5. African American slave
   good hunter
   helped Lewis and Clark explore the West

6. Shoshone Indian
   helped Lewis and Clark
   knew how to cross the Rocky Mountains

Journal Writing

Look at the list below. If you had gone with Lewis and Clark, which things would you have taken? Choose the five things you think are most important. In your journal, write a paragraph telling why you would have taken each one.

axe	rope	journal	matches	candles
soap	knife	blanket	animal trap	hat

The War of 1812

Find Out

❶ Why did Americans fight a second war against Great Britain?

❷ How did Tecumseh try to help Native Americans?

❸ How did the War of 1812 help the United States?

NEW WORDS

captured
freedom of the seas
navy

PEOPLE & PLACES

James Madison
Tecumseh
Dolley Madison
Fort McHenry
Baltimore
Francis Scott Key
Andrew Jackson

➤ Learning from Pictures Americans fought the British in the War of 1812 for freedom of the seas. Which ship won this battle at sea?

The United States and Great Britain were fighting again in the year 1812. Why did Americans fight a second war against the British?

Napoleon Bonaparte, the ruler of France, started a war against Great Britain in 1803. The United States wanted to trade with both Great Britain and France. British ships **captured** many American ships that sailed to France. The French did the same thing to ships that sailed to Great Britain. This made Americans very angry. Americans wanted **freedom of the seas**. "Freedom of the seas" means that ships can sail wherever they want.

The British angered Americans in another way. British ships stopped American ships on the ocean. British captains

James Madison

went on the American ships. These captains said that many of the Americans were really British people. They forced these Americans to sail on the British ships. The British made many Americans work for the British **navy**. Americans wanted to trade with France. They did not want their ships captured.

The French agreed to freedom of the seas. The British did not. In 1812 the United States began to fight Great Britain for freedom of the seas. This second war against Great Britain was called the War of 1812. James Madison was President during the War of 1812. He thought the United States would win the war quickly. But the American army and navy were small. The war did not end quickly. Americans fought against the British for more than two years.

During the War of 1812, the United States tried to capture Canada. Canada belonged to Great Britain. The British army in Canada was strong. The United States could not capture Canada.

A Native American leader named Tecumseh fought for the British during the War of 1812. Tecumseh lived on land between the eastern states and the Mississippi River.

Tecumseh

▲ **Tecumseh was killed in a battle during the War of 1812.**

81

Dolley Madison

He was angry because each year Americans took more land that belonged to Native Americans. The British promised Tecumseh that they would help the Native Americans get back their land. So Tecumseh and his people fought for Great Britain. He helped them win some battles in Canada. Tecumseh was killed in a battle during the War of 1812.

The American army had burned some buildings in Canada. The British army decided to burn the American capital city, Washington, D.C. President Madison was not in the city when the British army arrived.

Dolley Madison, the First Lady, was in the White House when Washington, D.C., began to burn. The brave First Lady stayed in the White House. She packed important government papers in a trunk. A famous painting of George Washington was in the White House. Dolley Madison left the burning city with the painting and the government papers. Very soon, British soldiers came to the White House and burned everything still inside. Dolley Madison had saved the painting of Washington and the government papers for the United States.

Dolley Madison saved important papers when the British marched into Washington, D.C. ➤

Andrew Jackson and his soldiers won the Battle of New Orleans. ▶

THE WAR OF 1812

CANADA

Washington, D.C.

MAP KEY
★ Battle site

New Orleans

Important battles

In 1814 the British tried to capture Fort McHenry. This fort guarded the port of Baltimore, Maryland. A large American flag flew over the fort. After the battle, an American named Francis Scott Key saw that this flag still flew over the fort. The flag showed that Americans had won the battle. Francis Scott Key wrote a song about the flag. His song was called "The Star-Spangled Banner." It became our country's song.

The British wanted to capture the port of New Orleans. Andrew Jackson was a general in the American army. He led 5,000 American soldiers in the Battle of New Orleans. These soldiers included people from Europe, Native Americans, slaves, and free African Americans. General Jackson won the Battle of New Orleans in January 1815. He did not know that the war had ended already. In December 1814 Great Britain and the United States had signed a peace treaty.

Nothing really changed much because of the War of 1812. Neither country won new land in the war. But Great Britain never again fought against the United States. Great Britain and other countries now knew that the United States was strong enough to fight for what it wanted.

Using Primary Sources

Chief Tecumseh's Speech, 1810

There were many groups of Native Americans that lived on land between the states and the Mississippi River. In the early 1800s, many of these groups were forced to sign treaties with Governor William Henry Harrison. In these treaties, Native Americans gave their land to the United States.

Tecumseh was the chief of the Shawnee, a group of Native Americans. He was very angry about the treaties. In 1810 Tecumseh met with Governor Harrison. Tecumseh told Harrison that the United States had no right to take land from Native Americans. Here is part of his speech.

Great Spirit important Native American god

race people

miserable unhappy

unite join together

> *Once . . . there was no white man on this continent. . . . All belonged to red men, children of the same parents, placed on it by the* **Great Spirit** *that made them, to keep it . . . , and to fill it with the same* **race**. *Once a happy race—since made* **miserable** *by the white people. . . . The way . . . to stop this evil is for all the red men to* **unite** *in claiming a common and equal right in the land . . . ; for it . . . belongs to all. . . .*
>
> *The white people have no right to take the land from the Indians, because they had it first; it is theirs. . . . All red men have equal rights to the . . . land. . . . It belongs to the first who sits down on his blanket or skins which he has thrown upon the ground; and till he leaves it, no other has a right.*

On your paper, write the answer to each question.

1. Who was Tecumseh?
2. To whom did Tecumseh give his speech in 1810?
3. What god did Tecumseh believe placed Native Americans on the land?
4. Who did Tecumseh say made Native Americans unhappy?
5. **Think and Write** How does Tecumseh describe life before Americans arrived? Why might Tecumseh believe that he and other Native Americans own the land they live on?

Using What You've Learned

Read and Remember

Choose the Answer Write the correct answers on your paper.

1. What country was Great Britain fighting in 1803?
   the United States   France   Spain

2. What did the United States fight Great Britain for in 1812?
   freedom of the seas   freedom of the press   freedom of religion

3. Who was President during the War of 1812?
   George Washington   Thomas Jefferson   James Madison

4. Who fought for Great Britain during the War of 1812?
   Tecumseh   Andrew Jackson   James Madison

5. What did Tecumseh want?
   to be rich   to get back Native American lands   to go to France

6. Who saved the painting of George Washington when the British burned Washington, D.C.?
   Dolley Madison   Molly Pitcher   Martha Washington

7. Which country won the battle at Fort McHenry?
   the United States   Great Britain   France

8. Who wrote our country's song, "The Star-Spangled Banner"?
   a British soldier   Francis Scott Key   Dolley Madison

9. Who won the Battle of New Orleans?
   James Armistead   Benjamin Franklin   Andrew Jackson

Journal Writing

It often took months for mail to get anywhere in the United States. Because of the slow mail, Andrew Jackson didn't know that the War of 1812 had ended. He and his soldiers fought the Battle of New Orleans. Imagine how he felt when he learned that the peace treaty had already been signed. Write four or five sentences in your journal that tell how Jackson must have felt.

Think and Apply

Drawing Conclusions Read each pair of sentences. Then look in the box for the conclusion you can make. Write the letter of the conclusion on your paper.

1. British ships captured American ships that were sailing to France.
   British captains forced American sailors to work on British ships.

2. African Americans fought in the United States Army.
   People from Europe fought for the United States.

3. Great Britain and the United States wanted peace.
   Both countries had won and lost many battles.

4. In December 1814 Great Britain and the United States signed a peace treaty.
   In January 1815 Andrew Jackson won the Battle of New Orleans.

Conclusions

a. Great Britain and the United States signed a peace treaty.

b. Americans wanted freedom of the seas.

c. Andrew Jackson did not know that the war was over.

d. Many people helped the United States in the War of 1812.

Sequencing Events

Number your paper from 1 to 5. Write the sentences to show the correct order.

The British burned Washington, D.C.

The United States began to fight Great Britain for freedom of the seas.

The British forced many Americans to work on British ships.

Andrew Jackson won the Battle of New Orleans.

Great Britain and the United States signed a peace treaty.

The Industrial Revolution

Find Out

❶ How did the Industrial Revolution begin in the United States?

❷ How did canals and railroads help the United States?

❸ How did the Industrial Revolution change the United States?

NEW WORDS

invented
Industrial Revolution
goods
cotton gin
mass production
steamboat
steam engine
canals
locomotives

PEOPLE & PLACES

Samuel Slater
Eli Whitney
Francis Cabot Lowell
Robert Fulton
Hudson River
Erie Canal
Lake Erie

Learning from Pictures During the Industrial Revolution, how might factory machines have been dangerous for workers?

In the 1700s most people wore clothes that were made by hand. They wore shoes that were made by hand, too. Then in the late 1700s the British **invented** machines to help them make cloth. Soon the British began to use the machines in factories. This was the start of the **Industrial Revolution**. The Industrial Revolution began in Great Britain.

The Industrial Revolution was different from the American Revolution. The Industrial Revolution was a change in the way **goods** were made. Before this revolution, most goods were made by hand at home. After the revolution began, machines in factories made many goods.

In 1790 the Industrial Revolution began in the United States. It brought many changes to American life.

87

Samuel Slater

Eli Whitney

Eli Whitney's cotton gin removed seeds from cotton quickly. ➤

Samuel Slater helped start the Industrial Revolution in the United States. Slater had grown up in Great Britain. He studied how the British built their machines for making cloth. Then he moved to the United States. He built new machines for spinning thread. In 1790 Slater and a partner built a factory where workers could use Slater's spinning machines. Soon the factory was making lots of thread.

Eli Whitney also changed the way goods were made. In 1793 Whitney invented a machine called the **cotton gin**. This machine helped cotton farmers. After cotton was picked, seeds had to be removed from the cotton plant. Before the cotton gin, workers removed the seeds by hand. After all the seeds were removed, cotton could be made into thread. It took a long time to remove the cotton seeds by hand. The new cotton gin removed the seeds quickly. Farmers began to grow much more cotton. The cotton was made into thread in factories.

Eli Whitney helped the Industrial Revolution in another way. He began **mass production**. In mass production, people or machines make many goods that are exactly alike. In 1798 the United States Army needed many new guns. Whitney showed how he could use his machines to make thousands of guns in one factory. All the guns were alike. They had the same parts. If a part for

"I gave you an account [report] of the success of my steam boats, which has been so great. . . ."

–Robert Fulton

one gun broke, the gun could be fixed with the same part for another gun. Soon many factories began using mass production. It became faster and cheaper to make goods.

Francis Cabot Lowell started a factory for making cloth in Massachusetts. Lowell was the first person to put all the machines for making thread and cloth in one factory. He needed workers for his factory. He hired young women to work in his factory. Lowell tried to give his workers good places to live. But the women had to work very hard. They had to work with dangerous machines. They worked in the factory from morning until night. Many other factories hired both women and children.

Most American factories were built near rivers. Water power from the rivers was used to run the machines. The rivers also were used to move factory goods from one place to another. Ships carried goods on rivers to many parts of the country.

People wanted to travel faster on rivers. In 1807 a man named Robert Fulton sailed a **steamboat** on the Hudson River in New York. A **steam engine** helped the boat move faster. By the 1820s there were many steamboats carrying people and goods on rivers.

▲ **In 1807 Robert Fulton sailed his steamboat, the Clermont, up the Hudson River.**

The Erie Canal helped ships travel all the way from the Atlantic Ocean to Lake Erie. ➤

Locomotive pulling train

Soon Americans needed more waterways to move goods. They began to build **canals**. These canals were waterways that joined rivers and lakes. The first big canal was built in New York. It was the Erie Canal. It was finished in 1825. Ships sailed from the Atlantic Ocean into the port of New York City. Then they sailed up the Hudson River. From there ships could sail on the Erie Canal all the way to Lake Erie. The canal was more than 350 miles long. Many new businesses, factories, and cities were built near the Erie Canal. The canal helped New York City become a very large city.

People wanted a better way to travel across land. Wagons were very slow. People began to build railroads. At first, horses pulled the trains. Soon people wanted faster trains. They built trains that were pulled by **locomotives**. Each locomotive had a steam engine. The steam engine made the locomotive move faster than trains pulled by horses.

The Industrial Revolution helped the growth of American cities. Before 1800, most people were farmers. Most people did not live in cities. In the 1800s more and more people began working in factories. Cities grew around these factories. As time passed, more Americans lived in cities. Fewer people lived on farms. The Industrial Revolution changed life in the United States.

Using What You've Learned

Read and Remember

Find the Answers Find the sentences below that tell about the Industrial Revolution. On your paper, write the sentences you find. You should find three sentences.

1. In the 1700s the British invented machines that changed how cloth was made.

2. Samuel Slater built spinning machines in the United States.

3. Cotton seeds are removed from the cotton plant after it is picked.

4. Mass production made it faster and cheaper to make goods.

5. Before 1800 most people were farmers.

Using Graphic Organizers

Cause and Effect Read each of the sentences under *Cause* below. Then read each of the sentences under *Effect*. Copy and complete the graphic organizer to match each cause on the left with an effect on the right.

Cause

1. It took a long time to pick seeds out of cotton, so _____

2. Francis Cabot Lowell needed workers for his cloth factories, so _____

3. More and more people began working in factories, so _____

Effect

a. he gave jobs to young women.

b. Eli Whitney invented the cotton gin.

c. cities grew around the factories.

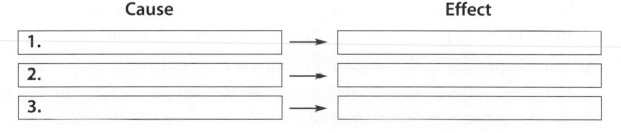

Cause		Effect
1.	→	
2.	→	
3.	→	

Journal Writing

The Industrial Revolution changed the United States in many ways. Write a paragraph in your journal that tells about two ways the United States changed.

Skill Builder

Reading a Line Graph A **line graph** shows how something changes over time. The line graph below shows how the population of New York City changed from 1790 to 1840. The Erie Canal was finished in 1825. The Industrial Revolution and the Erie Canal helped bring many people to the city. Study the line graph.

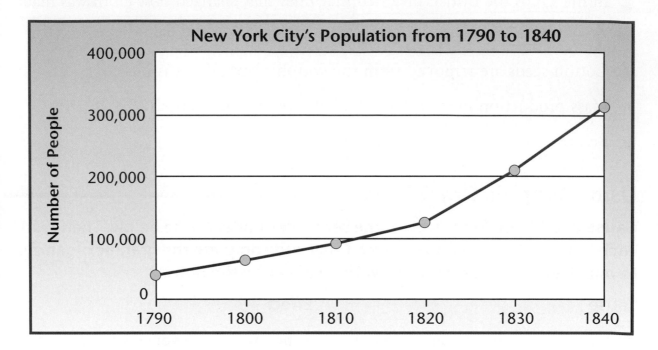

New York City's Population from 1790 to 1840

On your paper, write the number or words that answers each question.

1 What was New York City's population in 1810?
   61,000   96,000   124,000

2 In which year was the population about 203,000 people?
   1800   1830   1840

3 What does the line graph show that many people began to do?
   move to the city   move to farms   leave the nation

4 What happened to the population between 1790 and 1840?
   stayed the same   grew slowly   grew larger

5 What was the population by 1840?
   124,000   313,000   400,000

Andrew Jackson

Find Out

❶ How did Andrew Jackson become a hero?

❷ How did Sequoyah help the Cherokee?

❸ Why did Osceola fight against the United States Army?

NEW WORDS

border
Trail of Tears
tariffs

PEOPLE & PLACES

North Carolina
South Carolina
Creek
South
Cherokee
Alabama
Sequoyah
Indian Territory
Oklahoma
Osceola
Seminole

Andrew Jackson became President in 1829. He was called the "People's President."

Andrew Jackson was the seventh President of our country. He was born near the **border** between North Carolina and South Carolina in 1767. Jackson's father died before Jackson was born. In 1780 Jackson fought for America during the American Revolution. He was 13 years old. Jackson's two brothers died during the American Revolution. His mother also died during the war. Jackson had to live by himself when he was only 14 years old. After the war Jackson studied law and became a lawyer.

Andrew Jackson wanted to help his country during the War of 1812. A large group of Native Americans called the Creek lived in the South. The Creek helped the British during the War of 1812. Andrew Jackson led his soldiers against the Creek. Americans fought the Creek for many months.

Sequoyah with the Cherokee alphabet

Another group of Native Americans was the Cherokee. They helped Americans fight against the Creek. In March 1814 the Creek lost an important battle in Alabama. They surrendered to Andrew Jackson and stopped fighting. The Creek had to give most of their land in Alabama and Georgia to Americans. Jackson and his soldiers also fought American Indians in Florida. Florida belonged to Spain. In 1821 Spain sold Florida to the United States for five million dollars.

Andrew Jackson became a hero. People liked him because he won the battle against the Creek and the Battle of New Orleans. Andrew Jackson became President of the United States in 1829.

Sequoyah was a Cherokee who helped Americans fight the Creek. The Cherokee spoke their own language. The Cherokee, like other groups of Native Americans, did not have an alphabet for their language.

The United States fought many battles against Native Americans. ⱱ

Sequoyah decided to help his people learn to read and write. He carefully studied the Cherokee language. By 1821 Sequoyah had made an alphabet for the Cherokee language. His alphabet had 85 letters.

Sequoyah helped the Cherokee learn to read and write with his alphabet. The Cherokee started the first Native American newspaper. They printed books. The Cherokee started schools. Soon almost every Cherokee could read and write Sequoyah's alphabet.

Thousands of Native Americans lived in the Southeast. Many Americans wanted to own land in the Southeast. President Jackson and these Americans believed that Native Americans should move off the land. In 1830 Congress passed a law. It said Native Americans must move to land west of the Mississippi River. They had to move to an area called Indian Territory. Today much of this land is part of the state of Oklahoma. President Jackson worked to carry out the new law.

From 1831 to 1839, many thousands of Native Americans were forced to move west to Indian Territory.

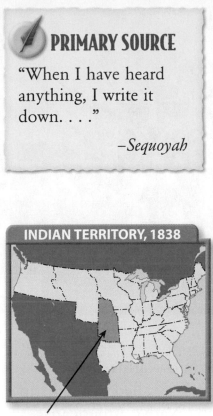

INDIAN TERRITORY, 1838

Native Americans were forced to move to Indian Territory.

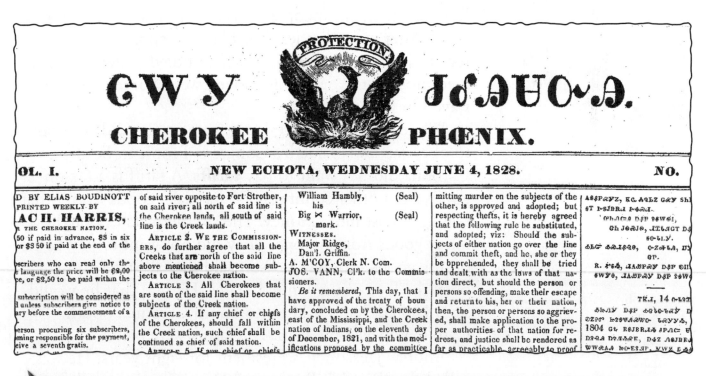

> **Learning from Pictures** The Cherokee started the first Native American newspaper. It was written in both English and Cherokee languages. About how old is this newspaper?

95

American soldiers captured many Seminole during battles in Florida.

Osceola

They did not want to leave their homes, farms, and villages in the Southeast. The Cherokee called the sad trip to the West the **Trail of Tears**. Many Native Americans became sick and died during the long, hard trip.

Osceola was a brave Native American who would not move west. Osceola was the leader of the Seminole in Florida. He led his people in battles against the American army. After many battles Osceola was captured. He was sent to jail. He became very sick and died. After Osceola died most of the Seminole moved west. Some Seminole stayed in Florida.

While Jackson was President, some states did not want to obey tax laws made by Congress. People in South Carolina did not want to pay **tariffs**. A tariff is a tax on goods from other countries. Tariffs make goods from other countries cost more money. The southern states bought many goods from Europe. They did not want to pay tariffs on the goods. Andrew Jackson said that all states must obey the laws of the United States. He said that he would send United States soldiers to South Carolina. South Carolina obeyed the laws. The tariffs were paid.

Andrew Jackson was President for eight years. He was called the "People's President." He believed that all people, both rich and poor, should work for their country. Jackson died in 1845.

Using Geography Themes

Movement: The Trail of Tears

The theme of **movement** tells how people, goods, and ideas move from one place to another. In the 1800s people traveled on horses, wagons, boats, or trains. Goods were sent on wagons, trains, or ships. Ideas were told by one person to another. Some ideas were shared in newspapers.

Read the paragraphs about the Trail of Tears. Study the picture below and the map on page 98.

In 1838 most Cherokee lived in Georgia and nearby states. Other Native Americans of the Southeast had been forced to move west to Indian Territory before 1838. The Cherokee were the last Native American nation to leave the Southeast.

In May 1838 the United States Army began to force about 17,000 Cherokee to leave their homes. The Cherokee were divided into groups. Some groups used land routes. They traveled through many states to reach Indian Territory. Many people walked to Indian Territory. Some rode on horses. Older people traveled in wagons. Other groups used a water route. They traveled in boats on different rivers to Indian Territory. Both routes were very dangerous.

In June 1838 the first group of Cherokee began the long trip west. The trip was more than 800 miles. The trip was hard. There was not

enough food and water. The winter was very cold. People did not have enough warm clothes and blankets. About 4,000 Cherokee died on the way to Indian Territory. The Cherokee called this hard trip the Trail of Tears. In March 1839 the last group on the Trail of Tears reached Indian Territory.

The Cherokee brought their language, religion, songs, and customs to Indian Territory. They continued to tell old Cherokee stories to their children. They started a Cherokee capital city called Tahlequah. Today more Cherokee live in Oklahoma than in any other state.

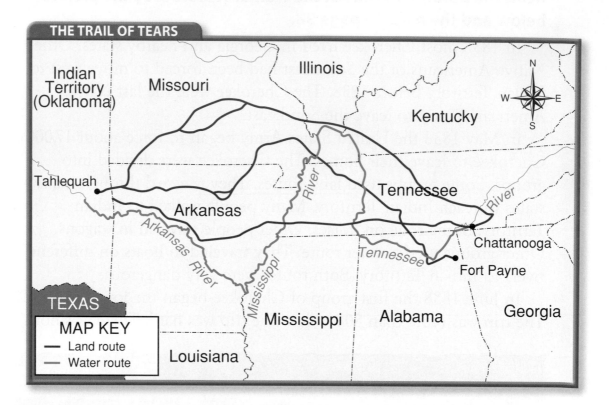

On your paper, write the answer to each question.

1. Some Cherokee rode horses along the land routes. How did other Cherokee travel on land?

2. What did Cherokee travel in if they took a water route?

3. How did children in Indian Territory learn old Cherokee stories?

4. Look at the map. What are five states the Cherokee traveled through on their land routes?

5. What were three rivers the Cherokee used on their water route?

Using What You've Learned

Read and Remember

Finish the Story Use the words in the first box to finish the first paragraph. Use the words in the second box to finish the second paragraph. On your paper, write the words you choose.

Paragraph 1	**Paragraph 2**
Creek	newspaper
Spain	west
five	Florida
Florida	Army
Territory	Osceola
Trail of Tears	alphabet
tariff	Cherokee

During the War of 1812, Andrew Jackson fought against a group of Native Americans called the __(1)__ . Jackson also fought against Native Americans in __(2)__ . In 1821 __(3)__ sold Florida to the United States for __(4)__ million dollars. As President, Jackson said all states must obey the __(5)__ laws. Jackson also forced Native Americans to move west to Indian __(6)__ . Many Native Americans became sick and died as they moved west. The Cherokee called the sad trip to the West the __(7)__ .

Two famous Native Americans lived during the time of Andrew Jackson. Sequoyah was a __(8)__ . He helped his people by making the first Native American __(9)__ . It had 85 letters. The Cherokee used it to print books and a __(10)__ . The famous leader of the Seminole in Florida was __(11)__ . This brave leader would not move __(12)__ . He fought many battles against the United States __(13)__ . After Osceola died, most Native Americans in __(14)__ were forced to move west.

Think and Apply

Fact or Opinion Read each sentence below. Write an **F** on your paper for each sentence that tells a fact. Write an **O** for each sentence that tells an opinion. You should find six opinions.

1. Andrew Jackson fought the Creek.

2. The United States paid too much money to Spain for Florida.

3. Sequoyah was a Cherokee.

4. Sequoyah spent too much time making the alphabet.

5. The Cherokee made the first Native American newspaper.

6. The Cherokee newspaper had many interesting stories.

7. Jackson believed that Native Americans should move west of the Mississippi River.

8. The Cherokee moved to Indian Territory.

9. Many Native Americans died during the long, hard trip to Indian Territory.

10. Osceola wanted to stay in Florida.

11. The United States Congress can write tax laws.

12. States should not have to pay tariffs.

13. Andrew Jackson was a better President than Thomas Jefferson.

14. Andrew Jackson was a good President.

Journal Writing

Imagine that you and your family are Native Americans. You are forced to move west. Think about how you would feel. In your journal, write four or five sentences telling about your feelings. Be sure to tell why you feel the way you do.

CHAPTER 16

Find Out

❶ What was education like in the early 1800s?

❷ How did some Americans help education?

❸ How did other Americans work for reform?

NEW WORDS

reform
education
abolitionists
mental illness

PEOPLE & PLACES

Horace Mann
Emma Willard
Mary Lyon
Mount Holyoke Female Seminary
Oberlin College
Ohio
Thomas Gallaudet
Connecticut
William Lloyd Garrison
Frederick Douglass
North
Dorothea Dix
Elizabeth Cady Stanton
Seneca Falls

Americans Work for Reform

Frederick Douglass worked to end slavery.

Should there be free schools for all children? Should there be laws to end slavery? Should men and women have the same rights? People asked these questions in the early 1800s. Many people answered "no" to these questions. Other people wanted to improve the country. These Americans began to work for **reform**.

In the early 1800s, there were no laws that said children must go to school. Many children worked on farms and in factories. Children from rich families went to fine private schools. But children from poor families did not attend good schools. They often went to public schools that had only one big classroom. All grades were in the classroom. These schools had only one teacher. There were few books. There were not very many high schools.

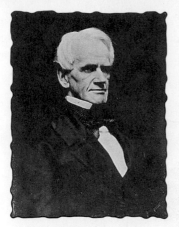

Horace Mann

Mary Lyon

Horace Mann worked to improve public schools in Massachusetts. He worked to have the state pay for children to go to public schools. People built bigger schools that had many classrooms. People built more high schools. Mann started the first school to teach people how to be good teachers. He also helped teachers earn higher pay.

Massachusetts had better schools because of Horace Mann. Other states began to improve their schools, too. States passed laws that said children must go to school.

At that time girls could not get the same **education** that boys could. Often they could only go to school if there was room. This was usually in the summer. Girls were not taught science or math. Girls were not allowed to go to college.

Emma Willard helped girls get a better education. She started the first high school for girls.

Mary Lyon also helped women get a better education. She decided to start a college for women. It was called Mount Holyoke Female Seminary. Mount Holyoke opened in Massachusetts in 1837. Women at Mount Holyoke studied the same subjects that men studied in other colleges.

Soon other colleges for women were started. Women were allowed to study in some colleges with men. Oberlin College in Ohio became the first college for men and women. It also had many African American students.

Mary Lyon began Mount Holyoke Female Seminary. It later became Mount Holyoke College.

Dorothea Dix

At first there were few schools for children with special needs. Thomas Gallaudet believed deaf children should go to school. In 1817 he started a free school for deaf children in Connecticut.

In the 1830s, there were more than two million African American slaves in the United States. Most of them lived in the South. Some Americans believed slavery was wrong. They wanted all slaves to be free. The people who worked to end slavery were called **abolitionists**. William Lloyd Garrison became an abolitionist leader. He published a newspaper about ending slavery.

Frederick Douglass was an African American abolitionist. Douglass had been a slave. He ran away to the North and became free. Douglass gave many speeches. Again and again he told people why slavery was wrong. Many people heard Frederick Douglass and became abolitionists.

Dorothea Dix was another American who worked for reform. Dix visited many jails. She worked to make jails better for prisoners. Dix also saw that many prisoners were in jails because they had **mental illness**. She said these people should not be in jail. Dix said people with mental illness should be treated in hospitals. She helped start hospitals to care for people with mental illness.

Learning from Pictures William Lloyd Garrison published this newspaper about ending slavery. Where was this newspaper published?

Elizabeth Cady Stanton spoke about women's rights at a meeting in Seneca Falls in 1848. ➤

Elizabeth Cady Stanton

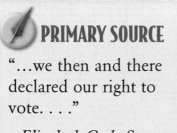

In the 1800s the fight for women's rights began. Some people felt that women were not treated fairly. Women were not allowed to vote. Married women had to give their money to their husbands. Women could not get good jobs. They could not become doctors or lawyers. Women who worked earned much less money than men did.

Some women abolitionists decided that women should have the same rights that men had. They wanted women to have the right to vote. Elizabeth Cady Stanton was an abolitionist. She was also one of the leaders in the fight for women's rights.

In 1848 Stanton helped plan the first large meeting about women's rights. The meeting was in Seneca Falls, New York. About 240 women and men came to the meeting. Stanton gave a speech. She said women should be allowed to vote. She told why women needed more rights. Frederick Douglass and other people joined the fight for women's rights. Slowly, women did win more rights. In Chapter 32 you will learn how women won the right to vote in 1920.

Many people in the United States worked for reform in the 1800s. They wanted Americans to have better lives.

Using What You've Learned

Read and Remember

Match Up Finish each sentence in Group A with words from Group B. On your paper, write the letter of each correct answer.

Group A

1 In the early 1800s, there were not enough good _____ .

2 Thomas Gallaudet started a free school for _____ .

3 Women could not become doctors or _____ .

4 Elizabeth Cady Stanton said women should be allowed _____ .

Group B

a. to vote

b. deaf children

c. public schools

d. lawyers

Think and Apply

Finding the Main Idea Read each group of sentences below. One of the sentences is a main idea. Two sentences support the main idea. On your paper, write the sentence that is the main idea in each group.

1 There were problems in American education in the 1800s.
There were no laws that said children must go to school.
There were few schools for children with disabilities.

2 Girls were not taught science and math.
Only boys were allowed to go to college.
Girls did not get the same education that boys did.

3 Emma Willard started the first high school for girls.
People tried to help girls get a better education.
Mary Lyon started Mount Holyoke Female Seminary.

4 William Lloyd Garrison began a newspaper about ending slavery.
Frederick Douglass spoke about why slavery was wrong.
Some Americans wanted to end slavery.

Skill Builder

Reading a Chart A chart lists a group of facts. Charts help you learn facts quickly. Read the chart below to learn how some Americans worked for reform in the 1800s.

Americans Who Worked for Reform in the 1800s		
Name	**Place**	**Important Work**
Horace Mann	Massachusetts	Mann improved education in public schools in Massachusetts.
Mary Lyon	Massachusetts	Lyon started Mount Holyoke Female Seminary for women.
Thomas Gallaudet	Connecticut	Gallaudet started the first school for deaf children in the United States.
Frederick Douglass	New York and other states	Douglass was an abolitionist. He worked to end slavery.
Dorothea Dix	Massachusetts	Dix helped start hospitals to treat people with mental illness.
Elizabeth Cady Stanton	New York	Stanton worked for women's rights.

On your paper, write the words that finish each sentence.

1. To read the names of people who worked for reform, read the chart from _____ .
   left to right   top to bottom   the middle

2. To learn all about Mary Lyon, read the chart from _____ .
   left to right   top to bottom   bottom to top

3. The person who improved public schools in Massachusetts was _____ .
   Thomas Gallaudet   Horace Mann   Dorothea Dix

4. The person who was an abolitionist was _____ .
   Mary Lyon   Dorothea Dix   Frederick Douglass

5. Elizabeth Cady Stanton worked for _____ .
   women's rights   better schools   hospitals for mental illnesses

Review

Study the time line on this page. Then use the words and date in blue print to finish the story. On your paper, write the words and date you choose.

cities	Louisiana	reform
1812	women's rights	doubled
Cherokee	Industrial Revolution	factory

Many changes took place in the United States as it grew. The United States __(1)__ its size when it bought __(2)__ from France in 1803. The United States showed it was strong when it fought a second war against Great Britain from __(3)__ to 1814. Many Americans wanted to own Native American land. Native Americans were forced to move west. The __(4)__ were forced to move to Indian Territory in 1838.

The __(5)__ began in the United States in 1790 when Samuel Slater built a __(6)__ for spinning thread. During the 1800s fewer people lived on farms. More Americans moved to __(7)__ . People built steamboats, canals, and railroads to help move goods. Many people worked for __(8)__ in the United States. Elizabeth Cady Stanton gave a speech about __(9)__ in Seneca Falls in 1848.

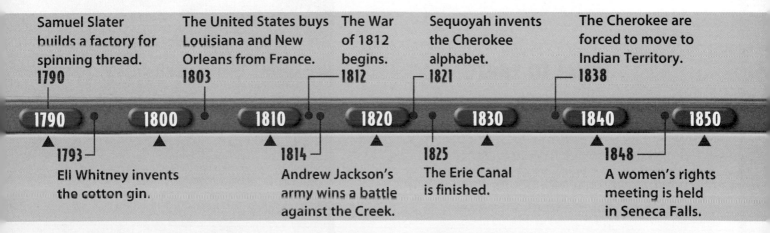

Samuel Slater builds a factory for spinning thread.
1790

The United States buys Louisiana and New Orleans from France.
1803

The War of 1812 begins.
1812

Sequoyah invents the Cherokee alphabet.
1821

The Cherokee are forced to move to Indian Territory.
1838

1790 1800 1810 1820 1830 1840 1850

1793
Eli Whitney invents the cotton gin.

1814
Andrew Jackson's army wins a battle against the Creek.

1825
The Erie Canal is finished.

1848
A women's rights meeting is held in Seneca Falls.

The Nation Grows and Divides

Stephen F. Austin starts an American colony in Texas.
1821

1820   1830

Suppose you are living in the United States in 1860. Everyone believes there will be a war between the northern states and the southern states. You must choose a side to fight for in this war. You might have to fight against your own family during the war. You might have to fight against your best friend. Thousands will die during the Civil War.

The years between 1821 and 1865 were years of great change. Many Americans moved west. Areas in the West became new states. The problem of slavery also grew. The northern states did not like slavery. The southern states said they needed slaves. In 1861 the terrible Civil War began.

Read to Learn

◗ What would you have done if you had lived between 1821 and 1865?

◗ Would you have moved west?

◗ Would you have fought for the northern states or for the southern states?

Texas wins independence from Mexico.
1836

Texas becomes a state.
1845

The United States wins the Mexican War.
1848

Abraham Lincoln becomes President. The Civil War begins.
1861

1840

1850

1860

1870

1843
People go to Oregon on the Oregon Trail.

1846
A treaty is signed about Oregon.

1850
California becomes a state.

1859
Oregon becomes a state.

1865
The Civil War ends.

CHAPTER 17

Independence for Texas

Find Out

❶ Why did Americans want to settle in Texas?

❷ What problems did Americans and Mexicans have in Texas?

❸ How did Texas become free from Mexico?

NEW WORDS

fort
Texas Revolution
republic

PEOPLE & PLACES

Moses Austin
Stephen F. Austin
Mexicans
German Americans
Asian Americans
Texans
Antonio López de Santa Anna
Alamo
Suzanna Dickenson
José Antonio Navarro
Lorenzo de Zavala
Sam Houston
San Jacinto River
Republic of Texas

➤ **Learning from Pictures How did Americans and Mexicans travel to Texas in the 1820s?**

Mexico belonged to Spain for 300 years. In 1821 Mexico became an independent country. At that time, Texas was part of Mexico.

Moses Austin wanted to start a colony for Americans in Texas. He died before he could start the colony. His son, Stephen F. Austin, decided to continue his father's plan to settle Texas. Few Mexicans lived in Texas. So the leaders of Mexico wanted Americans to move to Texas.

Stephen F. Austin started an American colony in Texas in 1821. The land was good for growing cotton and for raising cattle. African Americans, German Americans, and Asian Americans moved to Texas. Jewish Americans and many people from Europe also settled in Texas. More people from Mexico went to

Stephen F. Austin

live in Texas. By 1830 there were many more Americans than Mexicans in Texas. People who live in Texas are called Texans.

Many Mexicans were angry that Americans brought slaves to Texas. Mexican law did not allow slavery in Texas. Mexicans wanted the Americans to obey this law. The Americans did not listen.

Mexico's leaders were worried that Texas might want to become part of the United States. In 1830 Mexico made a new law. The law said that Americans could no longer come to live in Texas. Americans in Texas did not like this law.

Texans did not like other Mexican laws. They did not like the law that said Texans must speak Spanish. Another Mexican law said settlers must be Catholic. Texans wanted to help write laws for Texas. Mexico would not let the settlers make laws for Texas.

The Mexican government became angry with the new settlers. The government was angry that slaves were brought to Texas. Few Texans spoke Spanish. Many Texans were not Catholic.

▲ **Stephen F. Austin sold land to many families who wanted to move to Texas.**

Antonio López de Santa Anna

Suzanna Dickenson

José Antonio Navarro

Santa Anna and his soldiers attacked the Texans at the Alamo. ▶

Mexican soldiers went to Texas to force the Texans to obey Mexican laws. This made the Texans angry. Some Texans began to fight the Mexican soldiers.

Antonio López de Santa Anna was the Mexican president. He led his army against the Texans. In 1836 there were about 180 Texan soldiers in a mission called the Alamo. The Texans used the Alamo as a **fort**. Santa Anna and about 4,000 Mexican soldiers attacked the Alamo. The Texans were very brave. They fought for 13 days. Santa Anna won the Battle of the Alamo. His army killed every Texan soldier.

Some of the Texan soldiers had brought their wives and children to the Alamo. One of these wives was Suzanna Dickenson. After the battle, Santa Anna sent her to tell other Texans not to fight against Mexico.

Texan leaders met in March 1836 while the soldiers were fighting at the Alamo. The leaders wrote a declaration of independence for Texas. This declaration said that Texas was no longer part of Mexico.

Some Mexican Texans also wanted an independent Texas. José Antonio Navarro was a Mexican who was born

Santa Anna surrendered to Sam Houston after the battle at the San Jacinto River.

Lorenzo de Zavala

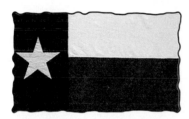

Texas flag

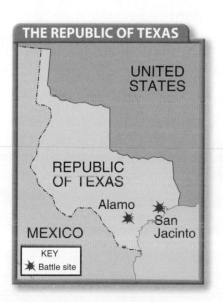

THE REPUBLIC OF TEXAS

UNITED STATES

REPUBLIC OF TEXAS

Alamo

San Jacinto

MEXICO

KEY
★ Battle site

Important battles

in Texas. He was a friend of Stephen F. Austin. He signed the Texas Declaration of Independence. He later helped write a new constitution for Texas. Lorenzo de Zavala was born in Mexico. He came to live in Texas with his family. De Zavala also signed the Texas Declaration of Independence. He told all Texans to fight for freedom.

Sam Houston became the general of the Texas army. He learned about the Battle of the Alamo from Suzanna Dickenson. Houston told his soldiers to remember the brave people who died at the Alamo.

On April 21, 1836, Sam Houston led the Texans against Santa Anna's army. They fought at the San Jacinto River. "Remember the Alamo!" Houston's soldiers shouted as they fought the Mexican soldiers. The battle lasted only 18 minutes. The Texans won. Antonio López de Santa Anna surrendered to Sam Houston. Texas was now free. The Texans called their war against Mexico the **Texas Revolution**.

Texas was no longer part of Mexico, and Texas was not part of the United States. Texas became a **republic**. A republic is an independent country. Sam Houston became the first president of the Republic of Texas. Lorenzo de Zavala became the vice president.

Texans wanted Texas to become part of the United States. But they would have to wait almost ten more years before Texas became a state.

113

Using Primary Sources

Letters from William Barrett Travis

William Barrett Travis led the Texan soldiers at the Battle of the Alamo. On March 6, 1836, Santa Anna and his large army captured the Alamo. They killed Travis and the other Texan soldiers. During Travis's last days at the Alamo, he wrote letters asking Americans and Texans to help. Here are parts of three of his letters.

promptly
soon

provisions
food

victory
a win

relief
help

peril
put in danger

> *February 23, 1836*
> *We have removed all our men into the Alamo. . . . We hope you will send us all the men you can spare **promptly**. . . . We have but little **provisions**. . . .*
>
> *February 24, 1836*
> *. . . The enemy has demanded a surrender. . . . I shall never surrender. . . . I call on you . . . to come to our aid. . . . **Victory** or Death. . . .*
>
> *March 3, 1836*
> *I am still here. . . . I have held this place 10 days against . . . 1,500 to 6,000, and shall continue to hold it till I get **relief** from my countrymen. . . .*
>
> *Make a declaration of independence, and we will then understand, and the world will understand, what we are fighting for. . . . Under the flag of independence, we are ready to **peril** our lives. . . .*

On your paper, write the answer to each question.

1. Where were Travis and his men on February 23, 1836?
2. On February 23 what did Travis say he hoped Texans would do?
3. What did the enemy want Travis to do on February 24?
4. How many days had Travis been inside the Alamo as of March 3?
5. **Think and Write** Travis and the Texan soldiers would not surrender at the Alamo. They were willing to fight for "Victory or Death." Why do you think they would do this?

Using What You've Learned

Read and Remember

Choose a Word Choose the best word or words in blue print to finish each sentence. On your paper, write the word or words you choose.

Sam Houston	**Santa Anna**	**Texas Revolution**
Alamo	**de Zavala**	**Stephen F. Austin**

1 _____ started an American colony in Texas.

2 The leader of the Mexican army was President _____ .

3 About 180 Texan soldiers died at the _____ .

4 José Antonio Navarro and Lorenzo _____ were Mexican Texans who signed the Texas Declaration of Independence.

5 The leader of the Texas army and the first president of the Republic of Texas was _____ .

6 The war for Texan independence was called the _____ .

Think and Apply

Understanding Different Points of View Mexicans and Texans had different points of view about Texas. Read the sentences below. On your paper, write **Texan** for the sentences that show the Texan point of view. Write **Mexican** for the sentences that show the Mexican point of view.

1 People in Texas should obey Mexican laws.

2 People in Texas should write their own laws.

3 Everyone in Texas must be Catholic.

4 Americans in Texas do not have to be Catholic.

5 Americans can bring slaves to Texas.

6 Americans cannot have slaves in Texas.

7 Americans should speak Spanish in Texas.

8 Americans can speak English in Texas.

The United States Grows Larger

Find Out

❶ What was Manifest Destiny?

❷ How did the Mexican War help the United States grow larger?

❸ How did Mexican Americans help the United States?

NEW WORDS

Manifest Destiny
citizens
Mexican Cession
Gadsden Purchase
property

PEOPLE & PLACES

James K. Polk
Rio Grande
Mexico City
Nevada
Utah
Arizona
Colorado
Mexican Americans

When the flag of the Republic of Texas was lowered, Texas became the twenty-eighth state in the United States.

In Chapter 17 you read that Texans won their war against Mexico and started a republic. Santa Anna had surrendered to the Texans. But Mexican leaders did not accept his surrender. The Mexicans said that Texas was still part of Mexico. Texans wanted Texas to become part of the United States. The Mexicans said there would be a war if Texas became part of the United States.

Many Americans wanted Texas to become a state. They believed in an idea called **Manifest Destiny**. Manifest Destiny meant the United States should rule land from the Atlantic Ocean to the Pacific Ocean. This idea also meant that the United States should become a larger and stronger country.

James K. Polk

LAND CLAIMED BY MEXICO

UNITED STATES

Texas land claimed by Mexico

Texas

Rio Grande

MEXICO

The United States and Mexico fought a war over Texas land.

James K. Polk became President in 1845. The new President believed in Manifest Destiny. He wanted Texas to become a state. He also tried to buy California and New Mexico from Mexico. But Mexico refused to sell its land.

In 1845 the United States Congress voted for Texas to become a state. This made the Mexican government very angry.

In 1846 a war started between the United States and Mexico. The two countries did not agree on the border for Texas. The United States said a river called the Rio Grande was the southern border for Texas. Mexico said the size of Texas should be smaller. The Mexicans said that much of the land north of the Rio Grande belonged to Mexico.

The United States and Mexico sent soldiers to the Rio Grande. The soldiers began to fight. This war was called the Mexican War. During the war American soldiers captured California and New Mexico. The Mexican soldiers were brave. They did not stop fighting. Americans and Mexicans continued to fight. In 1847 American soldiers went into Mexico. They captured Mexico City, the capital of Mexico. Soon the Mexicans surrendered. The war was over.

American soldiers stand in Mexico City after capturing this capital city of Mexico.

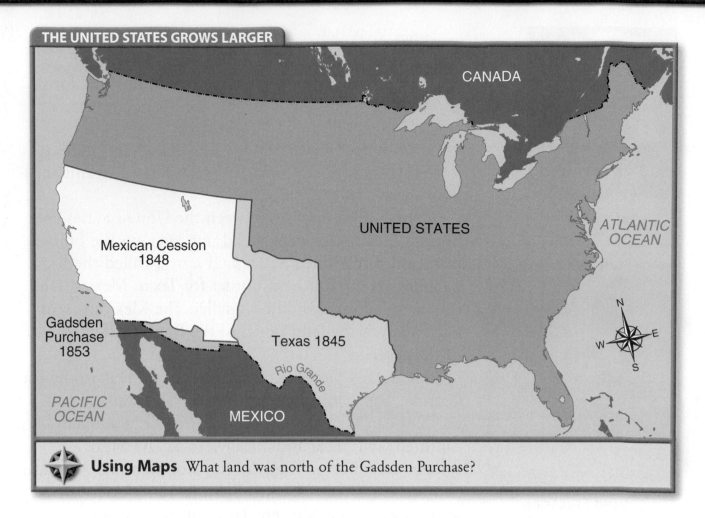

CANADA

UNITED STATES

ATLANTIC OCEAN

Mexican Cession 1848

Gadsden Purchase 1853

Texas 1845

Rio Grande

PACIFIC OCEAN

MEXICO

Using Maps What land was north of the Gadsden Purchase?

The leaders of the United States and Mexico signed a peace treaty in 1848. The treaty gave the United States a large area of Mexican land. It also said that Texas belonged to the United States. The Rio Grande became the border between Texas and Mexico. The treaty also said that Mexicans in the Southwest could become American **citizens**. The United States gave Mexico $15 million for land taken during the war.

The land that the United States got in 1848 was called the **Mexican Cession**. Find the Mexican Cession on the map above. The land from the Mexican Cession became California, Nevada, Utah, Arizona, and parts of New Mexico and Colorado. The United States now owned land from the Atlantic Ocean to the Pacific Ocean.

Americans wanted a railroad across the southern part of the United States. In 1853 the United States gave Mexico $10 million for the land in the **Gadsden Purchase**. Find the Gadsden Purchase on the map above. Years later, Americans built a railroad across the Gadsden Purchase.

PRIMARY SOURCE

"We must ever maintain . . . that the people of this continent alone have the right to decide their own destiny [future]."

–James K. Polk

Mexicans in the Southwest became American citizens after the Mexican War. They were called Mexican Americans.

Mexican Americans helped their new country. They taught Americans how to grow food on land where there was little rain. Mexican Americans helped build railroads for the United States. They helped other Americans look for gold and silver in the Southwest. They taught Americans how to be cowboys.

Mexican Americans helped the United States change a law that was unfair to women. Before the Mexican War, a married American woman could not own **property**. Her husband owned everything. Mexican law was fairer to women. Mexican women owned property together with their husbands. After the Mexican War, Americans changed their law so that women could own property with their husbands.

The land of the United States went from the Atlantic Ocean to the Pacific Ocean. The United States had become a strong country with a lot of new land and many new people.

Learning from Pictures Mexican Americans in the Southwest taught Americans many things, including how to be cowboys. What kind of clothing did a cowboy wear?

Using What You've Learned

Read and Remember

Choose the Answer Write the correct answers on your paper.

1. Which President believed in Manifest Destiny?
   James Madison   Andrew Jackson   James K. Polk

2. When did Texas become a state?
   1776   1845   1900

3. What city did American soldiers capture during the Mexican War?
   Boston   Washington, D.C.   Mexico City

4. Which river became the border for Texas?
   Mississippi River   St. Lawrence River   Rio Grande

5. How much did the United States pay for the Mexican Cession?
   $5 million $15 million $30 million

6. Which three states were among those made from the Mexican Cession?
   California, Nevada, Arizona   New York, New Jersey, Florida
   Texas, Mississippi, Oklahoma

7. What land did the United States buy in 1853?
   Louisiana Purchase   Gadsden Purchase   Florida

8. Why did the United States want the Gadsden Purchase?
   for its water   for a railroad   for a park

Skill Builder

Reviewing Map Directions Look back at the map on page 118. On your paper, write the word that finishes each sentence.

1. The Gadsden Purchase is _____ of Mexico.
   east   south   north

2. The Pacific Ocean is _____ of the Mexican Cession.
   southeast   east   west

3. The Rio Grande is _____ of the Gadsden Purchase.
   northwest   southwest   east

4 Mexico is _____ of the United States.

  south   north   west

5 Texas is _____ of the Gadsden Purchase.

  east   southwest   west

Using Graphic Organizers

Cause and Effect Read each of the sentences under *Cause* below. Then read each of the sentences under *Effect*. Copy and complete the graphic organizer to match each cause on the left with an effect on the right.

Cause

1 In 1845 many Americans believed their country should be larger, so _____

2 Texas became a state, so _____

3 In 1848 the United States got land in the Mexican Cession, so _____

4 Americans wanted to build a railroad across the southern part of the United States, so _____

Effect

a. they paid Mexico $10 million for land in the Gadsden Purchase.

b. Mexico said there would be a war with the United States.

c. the country's borders went from the Atlantic Ocean to the Pacific Ocean.

d. the United States Congress voted for Texas to become a state.

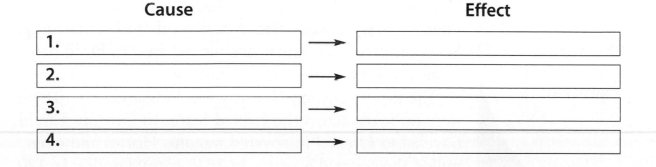

Cause		Effect
1.	→	
2.	→	
3.	→	
4.	→	

Journal Writing

Mexicans who lived in the Southwest became American citizens after the Mexican War. Write a paragraph in your journal that tells how Mexican Americans helped the United States.

On to Oregon and California

Find Out

❶ Why did people want to go to Oregon?

❷ How did people travel to Oregon in the 1840s?

❸ What happened after gold was found in California?

NEW WORDS

oxen
wagon train
Oregon Trail
coast
gold rush
pass

PEOPLE & PLACES

Oregon Country
Oregon
Independence, Missouri
Washington
Idaho
James Marshall
James Beckwourth
Beckwourth Pass

➤ **Learning from Pictures In what ways was the trip over the Rocky Mountains to Oregon hard?**

Many Americans wanted to move west to Oregon Country in the 1840s. Oregon had lots of trees for building new houses. Oregon had good land for farming. Soon thousands of Americans moved west to build new homes and farms in Oregon Country.

The trip to Oregon Country was long and slow. There were no roads across the United States to Oregon. Families traveled to Oregon in covered wagons. Horses and **oxen** pulled the covered wagons. In 1843 many families in 120 covered wagons met in Independence, Missouri. These 120 covered wagons made a **wagon train**. The covered wagons traveled together across the Great Plains and the Rocky Mountains to Oregon. The trail they followed became known as the **Oregon Trail**.

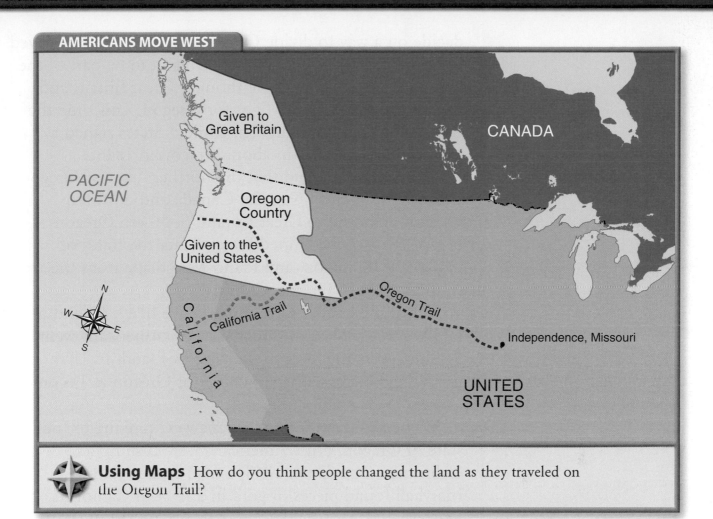

Using Maps How do you think people changed the land as they traveled on the Oregon Trail?

"The way looks pleasant . . . we are so near . . . the difficulties of an unheard-of journey for females."

–*Narcissa Whitman*

What was it like to travel on the Oregon Trail? Families woke up very early every day. Then people traveled as many hours as they could. At night they slept on the floors of their covered wagons. When it rained, wagon wheels got stuck in mud. Sometimes wagons turned over. Then people inside the wagons were hurt or killed. It was hard to find food on the way to Oregon. Many families were hungry. The wagons traveled across mountains, forests, and rivers. The long trip on the Oregon Trail took about six months.

At last the families reached Oregon Country. They had traveled nearly 2,000 miles. Soon thousands of other people went to Oregon on the Oregon Trail. Each year more people settled along the Pacific **coast**.

Oregon Country was much bigger than our state of Oregon today. Oregon Country included part of Canada. Great Britain and the United States had shared Oregon Country for many years. The two nations could not

123

decide on a way to divide Oregon. President Polk believed in Manifest Destiny. He wanted Oregon to be part of the United States. Many people thought Great Britain and the United States would fight for Oregon. This time the two nations did not fight. The United States signed a treaty with Great Britain about Oregon in 1846.

The 1846 treaty said that the northern part of Oregon Country was part of Canada. Canada and northern Oregon belonged to Great Britain. Southern Oregon became part of the United States. Later the states of Oregon, Washington, and Idaho were made from the southern part of Oregon Country.

The United States government gave free farmland to families that moved to Oregon. Many Americans went to Oregon on the Oregon Trail for free land. In 1859 the United States Congress voted for Oregon to become a state.

While thousands of Americans were moving to the state of Oregon, other Americans were rushing to California. One day in 1848, a man named James Marshall found pieces of gold in a river in California. Soon everyone knew that James Marshall had found gold.

People from all over the United States began moving to California. They wanted to find gold and become rich.

Many people moved to California to look for gold. ▽

James Beckwourth found a mountain pass that made it easier for Americans to travel west. ▶

We say that California had a **gold rush** in 1848 and 1849 because thousands of people went to find gold.

The gold rush brought many kinds of people to California. Many people came from Europe to look for gold in California. People came from China to find gold. Free African Americans also moved to California.

James Beckwourth made it easier for many people to travel west to California. Beckwourth was an African American. He moved west and lived with Native Americans. Tall mountains in the West made it hard to go to California. Beckwourth looked for an easier way to go across the mountains. At last Beckwourth found a **pass** through the mountains. Many people used this pass to reach California. Today that pass through the mountains is called the Beckwourth Pass.

Some people were lucky in California. They found gold and became rich. Most people did not find gold. Many people stayed in California. They built farms and factories. They started new cities. They built stores and houses. By 1850, 90,000 people were living in California. The United States Congress voted for California to become a state in 1850.

The California gold rush brought thousands of settlers to California. The Oregon Trail brought thousands of Americans to the Northwest. Every year more Americans moved west to California and Oregon.

Using Geography Themes

Human/Environment Interaction: The Gold Rush

The theme of **human/environment interaction** tells how people live in an area. People in cold areas wear coats. People near oceans might fish for their food. The theme also tells how people can change an area. People use the land to help them live and work. They cut down trees to build houses and roads. They build canals so that ships can reach rivers or lakes.

Read the paragraphs about California's gold rush. Study the photo below and the map on page 127.

Beginning in 1848, thousands of people rushed to California to search for gold. They started many mining camps. This gold rush changed California's land and rivers. The **environment** also changed how the **miners** lived.

When the gold rush began, people used their hands and tools to remove gold from rivers. Soon the gold in these rivers was gone. After 1850, miners began digging deep in the earth to find gold. Some miners built strong walls called **dams** to hold back the water in rivers. Then they dug deep into the ground where there had been water. Many miners dug tunnels to find gold. Others used huge amounts of water to break open mountain walls to find gold.

As the miners dug into the earth, dirt and rocks were dumped into rivers. The rivers became dirty. Most of the fish in the dirty rivers died.

The environment changed the lives of the miners. Miners spent most of their days searching for gold. At night, they often slept in tents on cold ground. When the fish died in the dirty rivers, miners had less food to eat. Sometimes the rivers spread lots of rocks over farmland. Farmers could not grow enough fruits and vegetables for miners to eat. Many miners became very sick because they did not eat well or sleep well.

Sutter Creek, California, was a mining town that began in 1848. The miners lived in tents. The town grew as more gold was found. The miners built houses. Today the gold is gone. Many people in Sutter Creek now sell wood from nearby forests to earn money.

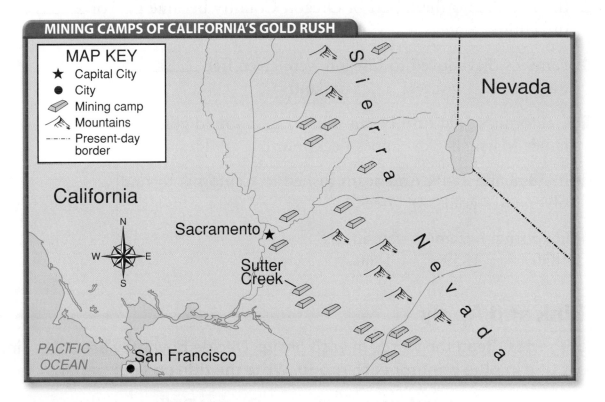

MINING CAMPS OF CALIFORNIA'S GOLD RUSH

MAP KEY
★ Capital City
● City
⬦ Mining camp
⛰ Mountains
--- Present-day border

Nevada

California

Sacramento

Sutter Creek

Sierra

Nevada

PACIFIC OCEAN

San Francisco

On your paper, write the answer to each question.

1. Where did people look for gold at the start of California's gold rush?
2. What are three things the miners did to the earth in order to find gold?
3. Why did the fish die in many of California's rivers?
4. How did the lives of miners change when many fish were gone?
5. Why couldn't farmers grow enough crops for miners to eat?
6. How do many people in Sutter Creek earn money today?

Using What You've Learned

Read and Remember

Finish the Sentence On your paper, write the date, word, or words that finish each sentence.

1 Thousands of Americans went to Oregon Country in the _____ .
1820s   1830s   1840s

2 The Oregon Trail began in _____ .
Philadelphia   New Orleans   Independence

3 In 1846 the northern part of Oregon Country became part of _____ .
the United States   Canada   Washington

4 Families that moved to Oregon were given free _____ .
wagons   houses   farmland

5 California's gold rush began when _____ found gold in a river.
James Marshall   James Beckwourth   President Polk

6 In 1848 and 1849, Americans rushed to California to find _____ .
silver   gold   trees

7 California became a state in _____ .
1850   1859   1860

Think and Apply

Categories Read the words in each group. Decide how they are alike. Find the best title in blue print for each group. Write the title on your paper.

James Beckwourth   **Oregon Trail**
California   **Gold Rush**

1 1848 and 1849
search for gold
brought thousands to California

2 African American
lived in the West
found a pass through the mountains

3 horses and oxen
covered wagons
went to Oregon

4 gold rush
new cities
90,000 people in 1850

Skill Builder

Reading a Historical Map The map below shows how the United States became a large country. Study each area and when it became part of the United States.

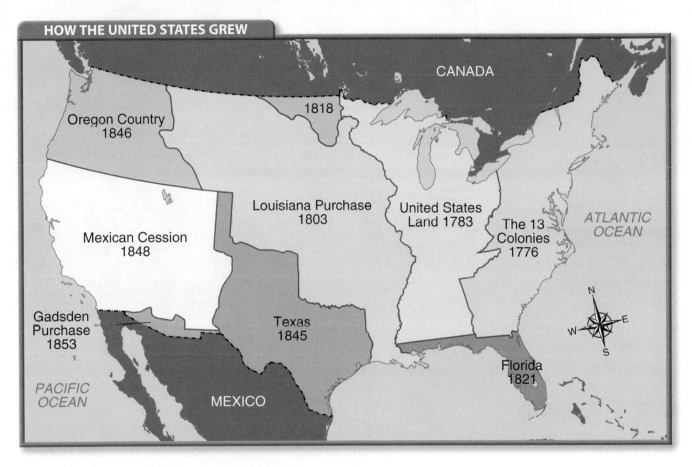

HOW THE UNITED STATES GREW

Write the correct answers on your paper.

1 What land made up the United States in 1776?
Texas   the 13 Colonies   Louisiana

2 What southeast land belonged to Spain until 1821?
Oregon Country   Texas   Florida

3 Which northwest land became part of the United States in 1846?
Oregon Country   Florida   Louisiana Purchase

4 What land did the United States get in 1848?
Mexican Cession   Louisiana Purchase   Texas

5 Which land did the United States buy in 1853?
Gadsden Purchase   Oregon Country   Texas

The Southern States Leave

Find Out

❶ Why were there more slaves in the South than in the North?

❷ Why did the South become angry with the North?

❸ What did the South do after Abraham Lincoln became President?

NEW WORDS

quarreling
plantations
sugar cane
escape
Fugitive Slave Act
Union

PEOPLE & PLACES

Harriet Tubman
Abraham Lincoln
Confederate States of America
Jefferson Davis

➤ **Learning from Pictures Who are these people on this plantation? What are they doing?**

The United States had become a large country after the Mexican War. But things were not going well in the United States. The northern states were **quarreling** with the southern states. The northern states were called the North, and the southern states were called the South. Why did the North and South quarrel?

An important problem was slavery. In the early days of our nation, there were slaves both in the North and in the South. But farms were small in the North. The North had many factories. Most people there did not need slaves on their farms and in factories. There were fewer slaves in the North.

In the South some people owned very large farms called **plantations**. The owners grew cotton, **sugar cane**, and tobacco on their plantations. Plantation owners needed many workers. Many plantation owners bought slaves to do the work. The plantation owners thought they could not grow crops without slaves.

A small group of rich plantation owners owned most of the slaves. Most people in the South did not own any slaves. But almost everyone in the South agreed that slavery should be allowed. The North did not agree.

After the Mexican War, more Americans moved to the West. People from the South started new plantations in the West. They wanted to bring their slaves. The northern states did not want slavery in the West.

The North and South began to quarrel. In the North many people said that all people should be free. They said that it was not right for one person to own another person. In the South people said that the Constitution allowed slavery. People in the South said that people in the North should not tell them what to do. The people in the North wanted to make new laws against slavery in the West. This made the South very angry.

Plantation owners in the South bought and sold slaves. ▽

Abolitionists helped many slaves escape to the North.

Harriet Tubman

The South was worried because many Americans had become abolitionists. They were working to end slavery. Some abolitionists wrote books and newspapers that told why slavery was wrong. Some people gave speeches against slavery. Other people helped slaves run away from their owners.

Harriet Tubman was one of the people who helped slaves become free. She had been a slave herself. She had run away to the North. In the North she was free. Tubman went back to the South and helped slaves **escape** to Canada. In Canada they were free. Harriet Tubman helped many people get their freedom.

In 1850 Congress passed a law about slaves who escaped to the North. It was called the **Fugitive Slave Act**. The new law said that slaves who ran away must be returned to the South. People who did not return them were punished. This new law made the North very angry with the South.

In 1861 a man named Abraham Lincoln became the President of the United States. What kind of man was Abraham Lincoln? He came from a poor family. He lived very far from school when he was young. He only went to school for about one year. Lincoln learned as much as he could by reading books. He grew up to be very tall, thin,

Abraham Lincoln came from a poor family. >

Abraham Lincoln

Jefferson Davis

and strong. He became a lawyer. Many people liked Lincoln because he was honest and smart.

President Lincoln believed that slavery was wrong. He promised he would not try to end slavery in the South. But he said slavery should not be allowed in the West. The North liked what Lincoln said, but the South did not. The South believed Lincoln would work to end slavery everywhere.

Seven southern states decided they no longer wanted to be part of the **Union**. The Union is another name for the United States. In 1861 these seven southern states started a new country. They called their country the Confederate States of America. The Confederate States wrote their own constitution. It had laws that allowed slavery. The Confederate States had their own flag and their own money. Jefferson Davis became the president of the Confederate States. Soon four other southern states joined the Confederate States.

President Lincoln said that the United States must be one country, not two. Would the Union and the Confederate States become one country again? Would it take a war to bring them together? Read Chapter 21 to find the answers to these questions.

Using Geography Themes

Region: The South in 1861

The theme of **region** tells how places in an area are alike. A region can be large or small. Places in a region might have the same weather or kind of land. People in a region might share customs, ideas, and ways of life.

Read the paragraphs about the South in 1861. Study the picture below and the map on page 135.

The South was a region with huge plantations. Plantations were the center of southern life. The South was a good place for farms and plantations. There was plenty of good soil. There were rain and a warm **climate** during most of the year. Plantation owners grew crops such as cotton, sugar cane, tobacco, and rice. Cotton was the most important crop. The South earned most of its money by selling its cotton.

Slaves did most of the farm work on the plantations. Plantation owners believed they could not grow cotton and other crops without the work of slaves. By 1861 one third of the people in the South were African American slaves.

The South was very different from the North. It did not have many big cities, factories, and railroads like the North. New Orleans was the biggest city in the South. But it was smaller than many cities in the North.

While many people in the North were moving to cities, most people in the South worked at farming. Many people owned small farms. Most of the farmers did not own slaves. But almost everyone in the South agreed that the region needed slavery.

In 1861 most people in the South said they would fight to keep their slaves and their way of life. Seven southern states decided to leave the United States. They did not want to be part of a country that might end slavery. They started a new country called the Confederate States of America. Later four other states joined the Confederate States.

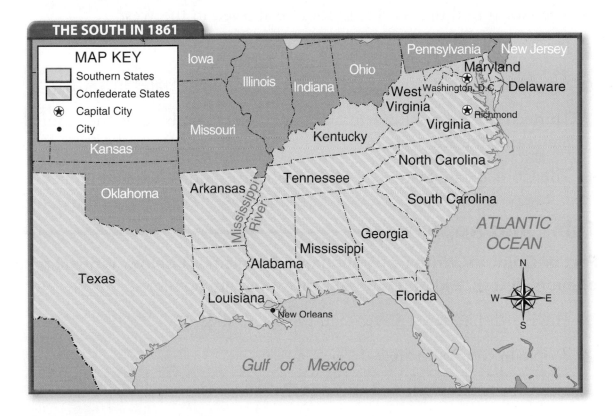

THE SOUTH IN 1861

MAP KEY
Southern States
Confederate States
★ Capital City
• City

On your paper, write the answer to each question.

1 Why was the South a good place for farms and plantations?

2 What was the most important crop in the South?

3 How was the South different from the North?

4 Why did some southern states start a new country?

5 Look at the map. Which four southern states did **not** join the Confederate States of America?

135

Using What You've Learned

Read and Remember

True or False On your paper, write **T** for each sentence that is true. Write **F** for each sentence that is false.

1. The North had small farms and many factories.

2. People grew cotton, sugar cane, and tobacco in the South.

3. Slaves worked on many plantations in the North.

4. The North said that slavery should be allowed in the West.

5. Harriet Tubman only helped three slaves escape.

6. Abraham Lincoln became President of the United States in 1861.

7. Thirteen northern states left the United States and became the Confederate States of America.

8. The Confederate States had their own constitution, flag, and money.

Think and Apply

Fact or Opinion Write **F** on your paper for each fact below. Write **O** for each opinion. You should find four sentences that are opinions.

1. The North had fewer slaves than the South did.

2. People in the South were the best farmers.

3. The Constitution allowed slavery.

4. People in the North should not tell people in the South what to do.

5. Abolitionists were working to end slavery.

6. The Fugitive Slave Act was not a good law.

7. President Lincoln did not want slavery in the West.

8. The southern states were wrong to leave the Union.

9. Jefferson Davis became president of the Confederate States.

Skill Builder

Reading a Bar Graph Graphs are drawings that help you compare facts. The graph on this page is a **bar graph**. It shows facts using bars of different lengths. The bar graph below shows the number of people who lived in the United States in 1860. Study the bar graph.

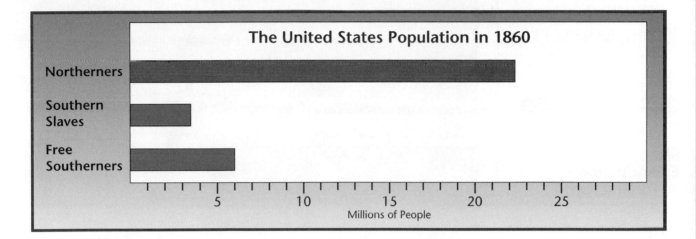

The United States Population in 1860

Northerners

Southern Slaves

Free Southerners

5   10   15   20   25

Millions of People

Write the correct answers on your paper.

1 About how many people lived in the North?
$3\frac{1}{2}$ million   6 million   22 million

2 About how many slaves lived in the South?
$3\frac{1}{2}$ million   6 million   22 million

3 Which group had the largest population?
Northerners   Free Southerners   Southern Slaves

4 Which group had about 6 million people?
Northerners   Free Southerners   Southern Slaves

5 What was the total number of people living in the South?
$3\frac{1}{2}$ million $9\frac{1}{2}$ million   16 million

Journal Writing

Harriet Tubman helped slaves escape. Why did she help them? Write a paragraph in your journal that tells why Tubman helped slaves.

The Civil War

Find Out

❶ What did the South fight for during the Civil War?

❷ What did the North fight for during the Civil War?

❸ Why did Robert E. Lee surrender?

NEW WORDS

Civil War
goal
Emancipation
 Proclamation
battlefields
destroyed
rebuild

PEOPLE & PLACES

Fort Sumter
Confederates
Robert E. Lee
Clara Barton
Ulysses S. Grant
Richmond

Many soldiers from both the North and the South died in the Civil War.

The South had started a new country called the Confederate States of America. President Lincoln did not want the North to fight against the South. He wanted the South to become part of the United States again. The South also did not want a war. But the South did not want to be part of the Union.

The United States Army owned a fort called Fort Sumter in South Carolina. South Carolina was one of the Confederate States. People who lived in the Confederate States were called Confederates. They said that the United States must give Fort Sumter to the Confederate States of America. But Union soldiers would not surrender Fort Sumter.

In 1861 Confederate soldiers began to shoot at Fort Sumter. A war between the North and South had begun.

Confederate battle flag

Robert E. Lee

This war was called the **Civil War**. The Civil War lasted four years. People in the South fought to have their own country, the Confederate States of America. The North fought so that all states would remain in the Union.

The Confederates thought they would win. They had many good army generals and brave soldiers. But the North was stronger than the South. The North had more people and more soldiers. The North had more money to pay for a war. The North had more railroads. Union soldiers traveled on these railroads to many places. The North had more factories, too. Northern factories made guns for the war. The South had few factories.

Robert E. Lee was the leader of the Confederate army. Lee loved the United States. He did not like slavery. He also loved his own state of Virginia. President Lincoln wanted Robert E. Lee to lead the Union army. But Lee would not fight against his family and friends in Virginia. Instead, he became the leader

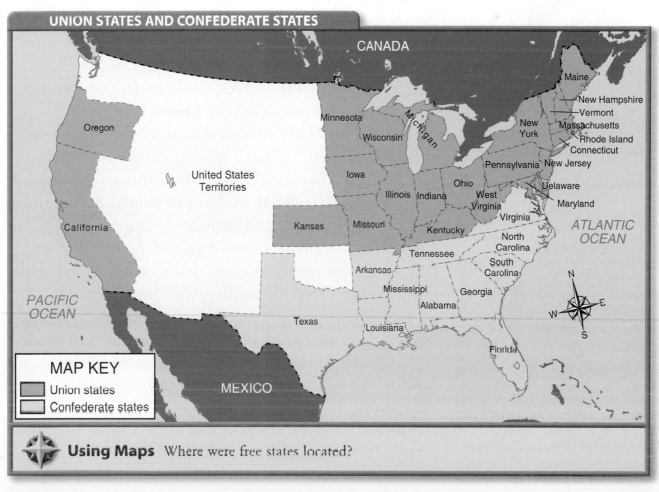

UNION STATES AND CONFEDERATE STATES

CANADA

Maine

New Hampshire

Vermont

Minnesota

Michigan

New York

Massachusetts

Rhode Island

Connecticut

Wisconsin

Oregon

Pennsylvania New Jersey

Iowa

Ohio

Delaware

United States Territories

Illinois Indiana

West Virginia

Maryland

California

Kansas

Missouri

Kentucky

Virginia

ATLANTIC OCEAN

North Carolina

Tennessee

Arkansas

South Carolina

PACIFIC OCEAN

Mississippi

Georgia

Alabama

Texas

Louisiana

Florida

MAP KEY

Union states

Confederate states

MEXICO

Using Maps Where were free states located?

Many African Americans joined the Union army and fought in the Civil War.

Clara Barton

THE CIVIL WAR

UNION STATES
Richmond, VA

CONFEDERATE STATES
Fort Sumter

KEY
★ Battle site

Major battles

of the Confederate army. General Lee was a good leader. He led the Confederate army for four long years.

President Lincoln had a **goal**. His goal was for the North and South to be one nation. He decided to help the Union win by working to end slavery. In 1862 he wrote a paper that said all slaves in the Confederate States were free. He wrote that the slaves would be free on January 1, 1863. The paper was called the **Emancipation Proclamation**. Many African American slaves left the South. Thousands of brave African Americans joined the Union army. They fought in many battles of the Civil War.

Women in the North and South helped during the war. They managed farms and factories. Some women became spies. Many women became nurses. Clara Barton was a famous Union nurse. She traveled to many **battlefields**. Clara Barton cared for soldiers who were hurt.

At the start of the Civil War, the South won many battles. After two years the South lost more and more battles. Most of the Civil War battles were fought in the South. The fighting **destroyed** houses, cities, and plantations in the South.

General Ulysses S. Grant was the leader of the Union army. He won many battles. In 1865 the Union soldiers captured Richmond, Virginia. Richmond was the

PRIMARY SOURCE

"I would save the Union. I would save it the shortest way under the Constitution."

–Abraham Lincoln, 1862

capital of the Confederate States. General Lee knew the Confederates could not win the war. There was very little food to eat in the South. Lee's army was hungry. The soldiers did not have enough guns. Lee did not want more people to die in the war. Lee surrendered to Grant in April 1865. The Civil War was over. Plans were made to return the Confederate States to the Union. General Lee returned to Virginia. He told the South to help the United States become a strong country.

President Lincoln was glad that the United States was one nation again. He was also unhappy. About 600,000 soldiers in the North and South had been killed. Thousands of other soldiers were badly hurt.

President Lincoln had new goals when the war ended. He wanted Americans to work together to **rebuild** the South. Lincoln wanted Americans in the North and South to like one another again.

President Lincoln never reached these goals. He was shot five days after the Civil War ended. President Lincoln died the next day. Americans in the North and South were sad because a great leader was dead.

People in the North and the South were united once again. It would take many more years to end the anger between the North and the South. But together they would continue to make the United States a great nation.

Ulysses S. Grant

141

Using What You've Learned

Read and Remember

Write the Answer On your paper, write one or more sentences to answer each question.

1. What did the North fight for in the Civil War?

2. What did the South fight for in the Civil War?

3. What was the Emancipation Proclamation?

4. How did women help during the Civil War?

5. Why did Clara Barton travel to many battlefields during the Civil War?

6. What was one reason General Lee surrendered to General Grant?

7. How many soldiers died in the Civil War?

8. What were President Lincoln's goals after the Civil War?

9. Why didn't President Lincoln reach his new goals after the war ended?

Match Up Finish each sentence in Group A with words from Group B. On your paper, write the letter of each correct answer.

Group A

1. The Civil War began when Confederate soldiers _____

2. The leader of the Confederate army was_____

3. When President Lincoln wrote the Emancipation Proclamation, _____

4. The leader of the Union army was _____

5. Most of the Civil War battles _____

Group B

a. General Ulysses S. Grant.

b. were fought in the South.

c. General Robert E. Lee.

d. began to shoot at Fort Sumter in South Carolina.

e. many African Americans who had been slaves left the South.

Think and Apply

Sequencing Events Number your paper from 1 to 5. Write the sentences to show the correct order.

In 1862 President Lincoln wrote the Emancipation Proclamation.

In 1861 Confederate soldiers attacked Fort Sumter.

President Lincoln was killed after the war ended.

The war ended when General Robert E. Lee surrendered to General Ulysses S. Grant.

In 1865 the Union captured the Confederate capital at Richmond, Virginia.

Drawing Conclusions Read each pair of sentences. Then look in the box for the conclusion you can make. On your paper, write the letter of the conclusion.

1. The Confederates wanted Fort Sumter in South Carolina.
   Union soldiers would not surrender Fort Sumter.

2. President Lincoln wanted Robert E. Lee to lead the Union army.
   Lee would not fight against his family and friends in Virginia.

3. The North had more factories and soldiers than the South did.
   The North had more money and railroads than the South did.

4. The Confederate soldiers did not have enough food.
   The Confederate soldiers did not have enough guns.

Conclusions

   a. The Confederates could not win the war.

   b. The North was stronger than the South.

   c. Confederate soldiers began to shoot at Fort Sumter.

   d. Lee decided not to lead the Union army.

Journal Writing

The Civil War was a long, hard war between the Union and the Confederate States. Write a paragraph about the Civil War in your journal. Tell how it began or how it ended. Write at least five sentences.

Skill Builder

Reading a Table A table lists a group of facts. You can compare facts by reading a table. Look at the table below. It compares the North and South before the Civil War. To learn facts about the North and the South, read the numbers listed beneath each heading. Read the table from left to right to find out what the numbers in the table stand for.

The North and South Before the Civil War		
	North	**South**
Money	$330,000,000	$47,000,000
Number of factories and shops	111,000	21,000
Miles of railroad track	22,000	9,000
Horses	3,400,000	1,700,000
Units of wheat	132,000,000	31,000

On your paper, write the number, word, or words that answers each question.

1 How many miles of railroad track did the South have before the Civil War?
22,000   9,000   111,000

2 How many factories and shops did the North have before the war?
3,400,000   21,000   111,000

3 How much money did the South have compared to the North before the war?
more   less   the same amount of

4 How many horses did the North have compared to the South?
more   fewer   the same number of

5 How many units of wheat for food did the North have compared to the South?
more   fewer   the same number of

6 Based on the chart, how would you compare the North to the South?
stronger than   weaker than   about the same as

Review

Study the time line on this page. Then use the words in blue print to finish the story. On your paper, write the words you choose.

slaves   Lincoln   state
Texas   California   Lee
Cession   Confederate   Civil War

In 1836 __(1)__ won a war for independence from Mexico. In 1845 Texas became a __(2)__ . The United States fought a war with Mexico. From that war the United States got the Mexican __(3)__ . Many Americans moved west. After the gold rush, __(4)__ became a state in 1850.

As the nation grew larger, the North and the South quarreled about slavery. In 1861 southern states started a new nation called the __(5)__ States of America. Later that year, the __(6)__ began. President Abraham Lincoln wrote the Emancipation Proclamation. This paper said that __(7)__ in the Confederate States were free. In 1865 General __(8)__ surrendered to General Grant. The Union had won the Civil War. A few days later, __(9)__ was killed.

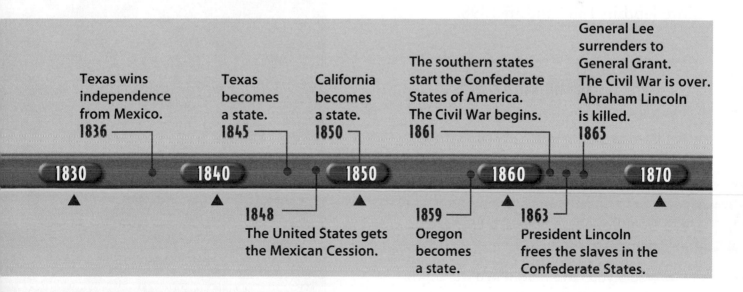

Texas wins independence from Mexico.
1836

Texas becomes a state.
1845

California becomes a state.
1850

The southern states start the Confederate States of America. The Civil War begins.
1861

General Lee surrenders to General Grant. The Civil War is over. Abraham Lincoln is killed.
1865

1830   1840   1850   1860   1870

1848
The United States gets the Mexican Cession.

1859
Oregon becomes a state.

1863
President Lincoln frees the slaves in the Confederate States.

After the Civil War

What was it like to live in the United States after the Civil War? For the first time, you could travel across the western part of the country by train. You might move west to the Great Plains. You might live in a small house that you helped your family build. All around your home you would see flat land and few trees. Your closest neighbor would be many miles away.

Life in the United States changed after the Civil War. In the North and in the South, people began to rebuild the country. People who had been slaves were now free. Many Americans moved west. Telephones and electric lights helped make life easier in the United States. The United States got more land in 1867 and in 1898.

Read to Learn

- What would you have done if you had lived in the United States after the Civil War?

- Would you have helped rebuild the South?

- Would you have helped build new railroads?

- Would you have fought in a war to win more land for your country?

The Civil War ends. Reconstruction begins.
1865

The first railroad that goes across the United States is finished.
1869

1860   1870

▲ 1862
Congress passes the Homestead Act.

1867
The United States buys Alaska. ▲

Thomas Edison invents the electric light bulb.
1879

Hawaii becomes part of the United States. The United States wins the Spanish-American War.
1898

1880

1890

1900

1910

1876
Alexander Graham Bell invents the telephone.

1882
Jan Matzeliger invents a machine for making shoes.

1896
Gold is found in Alaska.

1903
The Wright brothers fly the first airplane.

Find Out

❶ How was the South rebuilt?

❷ How did life change for African Americans after the Civil War?

❸ What laws were added to the Constitution to help African Americans?

NEW WORDS

Reconstruction
rejoined
equal rights
segregation
salaries

PEOPLE & PLACES

Booker T. Washington
Tuskegee Institute

Reconstruction

> **Learning from Pictures** How do you think families felt when soldiers returned home after the Civil War ended?

Americans in the North and South had hard work to do after the Civil War. Many cities and farms in the South were destroyed. The South had to be rebuilt. People in the North and South had to learn to like one another again.

The years after the Civil War were called the time of **Reconstruction**. Reconstruction began in 1865. It ended in 1877. During this time, the southern states **rejoined** the United States. The South was slowly rebuilt. Cities, farms, and roads were rebuilt. Southern farmers began to grow cotton again. Before the Civil War, the South had few factories. After the war, the South built more factories.

After the Civil War, about four million African American slaves became free people. African Americans in the South had many problems. Most of them did not know how to read or write. They had very little money. It was hard for them to find jobs.

After the war many African Americans still worked on large cotton plantations. But most plantation owners paid African Americans very little money for their work.

Voting for the first time

African Americans wanted to learn to read and write. Free schools were started. The first colleges for African Americans were built. Both children and adults went to school. Many adults went to school at night because they worked all day. Sometimes teachers from the North came to teach African Americans.

After the war United States senators and representatives wanted to help African Americans. They added three laws, or amendments, to the Constitution. The first law was the Thirteenth Amendment. It said that no one in the United States could own slaves. Never again would there be slavery in the United States. The second law was the Fourteenth Amendment. This law said that African Americans were citizens. It also said all people have **equal rights**. The third law to help African Americans was the Fifteenth Amendment. It said African American men could vote. At that time American women were not allowed to vote.

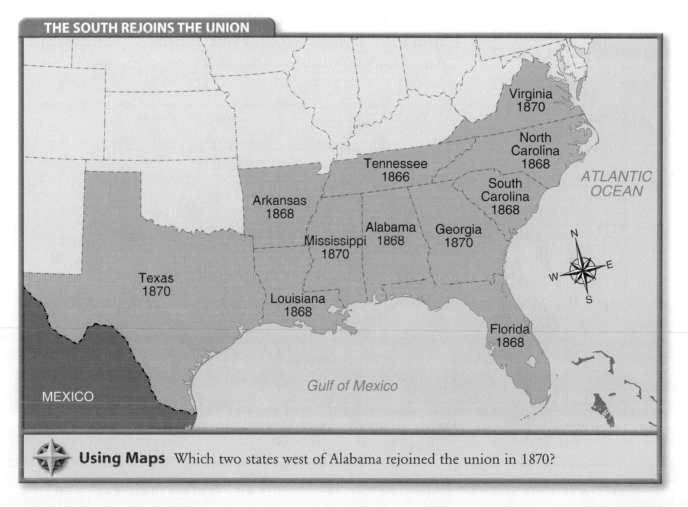

THE SOUTH REJOINS THE UNION

Using Maps Which two states west of Alabama rejoined the union in 1870?

Booker T. Washington

During Reconstruction, African Americans voted for the first time. By 1877 sixteen African Americans had become senators and representatives in Congress.

After the war people in the South wrote new laws that were not fair to African Americans. Other unfair laws were written after 1877. Some laws made it hard for African Americans to vote. Other laws allowed **segregation**. African Americans could not sit in train cars with white people. They could not go to white schools. There also were laws that made it hard for African Americans to get good jobs.

Booker T. Washington helped African Americans get better jobs. He had been a slave, but he became free after the Civil War. He became a teacher. In 1881 he started a school in Alabama for African Americans. His school was called the Tuskegee Institute. People could learn to do many kinds of work at Tuskegee. They could get better jobs and earn good **salaries**. Thousands of students have studied at the Tuskegee Institute.

Americans rebuilt the South. People in the North and South slowly began to like one another again. African Americans continued to work for equal rights.

▲ **These were the first African American senators and representatives in Congress.**

Using Primary Sources

Up from Slavery

In 1901 Booker T. Washington wrote a book about his own life. It was called *Up from Slavery*. In his book Washington wrote about his struggle to get to Hampton Institute, a school for African Americans.

fare
money paid for a trip

*The distance . . . to Hampton Institute is about five hundred miles. . . . I did not have enough money to pay my **fare** to Hampton. . . . By walking, begging rides both in wagons and in the cars, . . . after a number of days, I reached the city of Richmond, Virginia, about eighty-two miles from Hampton. . . . I was completely out of money. . . .*

At last . . . I could walk no longer. I was tired, I was hungry. . . . I . . . lay for the night upon the ground. . . . As soon as it became light . . . I noticed that I was near a large ship. . . .

The captain . . . told me . . . I could continue working for a small amount per day. . . .

I reached Hampton, with . . . fifty cents with which to begin my education. . . . [Hampton] seemed to me to be the largest and most beautiful building I had ever seen.

On your paper, write the answer to each question.

1. How did Washington travel to Richmond, Virginia?
2. How far was it from Richmond to Hampton?
3. Where did Washington sleep the first night in Richmond?
4. How much money did Washington have when he reached the Hampton Institute?
5. **Think and Write** Why do you think it was important to Washington to get to the Hampton Institute?

Using What You've Learned

Read and Remember

Finish the Story Use the words in blue print to finish the story. On your paper, write the words you choose.

vote   slavery   equal rights
fair   rebuilt   Reconstruction

The time of __(1)__ began after the Civil War. Southern cities were __(2)__ . The Thirteenth Amendment ended __(3)__ . The Fourteenth Amendment said all people have __(4)__ . The Fifteenth Amendment gave African American men the right to __(5)__ . But in the South people wrote laws that were not __(6)__ to African Americans.

Using Graphic Organizers

Main Idea and Supporting Details Read each group of sentences below. One of the three sentences is a main idea. The other two sentences support the main idea. Copy the chart twice. Then complete one chart for each group of sentences.

1. Many African Americans had little money.
   African Americans had many problems after they became free.
   It was hard for African Americans to find jobs.

2. Booker T. Washington started the Tuskegee Institute.
   At Tuskegee people learned to do many kinds of work.
   Booker T. Washington helped African Americans get better jobs.

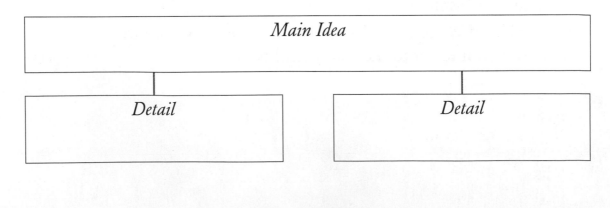

152

Americans Move West

Find Out

❶ How did the Homestead Act help Americans settle in the West?

❷ What problems did Native Americans have with the settlers of the Great Plains?

❸ How did railroads help Americans move west?

NEW WORDS

Homestead Act
weapons
reservations
immigrants
spike

PEOPLE & PLACES

Iowa
Ireland
Chinese

⟩ **Learning from Pictures** Why might life have been hard for settlers who went to live on the Great Plains?

The land between Iowa and the Rocky Mountains is called the Great Plains. In the 1840s and 1850s, many Americans traveled west across the Great Plains and the Rocky Mountains to California and Oregon. Not many Americans wanted to live on the Great Plains. There was very little rain. The land was flat, and there were few trees. Americans did not think they could grow food on the Great Plains.

In 1862 the United States senators and representatives in Congress wrote a new law. It was called the **Homestead Act**. The Homestead Act gave settlers free land on the Great Plains. The Homestead Act said settlers had to live on the land for five years. They had to build a house and a farm on the land. After five years, the settlers owned the land.

153

Wheat

The Homestead Act helped people who wanted to own land. Thousands of Americans moved to the Great Plains. After the Civil War, many African Americans also moved west to get free land. Farms were started on the Great Plains. Some farmers grew corn. Other farmers grew wheat. Flour is made from wheat. Breads and cakes are made from flour.

It was hard work to be a wheat farmer on the Great Plains. Sometimes there was not enough rain for the wheat to grow. There were terrible snowstorms in the winter. The farmers learned better ways to grow wheat. Today most of our wheat comes from the Great Plains.

After the California gold rush, people found gold and silver in other parts of the West. Thousands of Americans moved west to find gold and silver. They settled in areas that are now Nevada, Colorado, Idaho, and other states.

As Americans moved west, they settled on land where Native Americans lived. These Native Americans had always been buffalo hunters. Millions of buffalo lived on the Great Plains. The buffalo moved from place to place. Native Americans moved from place to place as they hunted buffalo.

Native Americans used every part of the buffalo they killed. They ate the meat. They made clothes from the animal skins. They also made tents from the skins. They made tools and **weapons** from the horns and bones.

Native Americans were not happy when farmers and miners settled on Native American land. As Americans

Farmers learned better ways to grow wheat on the Great Plains. >

Buffalo

moved west, they killed many, many buffalo. By 1900 most buffalo had been killed. Many Native Americans died because they had few other foods to eat.

As Americans moved west, there were many battles between settlers and Native Americans. Many settlers were killed. But many more Native Americans were killed.

The United States government forced Native Americans to stop moving from place to place. The government gave them lands to live on. These lands are called **reservations**. Many Native Americans became farmers on the reservations. They were not happy. They no longer could hunt buffalo. Their land was not good for farming. It was hard to grow enough food.

As Americans moved west, they needed better ways to travel. At first, people traveled with horses and covered wagons. Railroads would take Americans to the West faster. There were many railroads in the East. But there were no railroads across the West.

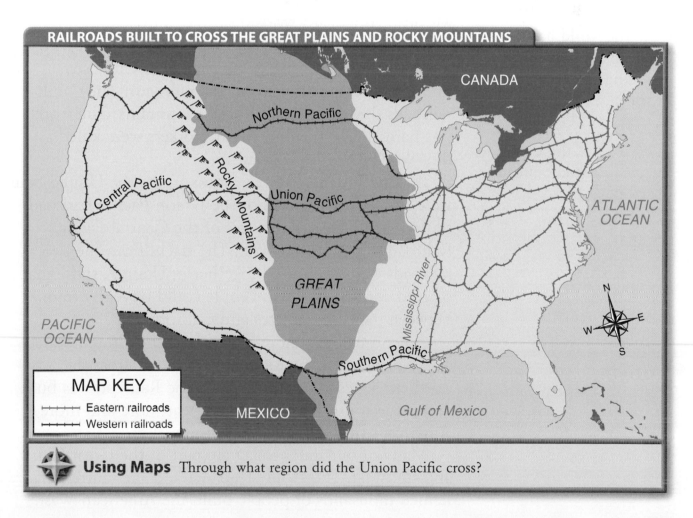

RAILROADS BUILT TO CROSS THE GREAT PLAINS AND ROCKY MOUNTAINS

CANADA

Northern Pacific

Central Pacific

Rocky Mountains

Union Pacific

ATLANTIC OCEAN

GREAT PLAINS

Mississippi River

PACIFIC OCEAN

Southern Pacific

N
W   E
S

MAP KEY
┼┼┼┼ Eastern railroads
┼┼┼┼ Western railroads

MEXICO

Gulf of Mexico

Using Maps Through what region did the Union Pacific cross?

After 1869 more people traveled west on the new railroads. ➤

After the Civil War, thousands of people helped lay railroad tracks across the West. African Americans and Mexican Americans worked on the railroads. **Immigrants** from Ireland also helped. Immigrants are people who move to another country. Thousands of Chinese immigrants came to work on the railroads. They built railroads through the tall Rocky Mountains. The work was hard and dangerous. Many workers were killed as they worked on the railroads.

In 1869 the first railroad tracks across the United States were finished. The tracks of the Union Pacific Railroad started in the East. The tracks of the Central Pacific Railroad started in the West. The tracks from the two railroads were connected together in Utah. A **spike** made of gold connected them. People could travel by train between the eastern states and California.

Americans built more railroads in the United States. The Northern Pacific Railroad was built across the northern states. The Southern Pacific Railroad was built across the southern states. Every year more and more Americans traveled west in trains.

Many of our states today are part of the Great Plains and the West. The Homestead Act and the railroads helped thousands of people build the American West.

Using Geography Themes

Region: The Great Plains

The theme of region tells how places in an area are alike. A region can be large or small. Places in a region might have the same weather or kind of land. People in a region might share customs, ideas, and ways of life.

Read the paragraphs about the Great Plains. Study the photo below and the map on page 158.

Imagine living on the Great Plains, where there are very few trees and little rain. This dry, flat region covers all or parts of 13 states. It also includes parts of Canada and northern Mexico. The Great Plains stretch as far east as Iowa and Missouri. To the west are the Rocky Mountains.

Tall grass grows in the eastern part of the Great Plains. Shorter grass covers the drier western part. Buffalo liked to eat the thick grass. That is why millions of buffalo once lived in the region.

The Homestead Act of 1862 gave thousands of settlers farmland in the Great Plains. It was difficult to plant seeds in the hard grass-covered soil. People found better ways to farm. Wheat and corn became two important crops on the Great Plains.

There were few trees for building houses. Settlers used **sod** to build houses. Sod is grass-covered land. People cut sod into large blocks. Then they stacked the blocks to make their houses.

Life was hard and lonely on the Great Plains. Neighbors were far away. Settlers had to make their own clothes. They had to work their own fields. Everyone in the family had a job to do.

Weather and insects also made life hard. Summers were very hot and dry. Winters brought terrible snowstorms. There were dangerous windstorms. Sometimes millions of grasshoppers attacked farms. These insects ate all the crops.

But the settlers worked hard. They turned the dry plains into an important farming region. Today the Great Plains region grows large amounts of wheat, corn, and other **grains** for the United States and many nations.

THE GREAT PLAINS

On your paper, write the answer to each question.

1. What kind of land does the Great Plains have?
2. How did settlers build houses in the region?
3. How did the weather make life hard for the settlers?
4. Why is the Great Plains an important farming region today?
5. Look at the map. Which four states are completely within the Great Plains region?

Using What You've Learned

Read and Remember

Match Up Each item in Group B tells about an item in Group A. On your paper, write the letter of the correct answer.

Group A

1. Homestead Act
2. wheat
3. buffalo
4. railroads
5. immigrants

Group B

a. used to make flour for bread

b. made it easier for people to travel west

c. hunted by Native Americans

d. gave people free land in the West

e. helped build railroads

Think and Apply

Cause and Effect Match each cause on the left with an effect on the right. On your paper, write the letter of the effect.

Cause

1. Americans did not want to live on the Great Plains, so _____

2. The Homestead Act gave settlers land, so _____

3. Buffalo moved from place to place, so _____

4. The United States government wanted Native Americans to live in one place, so _____

5. In 1869 two railroads were connected in Utah, so _____

Effect

a. Native Americans who hunted buffalo moved from place to place.

b. United States senators and representatives wrote the Homestead Act.

c. it forced Native Americans to live on reservations.

d. many Americans moved west to the Great Plains.

e. people could travel by train between the eastern states and California.

Skill Builder

Reading a Flow Chart   A **flow chart** is a chart that shows you facts in the correct order they occur. The flow chart on this page shows how wheat becomes flour for bread. Wheat kernels are the seeds of the wheat plant. Vitamins are added to food to make it better for people to eat.

Read the flow chart. On your paper, write the word that finishes each sentence below.

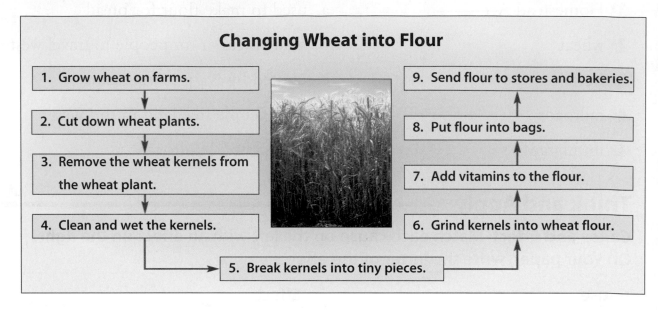

Changing Wheat into Flour

1. Grow wheat on farms.

2. Cut down wheat plants.

3. Remove the wheat kernels from the wheat plant.

4. Clean and wet the kernels.

5. Break kernels into tiny pieces.

6. Grind kernels into wheat flour.

7. Add vitamins to the flour.

8. Put flour into bags.

9. Send flour to stores and bakeries.

1 The first step is to _____ wheat.
cut   grow   shake

2 In Step 3 the wheat _____ are removed.
leaves   flowers   kernels

3 After grinding the kernels into flour, _____ are added.
vitamins   flavors   colors

4 Step 8 is to put flour into _____ .
wagons   bags   barns

Journal Writing

Imagine that you were a factory worker in the 1860s. You dream about owning your own farm. You learn about the Homestead Act and decide to move to the Great Plains. Write a paragraph in your journal that tells why you find it hard to live on the Great Plains.

CHAPTER 24

Find Out

❶ How did Alaska become part of the United States?

❷ How did Hawaii become part of the United States?

❸ How did the Spanish-American War help the United States get more land?

NEW WORDS

imperialism
icebox
battleship
Spanish-American War

PEOPLE & PLACES

Russia
Hawaiian Islands
Hawaii
Queen Liliuokalani
Cuba
Puerto Rico
Cubans
Guam
Philippines

The United States Gets More Land

▶ **Learning from Pictures** The United States bought Alaska from Russia in 1867. What resources does Alaska have?

The United States owned land from the Atlantic Ocean to the Pacific Ocean. But the United States had not finished growing. In 1867 the United States bought more land. In 1898 the United States owned even more land. How did the United States get more land?

After the Civil War, the United States wanted to rule more land. People in many countries believed in an idea called **imperialism**. Imperialism means one country rules other countries or colonies. The United States wanted to rule other countries, too.

The United States decided that it wanted to rule Alaska. Alaska is a large piece of land near northwestern Canada. The weather in Alaska is very cold much of the year. There is a lot of snow. A country called Russia is very close to Alaska. Russia owned Alaska. Russia wanted to sell Alaska

Native Americans in Alaska

to the United States. Some Native Americans lived in Alaska. Not many other people lived there.

In 1867 the United States bought Alaska from Russia for $7,200,000. Many Americans did not think the United States should buy Alaska. They said Alaska was a very big **icebox**.

In 1896 gold was found in Alaska. Soon there was a gold rush in Alaska. Thousands of people rushed to Alaska to find gold. Many people did not find gold. They found other things there. Alaska has furs and good fish. Alaska has oil. Oil makes our cars go. Oil helps us make electricity.

In 1959 Alaska became the forty-ninth state in the United States. It is also our largest state.

Many people wanted the United States to rule land in the Pacific Ocean, too. They wanted to trade more with Asia. They became interested in the Hawaiian Islands. These beautiful islands also are called Hawaii. Hawaii is over two thousand miles from California. The weather is

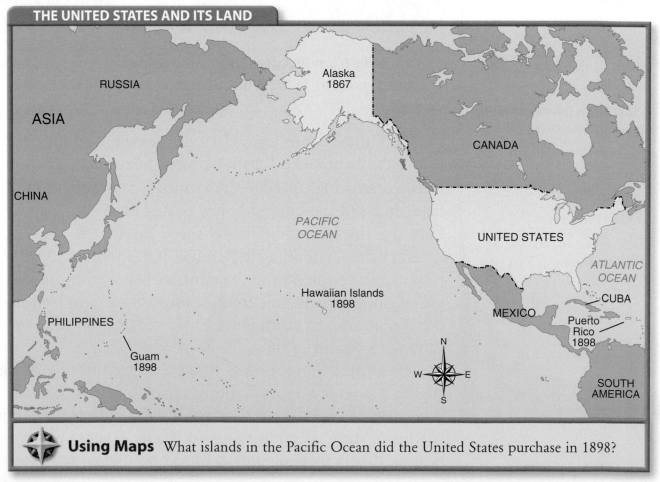

THE UNITED STATES AND ITS LAND

Using Maps What islands in the Pacific Ocean did the United States purchase in 1898?

The Hawaiian Islands have warm weather and good land for farming. ▷

Queen Liliuokalani

often sunny and warm. The land is good for farming.

In the 1820s many Americans went to Hawaii to build churches. Other Americans went to live and work in Hawaii. They grew sugar cane on large plantations. They wanted Hawaii to be part of the United States.

Hawaii was ruled by Queen Liliuokalani. She wanted Hawaii to be an independent country. In 1893 Americans sent ships, soldiers and guns to Hawaii. They forced the queen to end her rule. Hawaii became a republic in 1894. Then in 1898 the United States Congress decided to make Hawaii part of the United States. In 1959 Congress voted for Hawaii to become the fiftieth state.

The United States still had not finished growing. Cuba and Puerto Rico are island countries. Find them on the map on page 162. Both Cuba and Puerto Rico belonged to Spain.

The people of Cuba wanted their country to be free. They fought against Spain. Many Americans wanted the United States to help the people in Cuba fight for freedom. In 1898 the United States sent a **battleship**, the *Maine*, to Cuba. The ship blew up, and 260 Americans were killed. No one knew why the battleship blew up.

163

Soldiers from the United States fought Spanish soldiers in Cuba.

Raising the American flag on Cuba

Many angry Americans blamed Spain. They thought that Spanish soldiers had blown up the *Maine*. Today we know that the Spanish did not blow up the *Maine*.

In 1898 the United States decided to fight against Spain to help the Cubans become free. This war was called the **Spanish-American War**. The United States won every battle. American soldiers fought the Spanish in Cuba. American soldiers captured Puerto Rico from Spain.

Americans also fought the Spanish in the Pacific Ocean. Guam and the Philippines are island nations in the Pacific Ocean. Guam and the Philippines had belonged to Spain. American soldiers helped Guam and the Philippines become free from Spain. After a few months, Spain surrendered to the United States.

At the end of the war, Spain gave Cuba, Puerto Rico, Guam, and the Philippines to the United States. Cuba became an independent country in 1902. The Philippines belonged to the United States for almost 50 years. Today the Philippines is an independent country. Guam and Puerto Rico belong to the United States, but they are not states. The people of Guam and Puerto Rico are American citizens.

The United States had a lot of new land in 1898. It had bought some land and fought for other land. Other countries knew that the United States had become a very strong nation.

Using What You've Learned

Read and Remember

Choose the Answer Write the correct answers on your paper.

1. What do we call the idea that one country should rule other countries?
   imperialism   reconstruction   government

2. What country sold Alaska to the United States?
   Cuba   France   Russia

3. What did people rush to find in Alaska after 1896?
   furs   gold   snow

4. When did Hawaii become a state of the United States?
   1867   1898   1959

5. Where did people fight against Spain for freedom?
   Hawaii   Canada   Cuba

6. What was the *Maine*?
   a battleship   a train   a bridge

7. What country did the United States fight against in 1898?
   Great Britain   Russia   Spain

8. What island nation does not belong to the United States today?
   Guam   the Philippines   Puerto Rico

9. Where are people American citizens today?
   Guam and Puerto Rico   Cuba and the Philippines   Spain and Russia

Think and Apply

Fact or Opinion Write **F** on your paper for each fact below and on page 166. Write **O** for each opinion. You should find three sentences that are opinions.

1. The United States bought Alaska for $7,200,000.

2. Alaska is a big unfriendly icebox.

3. There is oil in Alaska.

4. Hawaii is over two thousand miles from California.

5 It was wrong for the United States to force Queen Liliuokalani to end her rule in Hawaii.

6 In 1898 American soldiers captured Puerto Rico from Spain.

7 Spain should not rule Guam and Puerto Rico.

8 Cuba became an independent nation in 1902.

Sequencing Events Number your paper from 1 to 5. Write the sentences to show the correct order.

Hawaii became a republic in 1894.

Many Americans were killed when the *Maine* blew up.

In 1867 the United States bought Alaska.

Alaska became the forty-ninth state in 1959.

The Spanish-American War began and ended.

Skill Builder

Using Map Directions Study the map on page 162. Choose a word in blue print to finish each sentence below. On your paper, write the word you choose.

Cuba   **west**   **southeast**   **northwest**   **Alaska**

1 The Hawaiian Islands are south of _____ .

2 The Philippines is _____ of Guam.

3 _____ is east of Mexico.

4 Alaska is near the _____ part of Canada.

5 Puerto Rico and Cuba are _____ of the United States.

Journal Writing

Many Americans did not think the United States should buy Alaska from Russia. Write a paragraph in your journal that tells why Alaska was worth buying.

CHAPTER 25

Find Out

❶ How have the electric light bulb and the telephone changed the United States?

❷ How did Jan Matzeliger change the way shoes were made?

❸ Why was the assembly line an important invention?

NEW WORDS

invention
skyscraper
assembly line
conveyor belt

PEOPLE & PLACES

Alexander Graham Bell
Scotland
Thomas Edison
Jan Matzeliger
Elisha Graves Otis
Orville Wright
Wilbur Wright
Kitty Hawk
Henry Ford
Garrett Morgan

New Inventions Change the United States

Thomas Edison invented many things, including the electric light bulb.

Two hundred years ago, Americans had very few machines to help them with their work. There were no telephones, cars, or electric lights. People traveled on horses. People used candles to light their homes. Americans learned to make new machines. A new machine is called an **invention**. The inventions made life easier and better for people.

Alexander Graham Bell made, or invented, the first telephone. He was an immigrant from Scotland. Bell was a teacher of children who were deaf. He taught them how to speak.

Alexander Graham Bell wanted to make a machine so that people who were far apart could talk to one another.

167

Alexander Graham Bell worked for years on his invention, the telephone. ▷

Thomas Edison's light bulb

Jan Matzeliger

Bell worked on his machine for two years. In 1876 his machine worked. Bell had made the world's first telephone. In a few years, there were telephones in most American cities.

A long time ago, American homes and streets were dark at night because there were no electric lights. Thomas Edison changed that. He invented the first electric light bulb. Thomas Edison started working on it in 1879. Finally, after many months, his bulb worked. It gave off light for a short time. Edison wanted his electric bulbs to burn for a long time. He continued to make different light bulbs. He learned how to make better bulbs that burned longer. The electric light bulb made our houses and streets bright at night.

A long time ago, people made most shoes by hand. Shoes were made to fit each person's feet. Jan Matzeliger changed the way shoes were made. In 1882 Matzeliger invented a special machine that could make shoes of many different sizes. Shoes could be made quickly in factories with Matzeliger's machine. Today most shoes are made in shoe factories with the kind of machine Matzeliger invented.

Before 1885 most buildings in the United States had only a few floors. In 1885 the first **skyscraper**, or very tall building, was built in the United States. This tall building had ten floors. No other building had so many floors!

The first American skyscraper was built in 1885.

Learning from Pictures The Wright brothers' airplane first flew at Kitty Hawk, North Carolina. How does this airplane compare with those today?

Americans were able to start building taller skyscrapers because of an earlier invention. That invention was the elevator. In the 1850s Elisha Graves Otis invented an elevator that moved people from one floor to another. Before long, many more skyscrapers were built.

Long ago people dreamed about traveling through the sky. Two brothers, Orville and Wilbur Wright, proved that people could fly in airplanes. The brothers spent two years building an airplane. At last they were ready to fly. They took their airplane to Kitty Hawk, North Carolina. On December 17, 1903, the Wright brothers flew through the sky! Their plane flew for less than one minute. After that, people began building better planes. They built planes that could fly for many hours.

For hundreds of years, people traveled on horses. Henry Ford helped change the way Americans traveled. In 1896 Ford made one of the first cars in the United States. Then in 1903 he started a factory that made cars. It was called the Ford Motor Company.

The assembly line in the Ford factory helped to make cars quickly. ➤

Henry Ford

Garrett Morgan

In 1913 Ford invented the **assembly line** to make cars in his factory. In the Ford factory, a moving **conveyor belt** carried the body of each car past the workers. Each worker put one part on the body of each car. Each worker stayed in one place and did the same job all day. In less than two hours, a car was put together.

Cars were made very quickly on the assembly line. Because cars were made quickly, they were not very expensive. In 1916 a new Ford car cost only $360. Millions of Americans bought Henry Ford's cars.

Every year more and more Americans bought cars. Since there were many cars on the street, traffic became a problem. Drivers did not know when to stop and when to go. Police officers directed some of the traffic, but they could not direct all of it. In 1923 a man named Garrett Morgan solved this problem. He invented the first traffic light in the United States.

People have better lives because of inventions like the telephone, the electric light bulb, and the traffic light. The assembly line changed the United States. Today factories everywhere make products quickly by using assembly lines. Inventions have improved life in the United States.

Using What You've Learned

Read and Remember

Choose a Word Choose a word in blue print to finish each sentence. On your paper, write the word you choose.

telephone	skyscraper	Wright
invention	shoes	Edison

1 A new machine is called an _____ .

2 Alexander Graham Bell invented the _____ , which allowed people who were far apart to talk to one another.

3 Thomas _____ tried to make electric light bulbs that would burn for a long time.

4 Jan Matzeliger invented a machine to make _____ quickly in factories.

5 In 1885 the very first tall building, or _____ , was built in the United States.

6 The _____ brothers flew the first airplane in 1903.

Using Graphic Organizers

Sequencing Events Read each of the sentences below. Copy and then complete the graphic organizer by listing the events in the correct order.

In 1896 Henry Ford built his first car.

In 1923 Garrett Morgan invented the traffic light to solve traffic problems.

Ford invented a way to make cars on an assembly line in the Ford factory.

For hundreds of years, people traveled on horses.

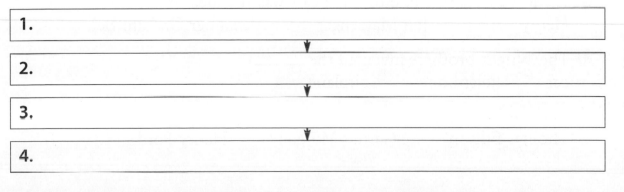

1.

2.

3.

4.

Skill Builder

Reading a Chart A **chart** lists a group of facts. Charts help you learn facts quickly. Read this chart to learn how inventions changed America.

Inventions Change America			
Inventor	Invention	Date	How the Invention Changed America
Alexander Graham Bell	telephone	1876	People who are far apart can talk to one another.
Thomas Edison	electric light bulb	1879	Electric lights are used to light homes, streets, schools, and offices.
Jan Matzeliger	shoe-making machine	1882	Shoes are made in shoe factories and sold in shoe stores.
Orville and Wilbur Wright	airplane	1903	People can travel by airplane.
Henry Ford	assembly line to make cars quickly	1913	People travel in cars instead of on horses.
Garrett Morgan	traffic light	1923	Traffic lights control traffic.

On your paper, write the word or words that finish each sentence.

1. To learn how the inventions changed America, read the chart from _____ .
   left to right   top to bottom   the middle

2. To learn information about Thomas Edison, read the chart from _____ .
   left to right   top to bottom   bottom to top

3. Using an assembly line to build cars was the idea of _____ .
   Henry Ford   Jan Matzeliger   Alexander Graham Bell

4. The Wright brothers invented the _____ .
   car   telephone   airplane

5. The traffic light was invented by _____ .
   Thomas Edison   Garrett Morgan   Henry Ford

Review

Study the time line on this page. Then use the words in blue print to finish the story. On your paper, write the words you choose.

Homestead Act	Reconstruction	Alaska
reservations	Hawaii	slaves
imperialism	Great Plains	Edison

During __(1)__ , southern states rejoined the United States. Congress passed three amendments to help African Americans. The Thirteenth Amendment said no one in the United States could own __(2)__ .

In 1862 Congress passed the __(3)__ . This law gave settlers free land on the __(4)__ . The settlers had fights with the Native Americans who lived on the Great Plains. Many Native Americans were forced to move to __(5)__ .

Many Americans wanted the United States to own more land because they believed in __(6)__ . In 1867 the United States bought __(7)__ . Then in 1898 __(8)__ became part of the United States.

In 1879 Thomas __(9)__ invented the electric light bulb. In 1882 Jan Matzeliger invented a new machine for making shoes. Inventions improved life in the United States.

| The Civil War ends. Reconstruction begins. | The first railroad across the United States is finished. | Thomas Edison invents the electric light bulb. | Hawaii becomes part of the United States. The United States wins the Spanish-American War. |
| 1865 | 1869 | 1879 | 1898 |

| 1860 | 1870 | 1880 | 1890 | 1900 | 1910 |

| 1862 | 1867 | | 1882 | 1903 | |
| Congress passes the Homestead Act. | The United States buys Alaska from Russia. | | Jan Matzeliger invents a machine to make shoes in factories. | The Wright brothers fly the first airplane. Henry Ford starts a car factory. | |

The United States Becomes a Modern Nation

Imagine what it was like to move to the United States in the year 1900. You might travel on a ship crowded with people. When you arrive, you might not know where to live or work. You might not know how to speak English. But you had come to the United States with a dream of a better life.

The United States was becoming a modern nation. Millions of immigrants arrived between 1840 and 1920. Businesses also changed. A small group of people controlled the country's largest businesses. Millions of people became factory workers. Cities grew larger. Many Americans worked to solve problems in the nation.

Read to Learn

◗ Who helped the new immigrants have a better life in the United States?

◗ Who were the people that controlled the oil and steel businesses?

◗ What important changes were made in American life?

◗ What was it like to live in the United States as it became a modern nation?

Oil is found in Pennsylvania.
1859

1840

1860

1863
John D. Rockefeller builds his first oil refinery.

Susan B. Anthony is arrested for trying to vote.
1872

Samuel Gompers helps start the American Federation of Labor (AFL).
1886

Andrew Carnegie owns most of America's steel companies.
1899

W.E.B. Du Bois helps start the NAACP.
1909

1880

1900

1920

1889
Jane Addams starts Hull House.

1906
Theodore Roosevelt helps get laws passed for safe meat, food, and medicine.

1911
The Supreme Court breaks up the Standard Oil Company.

HESTER ST.

175

Find Out

❶ Why did people want to come to America?

❷ Which groups of people came to America?

❸ What was it like to be an immigrant in America?

NEW WORDS

Great Irish Famine
reporter

PEOPLE & PLACES

Irish
Japan
Chicago, Illinois
Greece
Jews
Jacob Riis
Denmark

Starting a New Life in America

Learning from Pictures How do you think immigrants from Europe felt when they came to the United States to start a new life?

For hundreds of years, people have moved to America from many other countries. More than 25 million immigrants came to America from 1865 to 1915. Native Americans are the only Americans who lived in America long before other immigrants came.

Before 1880 most immigrants came to America from Great Britain, Germany, and other countries in northern Europe. Some people came to America for freedom of religion. Others came because they did not like the laws of their country. Most people came because they were poor. They thought they could earn more money in America.

In the 1840s many people in Ireland were starving. There was not enough food in Ireland. This time in Ireland became known as the **Great Irish Famine**. Thousands of Irish people came to the United States. They were hungry

ILLINOIS

Chicago

and poor. In America they helped build railroads. They worked in factories.

Thousands of immigrants from China came to the United States during the California gold rush. Many Chinese became miners. Others helped build railroads in the West. Many Chinese immigrants settled in California.

People from Japan also came to the United States. Most people from Japan settled in California and the West. Many of them worked on farms.

Many Mexicans in the Southwest became American citizens after the Mexican War ended in 1848. After 1880 more Mexicans moved to the United States. Others came after a war began in Mexico in 1910. Many Mexicans worked as farmers or miners in the United States. At first most Mexicans lived in the Southwest. Later, many moved to Chicago, Illinois, and to other large cities.

African Americans were different from other groups of immigrants. Beginning in 1619, many Africans were forced to come to America as slaves. Soon there were many more African slaves in America. Most slaves lived in the South. They became free after the Civil War ended. After the war thousands of African Americans moved to the North and to the West.

▲ **Many immigrants helped build our country's railroads.**

177

"Mama, America is wonderful. You would love it here. There are so many opportunities [chances] here."

—Josephine Roche, a young immigrant girl from Greece.

From the 1880s to the 1920s, other immigrant groups came to America. Many came from southern and eastern parts of Europe. Millions of people left Italy, Greece, Russia, and Poland. They did not have enough food in Europe. They traveled to America on large, crowded ships. Most of these immigrants were very poor.

Many Jewish immigrants came to the United States from Russia and Poland. The governments of those countries allowed people to kill Jews because of their religion. In the United States, Jewish immigrants were safe. They had freedom of religion.

Most of the immigrants from Italy, Greece, Russia, and Poland lived in large cities in the United States. Many of them settled in New York City. The immigrants had many problems in the United States. They had very little money. They had to learn to speak English. They lived in small, crowded houses. Many immigrants worked in dirty factories. Often they were paid very little money for their hard work. Many of their children had to work.

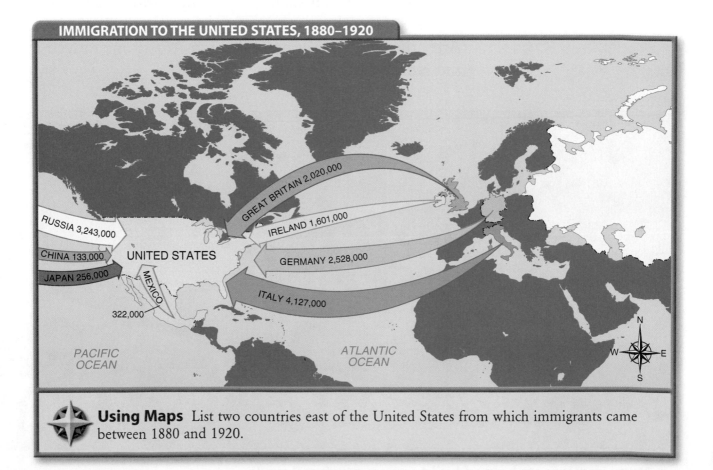

IMMIGRATION TO THE UNITED STATES, 1880–1920

RUSSIA 3,243,000
CHINA 133,000
JAPAN 256,000
UNITED STATES
MEXICO
322,000
GREAT BRITAIN 2,020,000
IRELAND 1,601,000
GERMANY 2,528,000
ITALY 4,127,000
PACIFIC OCEAN
ATLANTIC OCEAN

Using Maps List two countries east of the United States from which immigrants came between 1880 and 1920.

Immigrant families in New York City often lived crowded together. Children had to play in the streets. ➤

Jacob Riis

Jacob Riis took this photograph of immigrant children sleeping outside.

Immigrant children went to free schools in America. Their parents studied English in schools at night. Schools helped the immigrants become Americans. After immigrants lived in the United States for five years, they could become American citizens. Then they were allowed to vote.

Jacob Riis was an immigrant from Denmark. He became a newspaper **reporter** in New York City. Jacob Riis loved being an American. He wanted to help the many poor immigrants in American cities.

Riis wrote newspaper stories and a book about the new immigrants. He took photographs for his stories. His pictures showed the small, crowded houses where immigrants lived. His stories said that there were no parks where immigrant children could play. People learned about immigrant life from Riis's work. They wanted to help the immigrants. Better houses were built. Parks and playgrounds were built.

Millions of immigrants helped build America. Some became store owners and farmers. Others became government leaders. Some immigrants became teachers and doctors. Many immigrants worked in factories or built our railroads. Some immigrants became very rich.

Today our laws allow several hundred thousand immigrants to come to America every year. This year and every year, thousands of people from other countries will start a new life in America.

Using Geography Themes

Place: New York City, New York

The theme of place tells what makes an area different from all other areas. Place tells about an area's land, plants, and weather. It also tells about an area's people and what they built there.

Read the paragraphs about New York City. Study the photo and map.

New York City, New York, is a busy port on the Atlantic Ocean. Since 1790 the city has had the largest population in the United States. It has five **boroughs**, or parts. One borough is Manhattan.

From 1880 to 1920, more immigrants arrived in New York City than at any other time. They sailed on ships into the city's harbor. Many immigrants saw the Statue of Liberty as they arrived. The statue tells the world that the United States is a land of freedom.

Many immigrants settled in different neighborhoods of New York City. Many Italian immigrants lived in an area now called Little Italy. Jewish immigrants lived in a nearby neighborhood. Chinese immigrants settled in an area now called Chinatown. These neighborhoods help make New York City a very special place.

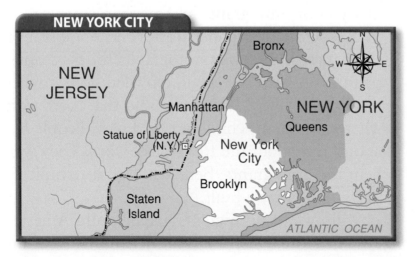

On your paper, write the answer to each question.

1. Since what year has the city had the nation's largest population?
2. What does the Statue of Liberty tell the world?
3. What are the names of two of New York City's neighborhoods?
4. Look at the map. What are the names of the city's five boroughs?
5. By what ocean is New York City?

Using What You've Learned

Read and Remember

Find the Answers Find the sentences that tell why people came to America. On your paper, write the sentences you find. You should find two sentences.

1 Native Americans lived in America long before other immigrants came.

2 Some people wanted freedom of religion.

3 Some people did not like the laws of their own country.

4 Many immigrants worked in dirty factories and earned little money.

5 There were no parks where immigrant children could play.

Using Graphic Organizers

Concept Web Read the words in each group. Decide how they are alike. Copy the chart three times. Then complete each chart by choosing the best title in blue print for each group. Write the title on the lines.

**Immigrant Life
Jacob Riis**

Chinese Immigrants

1 came during the gold rush
settled in California
helped build railroads

3 immigrant from Denmark
newspaper reporter
wrote stories about immigrants

2 studied English in schools
children worked in factories
crowded homes

Journal Writing

Immigrants came to the United States to find a better life. But many immigrants had problems in America. Write a paragraph in your journal that tells about problems that immigrants had.

181

Skill Builder

Reading a Bar Graph This bar graph shows how many immigrants came to the United States from five countries in 1900. Study the bar graph.

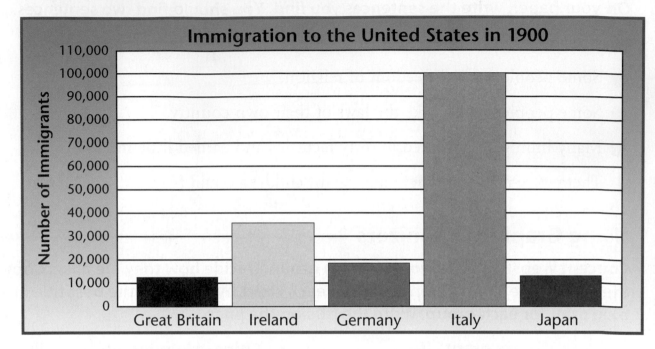

On your paper, write the number, word, or words that answer each question.

1 From what country did the largest number of immigrants come in 1900?
Ireland   Germany   Italy

2 What country had about the same number of immigrants as Great Britain?
Ireland   Japan   Italy

3 There were more German immigrants than what other group of immigrants?
Irish   British   Italian

4 About how many immigrants came from Italy?
10,000   50,000   100,000

5 How many immigrants came from Ireland?
more than 30,000   less than 30,000   exactly 30,000

6 There were fewer Irish immigrants than what other group of immigrants?
Italian   Japanese   German

Big Business Grows Bigger

Find Out

❶ What big business did Andrew Carnegie control?

❷ What big business did John D. Rockefeller control?

❸ Why did Congress write new laws about big business?

NEW WORDS

big business
ore
steel
steel mills
millionaire
drilled
oil refineries

PEOPLE & PLACES

Andrew Carnegie
Minnesota
John D. Rockefeller

Making steel was one big business that changed life in America.

Life in the United States changed after the Civil War. More and more Americans lived and worked in cities. Millions of Americans worked for factories, railroads, stores, and other kinds of businesses.

Sometimes one business owned many factories or smaller businesses. This is called **big business**. Sometimes one person would control a very large business. Railroads were an example of big business. At one time, one man controlled most of the railroads in the United States. He could decide how much money to charge people to use the railroads.

Before the Civil War, most machines were made of a metal called iron. Railroad tracks were made of iron. Iron is made from an **ore** found in the earth. Iron is not very strong. A man in Great Britain found a way to make iron

183

Andrew Carnegie

stronger. This new, stronger iron was called **steel**. Today railroad tracks and cars are made of steel.

Andrew Carnegie was an immigrant from Scotland. He moved to America when he was a young boy. When he grew up, he built factories in Pennsylvania for making steel. These factories are called **steel mills**. He called his steel mills the Carnegie Steel Company. Andrew Carnegie became very rich. He used his money to buy other steel companies. By 1899 Carnegie owned most of the steel mills in the United States. He became a **millionaire**.

Andrew Carnegie also owned railroads and ships for sending his steel to different places. He owned land in Minnesota where much of the iron for making steel was found. Carnegie was the "steel king."

In 1859 oil was found deep in the earth in Pennsylvania. Soon people **drilled** for oil all over the United States. Oil had to be cleaned before it could be used. Oil was cleaned in factories called **oil refineries**. In 1863 John D. Rockefeller built his first oil refinery. His business did well. He used his money to build more refineries. Rockefeller called his business the Standard Oil Company.

John D. Rockefeller sold his oil for less money than other oil companies. The other companies tried to sell

Learning from Pictures The steel mills of the Carnegie Steel Company were large and had many workers. What do you think it was like to live and work near a steel mill? ➤

John D. Rockefeller

their oil for less money, too. The other companies soon were losing money. Rockefeller bought the other oil companies. Soon Rockefeller owned almost all the oil companies in America. He also became a millionaire.

Andrew Carnegie and John D. Rockefeller paid their workers very low salaries. They did not treat their workers well. But they did use their money to help other people. They gave money to schools and churches. Andrew Carnegie used his money to build many libraries. He built more than 2,500 libraries. People still use many of the libraries that Carnegie started.

The big businesses of oil, steel, and railroads helped the United States become a nation with tall buildings and many factories. But many Americans thought that it was not right for a few companies to control all the oil, steel, and railroads in the United States. It was not right for a few people to decide how much Americans should pay for their oil, steel, and railroads. New laws were written in Congress. These laws said that a few companies could not control all the big businesses in the United States.

▲ **Tall wooden towers were used to drill deep into the ground to get to the oil.**

Using What You've Learned

Read and Remember

True or False On your paper, write **T** for each sentence that is true.
Write **F** for each sentence that is false.

1. When one business owns many factories or small businesses, it is called big business.

2. In 1859 steel was found deep in the earth in Pennsylvania.

3. Oil is cleaned in a refinery.

4. John D. Rockefeller owned almost all the oil companies in the United States.

5. Andrew Carnegie gave money to build libraries.

Using Graphic Organizers

Cause and Effect Read each of the sentences under *Cause* below. Then read
each of the sentences under *Effect*. Copy and complete the graphic organizer
to match each cause on the left with an effect on the right.

Cause

1. Steel is stronger than iron, so _____

2. Rockefeller and Carnegie wanted to help people, so _____

3. People said a few companies should not control all the oil, steel, and railroads in America, so _____

Effect

a. they gave money to schools, churches, and libraries.

b. Congress wrote laws to prevent a few companies from owning all the big businesses.

c. it is used for making railroad tracks and cars.

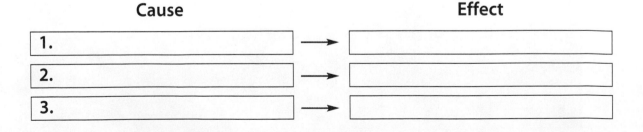

Cause		Effect
1.	→	
2.	→	
3.	→	

Skill Builder

Using a Map Key to Read a Resource Map A **resource map** shows where resources are found. Some resource maps show where natural resources are found. Natural resources are things we get from the earth. The resource map below shows where some natural resources are found that are used in making oil and steel. The **map key** tells you what each symbol on the resource map means. Study the map and the map key.

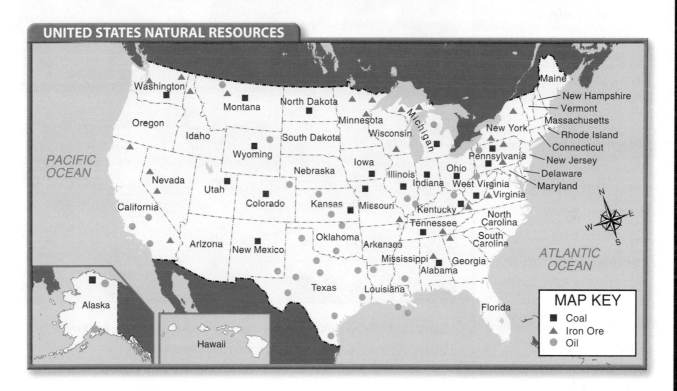

UNITED STATES NATURAL RESOURCES

MAP KEY
■ Coal
▲ Iron Ore
● Oil

On your paper, write the answer to each question.

1. What natural resource is shown as squares on the map?

2. What are three states that have coal?

3. What are three states that have iron ore?

4. Which natural resource does Texas have?

5. Which natural resource is found in New York?

6. What is one state that has coal, iron ore, and oil?

7. Which natural resource is found in California but not in Nevada?

Unions Help the Working People

Find Out

❶ What problems did factory workers have in the late 1800s and early 1900s?

❷ How did labor unions help workers?

❸ What kinds of laws were written to help workers?

NEW WORDS

working conditions
employers
labor unions
strike
American Federation of Labor (AFL)

PEOPLE & PLACES

Samuel Gompers
Mary Harris Jones
Lewis Hine

Many people worked long hours in dangerous factories. Many factory workers were immigrants.

Should small children work all day in dirty factories? Should factory workers work 12 to 15 hours every day? In the late 1800s and early 1900s, workers began to say no to these questions. They wanted better **working conditions**.

After the Civil War, more and more Americans became factory workers in cities. Some had been poor farmers. Many factory workers were immigrants. They often worked at factory jobs that paid very low salaries.

Life was hard for factory workers. They had to work 12 to 15 hours each day in dirty, dangerous factories. Most workers could not earn enough money for their families. Their young children had to work in factories, too. These children could not go to school. They had no time to

Learning from Pictures What was it like for children to work in factories?

play. Factory workers were afraid to ask their bosses, or **employers**, for more money. They were afraid of losing their jobs. Then they would have no money for their families at all.

Factory workers decided to help themselves. They started **labor unions**. A labor union is a group of workers who work together to make their jobs better. A union might ask for better salaries from the employer. It might ask for shorter working days or safer factories. The employer can say no to the union. Then the union members can decide to stop working until they get what they want. This is called a **strike**.

When union workers will not work because they want better salaries or other changes, we say that they are "on strike." Factory owners do not like strikes. Their factories cannot make goods when workers are on strike. Often employers will agree to what the workers want because the employers do not want their workers on strike. Labor unions have helped workers get better salaries and better working conditions.

Samuel Gompers was a famous union leader. He was a Jewish immigrant from England. Gompers started working in a factory when he was 13 years old because his family was very poor. Later he became a leader of the union in his factory.

189

Samuel Gompers

Samuel Gompers felt that workers all over the United States needed unions. He felt that new laws were needed to help working people. Gompers wanted laws that would not allow children to work. He wanted a law that said workers should work only eight hours a day. Many times the government would not allow workers to go on strike. Gompers wanted laws that would allow strikes.

In 1886 Gompers helped start the **American Federation of Labor (AFL)**. Many unions joined the AFL. Gompers was the president of the AFL for 37 years. He and the AFL tried to have new laws made to help workers. Samuel Gompers and the AFL helped unions go on strike for better salaries.

Most businesses did not want their workers to join unions. Many employers said they did not have enough money to pay better salaries. Employers refused to talk to union leaders. Slowly the AFL changed things. After many years employers learned to work together with union leaders. Workers worked fewer hours and were paid better salaries. As the years passed, more workers joined unions.

 **PRIMARY SOURCE**

"I want to live for one thing alone—to leave a better labor movement in America and in the world than I found it when I entered, as a boy."

—*Samuel Gompers*

Union workers tried to get better salaries by going on strike. A "scab" is someone who works when the union is on strike.

Photographs showed Americans the problems children had in factories like this coal factory. ➤

"Mother" Jones

Lewis Hine

Mary Harris Jones was an Irish immigrant who helped factory workers and miners. Many people called her "Mother" Jones because she was more than seventy years old. She traveled around the United States and helped miners start unions. She told them to go on strike for better salaries. She told factory workers to strike for shorter working days. People read about "Mother" Jones in their newspapers. They were told that new laws to help workers were needed.

By 1915 almost two million children were working in mines and factories. They were paid very little money. They had to work all day. Many children had to use dangerous machines.

Lewis Hine wanted to help the children who worked in factories. Hine was a photographer. He went into factories and took photographs. His pictures showed how terrible it was for children to be factory workers. His pictures were published in magazines and books. Many Americans learned from Hine's photographs about the problems children had. As time passed, new laws were written. These laws said children could not be factory workers.

Today we have many laws that help working people. Our laws allow union workers to go on strike. Most workers work only eight hours a day. Today millions of workers belong to labor unions.

Using What You've Learned

Read and Remember

Finish the Sentence On your paper, write the word or words that finish each sentence.

1 To get better salaries, factory workers started _____ .
labor unions   schools   new factories

2 Union workers who stop working because they want more money are _____ .
on vacation   on strike   on the job

3 In 1886 Samuel Gompers helped start the American Federation of _____ .
Labor   Miners   Factories

4 Lewis Hine used _____ to help children who worked in factories.
photographs   strikes   salaries

Think and Apply

Drawing Conclusions Read each pair of sentences. Then look in the box for the conclusion you can make. On your paper, write the letter of the conclusion.

1 Factory workers wanted safe factories.
Factory owners would not make changes when the workers asked.

2 Union workers sometimes asked for better salaries.
The employers did not always listen to the labor union leaders.

3 The AFL tried to have new laws made to help workers.
The AFL helped employers and union leaders work together.

4 "Mother" Jones helped miners start unions.
Lewis Hine took photographs of children in factories.

Conclusions

a. People wanted to help workers have better working conditions.

b. Factory workers started labor unions to help them get safe factories.

c. Union workers went on strike to get better salaries.

d. The AFL helped make life better for workers.

Skill Builder

Reading a Line Graph A **line graph** shows how something changes over time. The line graph on this page shows how many workers belonged to unions from 1900 to 2000. Study the line graph.

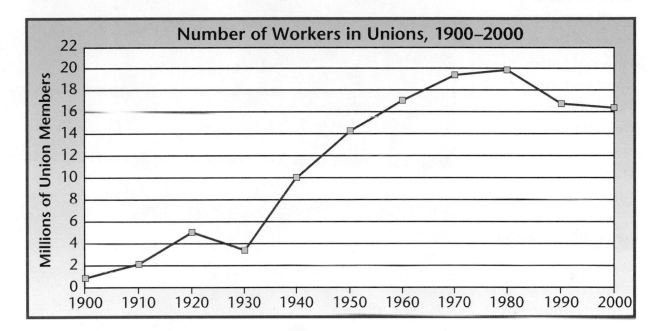

On your paper, write the dates, words, or numbers that answer each question.

1. The numbers on the left stand for how many union members?
   hundreds   thousands   millions

2. In which year did the smallest number of people belong to unions?
   1900   1930   1940

3. In which year did the largest number of workers belong to unions?
   1910   1930   1980

4. In 1920 about how many people belonged to unions?
   1 million   5 million   10 million

5. From 1930 to 1980, what happened to the number of people in unions?
   they became larger   they became smaller   they stayed about the same

6. From 1980 to 2000, what happened to the number of people in unions?
   they became larger   they became smaller   they stayed about the same

Women Work for a Better America

Find Out

❶ How did Susan B. Anthony and Jane Addams work to make America better?

❷ How did Lillian Wald and Janie Porter Barrett help people?

❸ How did Alice Hamilton help factory workers?

NEW WORDS

election
arrested
settlement house
lead
lead poisoning

PEOPLE & PLACES

Susan B. Anthony
Jane Addams
Hull House
Janie Porter Barrett
Locust Street Social Settlement House
Lillian Wald
Henry Street Settlement House
Alice Hamilton

Learning from Pictures How do you think Jane Addams is helping these children?

How can women get the same rights as men? How can we help new immigrants in our country? How can we help men, women, and children who work all day in factories? Many people asked these questions in the late 1800s. Six women found ways to help many Americans.

Susan B. Anthony worked for women's rights. She wanted women to have the right to vote in an **election**. She wanted women to be paid the same salaries as men were for the same job. She traveled with Elizabeth Cady Stanton throughout the United States. They made many speeches for women's rights.

In 1872 Susan B. Anthony tried to vote in an election. She was **arrested**. But Anthony and Stanton continued to

Susan B. Anthony

Janie Porter Barrett

Hull House was a settlement house in Chicago, Illinois.

work together for an amendment that would allow women to vote. Stanton died in 1902. Anthony died in 1906, fourteen years before a new amendment gave women the right to vote.

Jane Addams helped people in a neighborhood of immigrants in Chicago, Illinois. In 1889 she bought a large old house called Hull House. She bought Hull House with her own money and with money from other people. Addams helped Hull House become a **settlement house**. A settlement house is a house where workers help the people of a poor neighborhood.

Hull House helped the people of the neighborhood in many ways. Hull House workers took care of small children while their mothers were at work. Immigrants learned to speak English at Hull House. Addams helped them become American citizens. Addams started clubs and a summer camp for children. She started the first playground in Chicago.

Jane Addams worked to get new laws that would help immigrants, factory workers, and children. As time passed, new laws were written that helped these people.

People in other cities wanted to start settlement houses. Janie Porter Barrett was a teacher. In 1890 Barrett started the Locust Street Social Settlement House in Virginia. This house had clubs and classes for African

Lillian Wald started a kindergarten at the Henry Street Settlement House.

Lillian Wald

Alice Hamilton

Americans. Later, Barrett started a new school to help African American girls who had been in jail.

Lillian Wald was a nurse who started the Henry Street Settlement House in 1895. This house was in a crowded neighborhood in New York City. The Henry Street Settlement House had a kindergarten, clubs, English classes, and a library.

Lillian Wald also helped sick people. She thought nurses should visit sick people at home if they were too poor or too sick to go to a hospital. She started a visiting nurse program in New York City. Many nurses began helping sick people at home. Lillian Wald also thought there should be nurses in schools to help sick children. Other people liked Wald's idea. Soon there were nurses in New York's schools.

Alice Hamilton was a doctor who helped factory workers. She visited many paint factories. Paint had **lead** in it. Hamilton proved that many workers in paint factories had **lead poisoning**. Lead poisoning made workers very weak. Many of these workers died. Hamilton taught factory owners how to make their factories safer. She taught them how to keep the factory air clean.

These six women and many other people worked very hard to make important changes in the United States. They wanted to make the United States a better place to live.

Using Primary Sources

Twenty Years at Hull House

Jane Addams wrote a book called *Twenty Years at Hull House*. In it she told about her life and work at Hull House. She wrote that Hull House was in a neighborhood of poor immigrants. She also wrote about the problem of **child labor**, or working children. Many young children had to work all day in factories or mines. The paragraphs below are from Addams's book.

occupied
lived in

bear
put up with

employed
used

> *Between Halsted Street and the river live about ten thousand Italians. . . . To the south . . . are many Germans, and side streets are given . . . to Polish and Russian Jews. . . .*
>
> *The houses . . . were . . . built for one family and are now **occupied** by several. . . . Many houses have no water supply save the faucet in the back yard, there are no fire escapes. . . .*
>
> *Our very first Christmas at Hull House, . . . a number of little girls refused the candy which was offered them . . . , saying simply that they "worked in a candy factory and could not **bear** the sight of it." We discovered that for six weeks they had worked from seven in the morning until nine at night. . . .*
>
> *I remember a little girl of four who pulled out . . . threads hour after hour, sitting on a stool at the feet of her . . . mother. . . . The only child labor law in Illinois . . . had been . . . [for] children **employed** in mines.*

On your paper, write the answer to each question.

1. Which groups of immigrants lived near Hull House?

2. What were some problems with the houses in the neighborhood?

3. Why wouldn't the little girls eat candy at Christmas?

4. What hours did the little girls work?

5. **Think and Write** How do you think Hull House made life better for children who had worked in factories?

Using What You've Learned

Read and Remember

Who Am I? Read each sentence. Then look at the names in blue print. Decide which person might have said the sentence. On your paper, write the name of the person you choose.

Alice Hamilton	Jane Addams	Susan B. Anthony
Janie Porter Barrett	Lillian Wald	Elizabeth Cady Stanton

1. "I gave speeches about women's rights with Susan B. Anthony."

2. "I was arrested when I tried to vote."

3. "I started Hull House and worked for new laws to help immigrants, workers, and children."

4. "I started the Locust Street Social Settlement House to help African Americans in Virginia."

5. "I started the visiting nurse program in New York City."

6. "I worked to stop lead poisoning in paint factories."

Think and Apply

Fact or Opinion Write **F** on your paper for each fact below. Write **O** for each opinion. You should find three sentences that are opinions.

1. Susan B. Anthony should not have tried to vote in an election.

2. Immigrants learned to speak English at Hull House.

3. Jane Addams started the first playground in Chicago.

4. The Locust Street Social Settlement House had the best classes.

5. Janie Porter Barrett helped start a school for African American girls who had been in jail.

6. Lillian Wald started the Henry Street Settlement House in New York City.

7. Paint factories are too dangerous to work in.

Working for Reform After 1900

Find Out

1 Who were some of the progressive leaders in the early 1900s?

2 How did Theodore Roosevelt try to solve some of America's problems?

3 Why was the NAACP started?

NEW WORDS

progressives
inspected
muckrakers
industry
Pure Food and
 Drug Act
conservation
natural resources
acres
discrimination

PEOPLE & PLACES

Florence Kelley
Theodore Roosevelt
Ida Tarbell
Upton Sinclair
W.E.B. Du Bois

President Theodore Roosevelt (at left) and others worked to protect America's beautiful land.

Imagine being ten years old and working in a coal mine. Imagine eating bad meat from a dirty factory. Imagine having to go to a certain school because of the color of your skin. These were some of the problems Americans faced in the early 1900s. Many people wanted to make life better in the United States. These people who worked for reform were called **progressives**.

Florence Kelley was a progressive leader who worked to end child labor. She also helped factory workers. She helped Illinois pass a law in 1893 that said children under 14 could not work in factories. She **inspected** Illinois factories to make sure they were safe. Throughout the early 1900s, Kelley continued to help workers. She asked people to buy goods from safe factories that did not use child labor. She started groups that worked against child labor.

Florence Kelley

Theodore Roosevelt

Ida Tarbell wrote how Standard Oil used unfair ways to control America's oil business. ➤

She asked the Supreme Court to agree to a law for women workers. The law said employers could not make women work more than 10 hours a day.

In 1901 Theodore Roosevelt became President of the United States. He was a President who worked for reform. In 1902 a coal miners' union went on strike in Pennsylvania. The miners wanted better salaries. They wanted a shorter working day. President Roosevelt helped end the strike. He said the mine owners must work with the union to give the workers better working conditions. Theodore Roosevelt became the first President to help a labor union.

A group of progressives called **muckrakers** worked to correct problems in American life. They did this by writing about the problems in books, magazines, and newspapers. Americans became angry when they learned about the problems. They asked the government to make changes.

In Chapter 26 you read about Jacob Riis. Riis was a muckraker who tried to help poor immigrants. His book, photographs, and newspaper stories showed many problems in immigrant life.

Ida Tarbell was another muckraker. She wanted the government to do more to control big business. Tarbell wrote a book about John D. Rockefeller's Standard Oil Company. She wrote that Standard Oil used unfair ways to control most of the oil business in the United States.

Learning from Pictures Upton Sinclair's book told about problems in America's meat industry. What kind of factory conditions do you think these workers faced?

Upton Sinclair

In 1911 the Supreme Court ruled that it was against the law for the Standard Oil Company to control America's oil. Thirty-three smaller companies were formed from the Standard Oil Company. Standard Oil no longer controlled America's oil.

Upton Sinclair also was a muckraker. He wrote a book about problems in America's meat **industry**. The working conditions were terrible. The factories were very dirty. Rats ran everywhere, even on the meat. The factories sold bad meat and meat that had fallen on the dirty floors.

President Roosevelt decided new laws were needed to protect the country's meat. In 1906 a law was passed that said people from the government must check all meat factories. In that same year, Congress passed the **Pure Food and Drug Act**. This new law said all food and all medicine must be made in clean factories. The food and medicine must be safe for people to use.

President Roosevelt worked for reform in another way. He worked for **conservation**. Conservation means protecting **natural resources**. Natural resources are things we get from the earth. Animals, forests, metals, and water are some of our natural resources.

President Roosevelt believed Americans must protect their natural resources. He knew Americans were chopping down too many forests. He worked with

African American children had to go to separate schools from white children.

W.E.B. Du Bois

Congress to pass laws to protect the forests. After that, businesses had to obey laws about how and where trees could be cut down. Roosevelt helped protect about 150 million **acres** of land. People could enjoy America's beautiful land and water in new, large parks.

African Americans fought hard for reform. In 1909 W.E.B. Du Bois helped start a group called the National Association for the Advancement of Colored People, or NAACP. This group worked hard to end **discrimination** against African Americans in the United States. Discrimination is the unfair difference in the way people are treated. Discrimination against African Americans was present in many places. In the South it was difficult for African Americans to find work. African Americans could not vote. African American children were not allowed to go to the same schools as white children.

Jane Addams, Florence Kelley, and other important leaders worked with Du Bois. Du Bois and the NAACP worked to win equal rights for African Americans. It would be a long, hard struggle. You will read more about this struggle in Chapters 37 and 38. The NAACP continues to work for equal rights today.

Many Americans worked for reform in the early 1900s. They helped solve important problems for the nation.

Using What You've Learned

Read and Remember

Write the Answer On your paper, write a sentence to answer each question.

1. How did Florence Kelley help women workers?

2. How did President Theodore Roosevelt help the coal miners' union?

3. What was a muckraker?

4. What did the Supreme Court decide about Standard Oil in 1911?

5. What did Upton Sinclair write about?

6. What was the Pure Food and Drug Act?

7. How did President Roosevelt help conservation?

8. What was one example of discrimination against African Americans in the South?

9. Which progressive leader worked with W.E.B. Du Bois and Jane Addams at the NAACP?

Think and Apply

Categories Read the words in each group. Decide how they are alike. Choose the best title in blue print for each group. Write the title on your paper.

Muckrakers
Florence Kelley

W.E.B. Du Bois
Theodore Roosevelt

1. President of the United States
   wanted laws for safe meat, food,
      and medicine
   worked for conservation

2. fought against child labor
   checked factory safety
   helped working women

3. fought against discrimination
   helped start the NAACP
   worked for equal rights for
      African Americans

4. Jacob Riis
   Ida Tarbell
   Upton Sinclair

Skill Builder

Reading a Circle Graph A **circle graph** shows how all of something is divided into parts. The parts add up to 100 percent, or 100%. This circle graph tells about American workers in 1910. Many Americans did factory work and other jobs. Some people did farm work. Some people did not have jobs.

American Workers in 1910

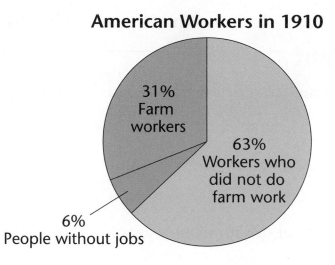

31% Farm workers

63% Workers who did not do farm work

6% People without jobs

Study the circle graph. Choose a word in blue print to finish each sentence. On your paper, write the word you choose.

smallest	**farm**	**six**
half	**factory**	**largest**

① In 1910, _____ percent of Americans did not have jobs.

② In 1910, 31 percent of American workers did _____ work.

③ The _____ group was workers who did not do farm work.

④ People who did not have jobs were the _____ group.

⑤ The largest group included _____ workers.

⑥ Less than _____ of the working people did farm work.

Journal Writing

Choose a person who worked for reform in the early 1900s. In your journal, write a paragraph about his or her work. Tell why the work was important.

Review

Use the words in the first box to finish the first paragraph. Use the words in the second box to finish the second paragraph. On your paper, write the words you choose.

Paragraph 1	Paragraph 2
reporter	Hull House
big business	equal rights
steel	Lillian Wald
immigrants	muckrakers
problems	lead
labor unions	Theodore Roosevelt
oil	Upton Sinclair

From the 1880s to 1920, millions of __(1)__ came to the United States. Jacob Riis was a newspaper __(2)__ . He wrote about __(3)__ in immigrant life. Andrew Carnegie was an immigrant from Scotland. By 1899 Carnegie owned most of the __(4)__ mills in the United States. John D. Rockefeller helped __(5)__ grow bigger. His company owned many __(6)__ refineries. Most factory workers did not earn much money. Factory workers started __(7)__ to get better salaries.

In 1889 Jane Addams started __(8)__ to help people in Chicago. __(9)__ started the Henry Street Settlement House. Alice Hamilton worked to help factory workers be safe from __(10)__ poisoning. President __(11)__ helped get laws passed for safe meat, food, and medicine. Jacob Riis, Ida Tarbell, and __(12)__ were progressive writers called __(13)__ . They worked to solve problems in the United States. W.E.B. Du Bois helped start the NAACP. Du Bois and the NAACP worked toward __(14)__ for African Americans.

Problems at Home and Across the Sea

World War I begins. 1914

The United States begins to fight in World War I. 1917

World War I ends. 1918

1910   1920

1920 — The Nineteenth Amendment is added to the Constitution to allow women to vote.

What was it like to live during World War II? If you were in the United States, you might have read in newspapers about battles being fought. American soldiers were fighting all over the world. There were battles on islands in the Pacific Ocean. There were battles in Europe and in the deserts of Africa.

The United States had to solve big problems between 1914 and 1945. One problem was World War I. Then the 1920s brought many changes to American life. In 1929 the Great Depression began. Millions of people became very poor. Finally World War II began. Thousands of Americans died during this long, terrible war.

Read to Learn

- What would you have done if you had lived in the United States between 1914 and 1945?

- Would you have worked for an amendment that would allow women to vote?

- Would you have had to struggle to get food for your family during the Great Depression?

- Would you have joined the army to fight in World War II?

The stock market crashes. The Great Depression begins.
1929

World War II begins.
1939

World War II ends.
1945

1930

1940

1950

1927
Charles Lindbergh flies across the Atlantic Ocean.

1933
Adolf Hitler becomes the leader of Germany.

1941
Japan attacks the United States at Pearl Harbor. The United States begins to fight in World War II.

World War I

Find Out

❶ What were the causes of World War I?

❷ How did Americans help the Allies during the war?

❸ Which side won World War I?

NEW WORDS

building armies
Allies
Central Powers
neutral
declared war
submarines
sunk
Liberty Bonds

PEOPLE & PLACES

Austria-Hungary
Serbia
Woodrow Wilson
Paris

➤ **Learning from Pictures How are the soldiers' clothes from World War I different from the clothes soldiers wear today?**

In 1914 a war began in Europe. Millions of soldiers from many countries fought in this war. This war was called the Great War then. It is now known as World War I. How did this war begin?

Many countries in Europe were **building armies**. Each country wanted to have the strongest army with the most soldiers. Imperialism became important, too. You read about imperialism in Chapter 24. Countries such as Germany and Great Britain wanted to win control over other countries.

Some countries in Europe joined together into two groups. One group was called the **Allies**. Great Britain, France, Russia, and some other countries were the Allies. These countries promised to help one another during a war.

The other group of countries was called the **Central Powers**. Germany, Austria-Hungary, and some other countries were part of the Central Powers. The Central Powers promised to help one another during a war.

Some countries did not want to help the Allies or the Central Powers. These countries were **neutral**. During the war the neutral countries did not fight for the Allies or for the Central Powers. The map below shows the Allies, the Central Powers, and the neutral countries of Europe during World War I.

One day in 1914, the prince of Austria-Hungary was shot and killed by a person from Serbia. Austria-Hungary **declared war** on Serbia. Russia sent its army to help Serbia. Russia was one of the Allies. The Allies had to keep their promise to help Russia in a war. All the Central Powers had to keep their promise to help Austria-Hungary fight. World War I had begun.

At the start of the war, the United States decided it would be a neutral country. Most Americans did not want to fight in a war that was across the Atlantic Ocean. But

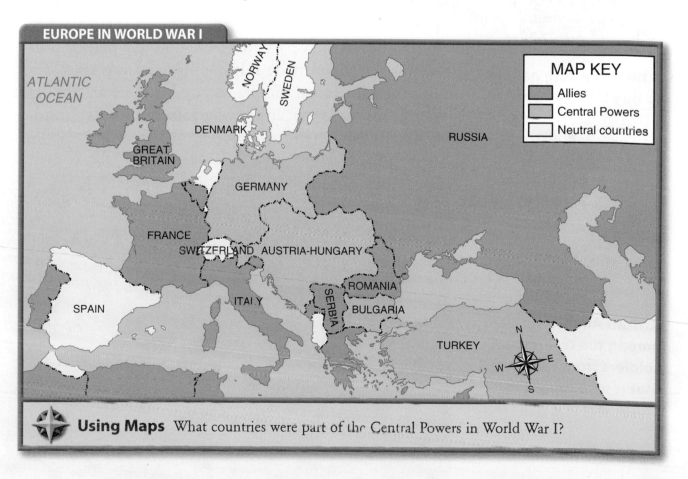

EUROPE IN WORLD WAR I

MAP KEY
- Allies
- Central Powers
- Neutral countries

ATLANTIC OCEAN
NORWAY
SWEDEN
DENMARK
GREAT BRITAIN
GERMANY
RUSSIA
FRANCE
SWITZERLAND
AUSTRIA-HUNGARY
ROMANIA
SPAIN
ITALY
SERBIA
BULGARIA
TURKEY
N W E S

Using Maps What countries were part of the Central Powers in World War I?

World War I poster

A poster asking people to buy Liberty Bonds

the United States had become good friends with Great Britain and France. Great Britain and France were part of the Allies. The United States did not want to fight, but most Americans wanted the Allies to win. The Allies did not have enough food or weapons. The United States sent ships filled with food and weapons to the Allies.

Germany did not want the United States to help the Allies. In 1917 German **submarines** attacked American ships. Submarines are ships that travel underwater. Many American ships were **sunk**. The United States was angry that Germans had killed many Americans at sea. Woodrow Wilson was the President of the United States. He wanted Americans to help the Allies win the war. In April 1917, Congress voted to declare war on Germany.

During World War I many Americans began to hate the people and the language of Germany. There were millions of German Americans who were good American citizens. But many people were unfair to German Americans during World War I. Many German Americans lost their jobs. Many high schools stopped teaching the German language.

Americans in every part of the country helped during the war. Factories made ships, guns, and airplanes. The government needed money to pay for the war. President Wilson asked Americans to buy **Liberty Bonds**. Bond money helped pay for the war.

African Americans were among the two million soldiers from the United States who fought in World War I. ➤

American soldiers marched through Paris after helping the Allies save the city.

Woodrow Wilson

Americans also knew that the Allies needed a lot more food. So Americans ate less wheat, meat, and sugar. They sent wheat, meat, and sugar to the Allies.

About two million American soldiers went to fight in Europe. They helped the Allies win the war. The German soldiers were fighting in France. They tried to capture Paris. The Allies could not stop the German soldiers by themselves. The Americans helped the Allies. Together they pushed the German army away from Paris. Paris was saved.

The Allies and the American soldiers continued to fight against the German army. The German army became weaker and weaker. Finally, Germany and the Central Powers surrendered. World War I ended on November 11, 1918. The Allies had won. American soldiers crossed the Atlantic Ocean and went home to the United States.

Americans were happy that the world had peace. They were also sad because more than 100,000 American soldiers had been killed during the war. President Wilson wanted the world to have peace for a long time. He went to France to help write a peace treaty. He wanted Americans to work for world peace.

The Allies made Germany pay billions of dollars to the countries it had attacked during the war. Soon Germany would fight again. There would be another world war. You will read about this war in Chapters 34 and 35.

Using What You've Learned

Read and Remember

Finish the Story Use the words and dates in blue print to finish the story. On your paper, write the words and dates you choose.

surrendered	1917	neutral	Allies
Woodrow Wilson	Paris	American	1914

World War I began in __(1)__ . During the war __(2)__ was the President of the United States. At first the United States wanted to stay __(3)__ . But Americans wanted the __(4)__ to win. Then German submarines sank __(5)__ ships that were sailing to the Allies. The United States went to war against the Central Powers in __(6)__ . American soldiers helped the Allies save the city of __(7)__ . In 1918 Germany and the Central Powers __(8)__ .

Using Graphic Organizers

Main Idea and Supporting Details Read each group of sentences below. One of the three sentences is a main idea. The other two sentences support the main idea. Copy the chart five times. Then complete one chart for each group of sentences.

1. Some nations in Europe promised to fight for one another in a war.
   Germany and Austria-Hungary were part of the Central Powers.
   Great Britain, France, and Russia were three of the Allies.

2. World War I began after a person from Serbia killed the prince of Austria-Hungary.
   The Central Powers began to help Austria-Hungary fight against Serbia.
   Russia and the Allies began to fight for Serbia.

3. The United States sent food to the Allies.
   The United States sent weapons to the Allies.
   The United States wanted to help the Allies win the war.

4 Americans bought Liberty Bonds to help pay for the war.

Americans wanted to help during the war.

Americans ate less wheat in order to send more to the Allies.

5 Germany surrendered to the Allies.

American soldiers helped the Allies push the German army away from Paris.

The German army became weaker and weaker.

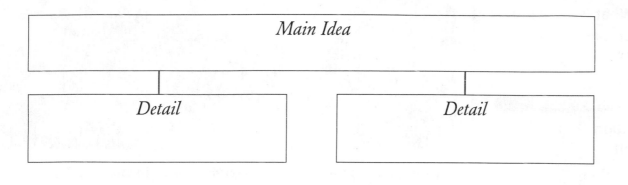

Skill Builder

Reading a Historical Map The **historical map** on page 209 shows Europe during World War I. Study the map and the **map key**. On your paper, write a sentence to answer each question.

1 Name four countries on the map that were Allies.

2 Name three countries on the map that were Central Powers.

3 Name four neutral countries on the map.

4 Which of the Allies was the largest country?

5 Which one of the Allies was east of Germany?

Journal Writing

Many Americans did not like Germany and the German language during World War I. Many German Americans who were good American citizens lost their jobs. Write four to five sentences in your journal that tell why it was unfair for German Americans to lose their jobs.

The 1920s Bring Change

Find Out

❶ How did life improve for Americans in the 1920s?

❷ What was the Harlem Renaissance?

❸ What were some problems in the 1920s?

NEW WORDS

isolation
credit
interest
popular
jazz
Harlem Renaissance
communism

PEOPLE & PLACES

Babe Ruth
Harlem
Langston Hughes
Charles Lindbergh
Ku Klux Klan
Soviet Union
Communists

Americans enjoyed listening to the radio in the 1920s.

The years between 1920 and 1930 were a time of many changes. These changes included new laws and new ways to have fun. They also included serious problems.

The United States had become a world leader after World War I. But most Americans wanted the United States to take care of its own problems. They did not want the United States to have to fight in another war in Europe. The 1920s became a time of **isolation** for the United States.

During World War I, many women took over factory jobs when men left to become soldiers. Women made weapons and airplanes. But they still were not allowed to vote. Finally, in 1920 the Nineteenth Amendment was added to the Constitution. It said women in every state could vote. That year women voted for the first time.

Women changed their lives in other ways during the 1920s. Women began to work at different jobs. Many women cut their hair short and wore much shorter skirts.

Machines for the home made life easier for people in the 1920s. Everyone wanted new washing machines and

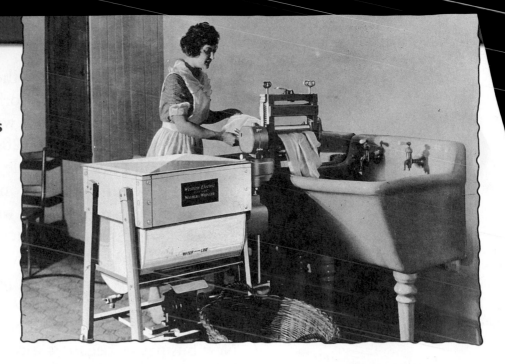

▶ **Learning from Pictures** How are washing machines from the 1920s different from washing machines today? ▶

Dancers in the 1920s

Babe Ruth

refrigerators. But many people did not have enough money to buy them. People began to buy new machines on **credit**. They only paid a small part of the machine's price. Then they took the machine home. Each month they paid part of the cost plus **interest**. They did this until they had completely paid for the machine. In the 1920s millions of Americans were in debt because they bought products with credit.

Radio became **popular** in the 1920s. Americans listened to stories, music, sports, and news on their radios. **Jazz** music became popular. It was started by African American musicians. Americans also enjoyed new kinds of dances.

Millions of Americans began going to movies in the 1920s. At first movies had pictures without sound. Then in 1927 the first movie with sound was made. It was called a "talkie."

Baseball and other sports were very popular in the 1920s. People enjoyed listening to ball games on their radios. A baseball player named Babe Ruth hit more home runs than any other player did. He became an American hero.

Between 1910 and 1930, thousands of African Americans left the South. Many moved to northern cities during World War I to get factory jobs. After the war, other African Americans also moved north to find better jobs.

Langston Hughes

The 1920s were the years of the **Harlem Renaissance**. Harlem was a very large neighborhood in New York City. Many African American artists, writers, and musicians lived in Harlem. During the 1920s they created new art, music, books, and poems. People enjoyed their work throughout the country. Langston Hughes was one of the most famous African American writers. He wrote poems and books about African American life.

In the 1920s the United States became a nation where people traveled in cars. In 1925 people could buy a new Ford car for only $300. By 1929 there were more than 23 million cars on the road.

New businesses began as more people bought cars. Some businesses made glass windows for cars. Others made tires for cars. New hotels opened because people used their cars to take vacations. Thousands of gas stations opened because every car needed gas. New highways were built across the nation. By the end of the 1920s, a person could drive on a highway from California to New York.

Airplane travel became more important. Planes were built that could fly farther. In 1927 Charles Lindbergh became the first person to fly alone across the Atlantic Ocean. His plane left from New York. Lindbergh flew all day and all night. After 33 hours, he landed safely in Paris. He became a hero.

Charles Lindbergh was the first person to fly alone across the Atlantic Ocean.

Farmers could not sell all their crops after the war. ➤

Some changes during the 1920s were not good. Farmers had grown a lot of crops during World War I. After the war they could not sell all their crops. Many farmers lost their farms because they could not earn enough money.

Another problem was the growth of a group called the Ku Klux Klan. Klan members wore white robes and hoods. Klan members attacked and sometimes killed African Americans, Catholics, Jews, and immigrants. More than four million people belonged to the Ku Klux Klan in the 1920s.

The fear of **communism** was another problem. Russia, the world's largest nation, had become a Communist nation. In a Communist nation, the government owns land and businesses. There is little freedom. In 1922 Russia and some other nations formed a larger Communist nation. It was called the Soviet Union. Millions of Americans feared that Communists would try to win control of the United States.

World War I and the fear of communism changed how many Americans felt about immigrants. In 1921 and 1924, Congress passed two laws to limit the number of immigrants. Few people from Asia and the southern and eastern parts of Europe were allowed to come to America.

For millions of Americans, the 1920s were an exciting time. But in 1929 life changed in the United States and across the world. Read Chapter 33 to learn how 1929 was the start of hard, hungry years for most Americans.

Using Geography Themes

Movement: Airmail Across the United States

The theme of movement tells how people, goods, and ideas move from one place to another. People and goods might travel by car, boat, train, or airplane. People can tell ideas to one another. In the 1920s many Americans learned about new ideas from the radio and from newspapers and books. Today people also learn about ideas through television and computers.

Read the paragraphs about airmail. Study the photo below and the map on page 219.

Before 1918 all mail between New York and California traveled on trains. Americans decided airplanes could move mail faster. Using planes to fly the mail was called **airmail**.

In 1918 airmail began between New York City and Washington, D.C. The trip between the two cities was 218 miles. But airplanes at that time could not fly that many miles without stopping for fuel, or oil and gas. So the airplanes flew from New York City to Philadelphia. Then they flew from Philadelphia to Washington, D.C.

In 1920 Americans began to use airmail between New York and California. The airplanes landed for fuel in many cities as they flew west. At that time, pilots could not fly across the country at night. So airplanes carried mail during the day. The airplanes landed near railroad stations. Then trains carried the mail during the night.

In 1921 people began to fly mail across the country both day and night. On February 21, 1921, an airplane with mail left San Francisco, California, at 4:30 A.M. The sky was very dark. The pilot landed the plane in Reno, Nevada. The mail was moved to another plane, and the new pilot took off. From one city to another, different planes moved the mail east across the country. At night, pilots used city lights to help guide them. At times terrible storms or thick fog made flights dangerous.

But finally, on February 23, 1921, the mail arrived in New York City. The trip east had taken about 33 hours. That was 75 hours less than the fastest train trip. The mail had traveled 2,666 miles. After 1921 more and more airplanes carried airmail. Soon, there were many more airmail routes. Faster and safer airplanes were built. Today millions of letters are flown across the country every day.

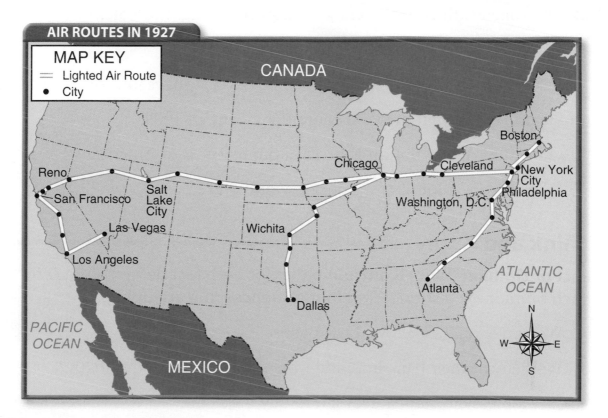

AIR ROUTES IN 1927

MAP KEY
= Lighted Air Route
• City

On your paper, write the answer to each question.

1. Before 1918 how did people move mail across the country?
2. Where did airplanes have to stop between New York City and Washington, D.C., in 1918?
3. In 1920 how did people move mail during the night?
4. How far did the mail travel between San Francisco and New York City on the February 1921 trip?
5. Look at the map. What are four cities where pilots landed as they flew east from San Francisco to New York?
6. From which city did people fly mail to Las Vegas in 1927?

Using What You've Learned

Read and Remember

Find the Answers Find the sentences below that tell about the 1920s. On your paper, write the sentences you find. You should find four sentences.

1 Americans wanted the United States to be isolated from Europe after World War I.

2 The Nineteenth Amendment gave women the right to vote.

3 People bought new machines on credit.

4 Before cars were invented, most people traveled in wagons or trains.

5 Henry Ford started the Ford Motor Company in 1903.

6 Communism and the Ku Klux Klan brought fear to Americans.

7 Farmers grew a lot of crops during World War I.

Think and Apply

Fact or Opinion Write **F** on your paper for each fact below. Write **O** for each opinion. You should find four sentences that are opinions.

1 Women should be allowed to vote.

2 Women cut their hair short and wore shorter skirts in the 1920s.

3 It is too easy to stay in debt if you buy on credit.

4 African Americans started a new kind of music called jazz.

5 Babe Ruth was a greater hero than Charles Lindbergh was.

6 Langston Hughes wrote poems during the Harlem Renaissance.

7 Millions of people bought cars in the 1920s.

8 The Ford Motor Company built the best cars.

9 In 1922 Russia and some other nations formed the Soviet Union.

10 Few Asians and people from the southern and eastern parts of Europe were allowed to come to the United States in the 1920s.

Skill Builder

Reading a Time Line A **time line** is a drawing that shows years on a line. Look at this time line. It shows one decade, the 1920s. A decade is ten years. Read the time line from left to right.

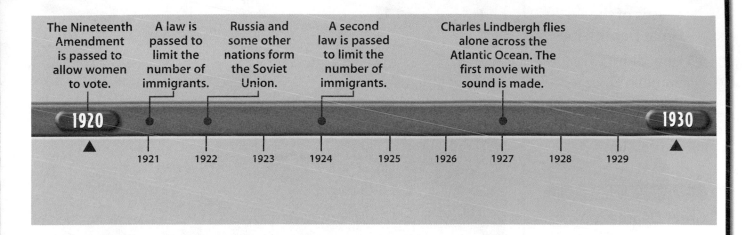

Study the time line. On your paper, write the best answer to each question.

1 In 1922 what did Russia and some other nations form?
the Nineteenth Amendment   an isolation treaty   the Soviet Union

2 In which years were laws passed to limit the number of immigrants?
1920 and 1922   1921 and 1924   1928 and 1929

3 In which year did Charles Lindbergh fly alone across the Atlantic Ocean?
1924   1926   1927

4 When was the Nineteenth Amendment passed compared to when the first movie with sound was made?
before   after   the same year

Journal Writing

The 1920s brought many changes to American life. There were new ways to have fun. People enjoyed listening to the radio and trying new dances. Jazz music, sports, and movies also became popular. Choose two of the ways people had fun in the 1920s. Write four to five sentences about them in your journal.

The Great Depression

Find Out

❶ How did the Great Depression hurt Americans?

❷ What were the causes of the Great Depression?

❸ How did Franklin D. Roosevelt try to end the depression?

NEW WORDS

Great Depression
depression
shares of stock
stock
stock market
crashed
drought
Dust Bowl
elected
New Deal

PEOPLE & PLACES

Herbert Hoover
Franklin D. Roosevelt

Many people lost everything they owned after the stock market crashed in 1929.

The year was 1930. Most Americans had little money. Many people did not have money to buy bread, even though a loaf of bread cost only five cents. Americans were living through the years of the **Great Depression**.

The Great Depression was not the nation's first depression. But it was the longest and hardest **depression**. It lasted more than ten years. It started in the United States. Then the depression spread to Europe and other countries. Millions of Americans lost their jobs. Many people did not have enough money to pay for food, clothes, or homes.

The Great Depression began in 1929. At that time many Americans had been buying **shares of stock**. Buying a share of stock means owning a small part of a business. When the business makes money, your **stock** makes money.

The stock market is where shares are bought and sold. >

Many people lost their homes.

Then you can sell your stock and get back more money than you paid for it. Sometimes a business might not do well. Then the owners of the stock sell the stock for less money than they paid for it.

Americans bought and sold stock on the **stock market**. They bought stock in many businesses. They thought the price of their stock would rise. Then they could sell their stock and get rich quickly. Many Americans did not have enough money to buy the stock they wanted. They borrowed money from banks to buy stock. The banks bought stock, too.

On October 29, 1929, the stock market **crashed**. The price of most stocks on the stock market became very, very low. On that day almost everyone wanted to sell their shares of stock. No one wanted to buy shares of stock. Shares were sold for much less money than people had paid for them. People lost millions of dollars. They couldn't pay back the money they had borrowed from banks to buy stocks. Banks lost even more money because they had bought stocks, too. The money that banks lost was the money that people had saved in the banks. Suddenly, many people became very poor when the stock market crashed.

Three other problems helped cause the Great Depression. The first problem was that factories were making too many products. Americans could not buy all the things that were being made. Factory owners sold

223

Winds blew thick dust across the Great Plains.

Herbert Hoover

their products for less and less money. Many factories were forced to close. Many workers lost their jobs.

Low salaries were the second problem. Workers were not earning enough money. They could not buy farm crops and factory products. Everything became cheaper and cheaper. Soon almost everyone was losing money.

The third problem was that farmers grew more crops than they could sell. The farmers had to sell their crops for less than they had spent to plant the crops. Many farmers did not earn enough to pay for their farms.

But soon many farmers had another problem. A long **drought** began in the Great Plains. Very little rain fell. Winds blew thick dust everywhere. The area became known as the **Dust Bowl**. Farmers in the Dust Bowl could not grow crops. Many farmers moved to other areas.

Herbert Hoover was President of the United States when the Great Depression started. The depression grew worse each year. Hoover was not popular. Americans felt he did not do enough to end the depression. In 1932 Americans **elected** a new President.

Franklin D. Roosevelt became President in 1933. Roosevelt promised a **"New Deal"** for America. He promised to try to end the depression.

Learning from Pictures Why do you think these people are waiting in line for something to eat during the depression?

The New Deal put people back to work. ➤

Franklin D. Roosevelt

Roosevelt and the New Deal helped the United States. The President knew the nation needed strong, safe banks. Roosevelt forced all banks to close for a bank holiday. After eight days, only safe banks were allowed to open. Americans began to put money in banks again.

Nearly thirteen million workers were without jobs when Roosevelt became President. Roosevelt worked with Congress to make new jobs for Americans. The government paid people to build roads, bridges, and parks. Americans built new schools and buildings. Millions of trees were planted across the nation.

Roosevelt also helped farmers. New laws helped farmers borrow money for their farms. Farmers were paid to grow less food. Food prices became higher because there was less food to buy. Roosevelt also found ways to help farmers in the Dust Bowl. Slowly farmers began to earn more money.

Franklin D. Roosevelt was a very popular President. He was the only President to be elected four times. Roosevelt and the New Deal gave jobs to millions of workers. But Roosevelt could not end the depression.

World War II ended the depression. This terrible war began in 1939. There were many new jobs because of the war. Men and women worked in factories making weapons, ships, and airplanes for the war. But Americans would never forget the hard, hungry years of the Great Depression.

Using What You've Learned

Read and Remember

True or False On your paper, write **T** for each sentence that is true. Write **F** for each sentence that is false.

1. When you buy a share of stock, you own a small part of a business.

2. Americans loved President Hoover.

3. Roosevelt worked with Congress to make new jobs for Americans.

4. The depression ended in one year.

5. World War II ended the Great Depression.

Using Graphic Organizers

Cause and Effect Read each of the sentences under cause below. Then read each of the sentences under effect. Copy and complete the graphic organizer to match each cause on the left with an effect on the right.

Cause

1. Too many people decided to sell their stocks on October 29, 1929, so _____

2. During the depression most Americans had very little money, so _____

3. Winds blew dust all over the Great Plains, so _____

Effect

a. it was hard to pay for food, clothes, and homes.

b. the stock market crashed.

c. farmers there could not grow crops.

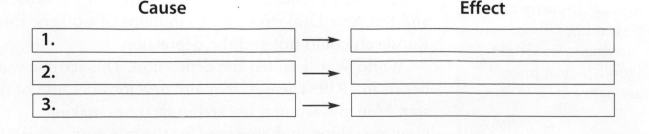

Cause		Effect
1.	→	
2.	→	
3.	→	

Skill Builder

Using a Map Key President Roosevelt started the Tennessee Valley Authority, or TVA, to help end the depression. There had been many floods on the Tennessee River. The TVA built forty dams on rivers to control the floods. Thousands of people had jobs while they built the dams. The dams made electricity for many people in nearby states.

Study the map below. Use the **map key** to learn where dams were built and where people got electricity. Find the three sentences below that tell something true about the TVA map. On your paper, write the sentences you find.

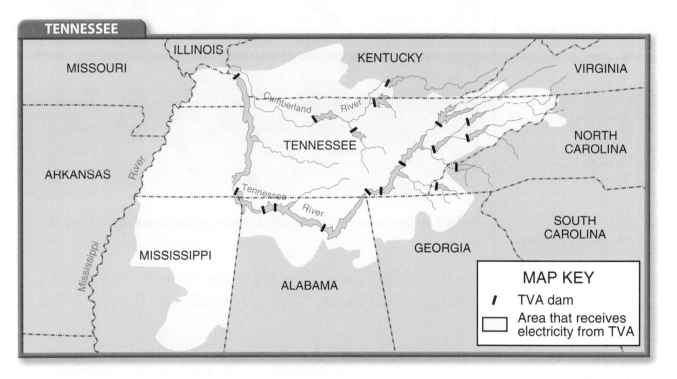

TENNESSEE

MISSOURI

ILLINOIS

KENTUCKY

VIRGINIA

Cumberland River

TENNESSEE

NORTH CAROLINA

ARKANSAS

Tennessee River

Mississippi River

MISSISSIPPI

GEORGIA

SOUTH CAROLINA

ALABAMA

MAP KEY

/ TVA dam

☐ Area that receives electricity from TVA

1 Tennessee, Mississippi, and Alabama receive electricity from the TVA.

2 Florida and New York receive electricity from the TVA.

3 Kentucky, Virginia, and Georgia receive electricity from the TVA.

4 The TVA built most of its dams in Alabama.

5 The TVA has dams on the Cumberland and Tennessee rivers.

Journal Writing

Study the photograph at the bottom of page 224. Write one or two sentences that tell about the photograph. Then write two or three sentences that tell what the photograph shows about the Great Depression.

World War II Begins

Find Out

❶ Why did World War II begin?

❷ What was the Holocaust?

❸ What happened at Pearl Harbor in 1941?

NEW WORDS

dictator
conquer
bombs
Axis countries
appeasement
concentration camps
Holocaust
naval base

PEOPLE & PLACES

Adolf Hitler
Austria
Czechoslovakia
Winston Churchill
Japanese
Pearl Harbor

Adolf Hitler was the ruler of Germany during World War II.

World War I ended in 1918. For many years there was peace in Europe. Why did World War II begin 21 years later?

After World War I, Great Britain and France forced Germany to sign a treaty. Germans hated the treaty. It blamed Germany for World War I. It forced Germany to give its colonies to Great Britain and France. Life became very hard in Germany during the Great Depression. The German people wanted a new leader who would make them feel proud. In 1933 Adolf Hitler became the leader of Germany.

Adolf Hitler was a **dictator**. He had full power to rule Germany. Many people who spoke against Hitler were killed. He said that Germany would **conquer** and rule much of Europe. Many Germans liked what Hitler said. Germany got ready for another war. Germans built airplanes, **bombs**, tanks, and ships.

German airplanes

Italy and Japan also wanted to conquer and rule other countries. Germany, Italy, and Japan were called the **Axis countries**. They promised to help one another during a war. Great Britain, France, and some other countries were called the Allies. Some countries were neutral countries. They did not fight for the Axis countries or for the Allies.

In 1938 Adolf Hitler began to conquer Europe. He forced Austria to become part of Germany. Then he conquered the western part of Czechoslovakia. Great Britain and France had promised to help Czechoslovakia during a war. But Hitler said he would not attack any more countries in Europe. Great Britain and France gave in to Hitler in order to prevent a war. This was called **appeasement**.

In September 1939 Germany attacked Poland. This time Great Britain and France sent soldiers to help Poland. World War II had begun. But the German army quickly conquered Poland. Then Germany attacked other countries in Europe.

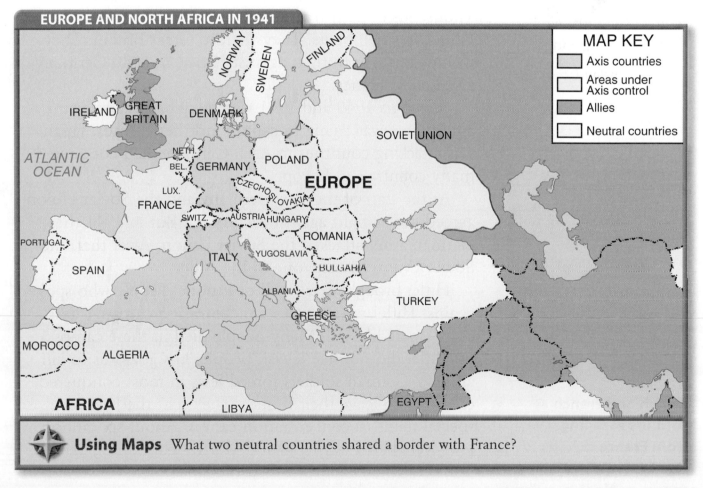

EUROPE AND NORTH AFRICA IN 1941

MAP KEY
- Axis countries
- Areas under Axis control
- Allies
- Neutral countries

Using Maps What two neutral countries shared a border with France?

229

Children were among the millions of people killed in the Holocaust. ➤

British and French soldiers escaping from France

The French and British armies were not strong enough to stop the German army. Germany attacked France. German soldiers quickly captured the city of Paris. Thousands of British and French soldiers escaped from France in small boats. They went to Great Britain. They would continue to fight against Hitler. In 1940 Germany ruled all of France.

The years 1940 and 1941 were very bad years for the Allies. Italy was trying to capture northern Africa. Japan was attacking countries in Asia. Germany had conquered many countries in Europe.

At the start of the war, Germany and the Soviet Union agreed not to fight against each other. But in 1941 the German army attacked the Soviet Union. After that, the Soviet Union became one of the Allies.

Hitler brought fear to all of Europe. People who spoke against Hitler were sent to **concentration camps**. These camps were like jail. Many people died in these camps.

Hitler did not like Jewish people. His goal was to kill all Jews. German soldiers forced Jews in most conquered countries to leave their homes. They sent the Jews on special trains to concentration camps. About six million Jews were killed during World War II. This killing of millions of Jews is now called the **Holocaust**.

Learning from Pictures
How can you tell that
Winston Churchill was
an excellent leader?

HAWAII

PACIFIC
OCEAN

Pearl Harbor

Millions of other people also were killed by Germans. Most were killed in the concentration camps. Never before had so many been killed because of one leader.

Great Britain was the only country in Europe that could fight against Hitler. The British had an excellent leader. His name was Winston Churchill. He believed that people in many nations would lose their freedom if Hitler won the war. Churchill said that Great Britain would never surrender to Hitler. In 1940 Germany tried to conquer Great Britain. German planes dropped thousands of bombs on British cities. Brave British pilots shot down hundreds of German planes. Great Britain remained free.

Franklin D. Roosevelt was the President of the United States. He knew Great Britain needed help to fight against Germany. The United States gave loans to Great Britain. The United States also sent food, weapons, and money.

On December 7, 1941, the Japanese attacked American planes, ships, and soldiers at Pearl Harbor. Pearl Harbor was an American **naval base** in Hawaii. The Japanese killed more than 2,000 American soldiers. They destroyed many American ships and airplanes. Americans were very angry. The next day, the United States declared war on Japan. A few days later, Italy and Germany said they were at war with the United States.

The Axis countries were winning the war in 1941. Read Chapter 35 to learn how the United States helped the Allies win the war.

The Japanese destroyed
many American ships at
Pearl Harbor.

Using Primary Sources

A World War II Political Cartoon

Political cartoons are pictures made by artists. Sometimes a political cartoon shows the artist's opinion about an event or a person. The political cartoon below is about the start of World War II.

The **swastika** was the symbol of Adolf Hitler's Germany. In the cartoon, the artist used a rolling swastika to show that Germany was planning a new attack in Europe.

Study the political cartoon. On your paper, write the answer to each question.

1 Toward what country was the swastika rolling?

2 From the cartoon, what do you think Germany planned to do?

3 Read page 229 again. In what year do you think this event took place?

4 Did the artist think Europe was a peaceful or a dangerous place?

5 **Think and Write** How did the artist show that Germany was very powerful?

232

Using What You've Learned

Read and Remember

Choose the Answer Write the correct answers on your paper.

1. Which word tells why the Allies did not fight Hitler when he conquered Czechoslovakia?

   appeasement   isolation   imperialism

2. When did World War II begin?

   1918   1939   1941

3. How many Jews were killed during the Holocaust?

   1 million   6 million   10 million

4. Which country was not captured by Adolf Hitler's army?

   Great Britain   France   Poland

5. Which country attacked the American naval base at Pearl Harbor?

   Italy   Germany   Japan

6. When did the United States begin to fight in World War II?

   1939   1941   1945

Think and Apply

Understanding Different Points of View The countries fighting in World War II had different points of view about the war. Read the sentences below. On your paper, write **Allies** for each sentence that shows the Allies' point of view. Write **Axis** for each sentence that shows the Axis countries' point of view.

1. Germany should have a large army.

2. Germany and Italy have a right to conquer other countries.

3. Great Britain and France should help Poland.

4. The United States should help the Allies.

5. Americans should not send food or weapons to Great Britain.

6. Japan should not conquer countries in Asia.

233

Skill Builder

Reading a Chart This **chart** gives information about some of the countries that fought in World War II. Study the chart.

Nations at War		
Allies	**Axis Countries**	**Neutral Countries**
United States	Germany	Switzerland
Great Britain	Italy	Sweden
France	Japan	Spain
Soviet Union		Portugal
China		Turkey
Australia		Ireland
Canada		
Mexico		

On your paper, write the word or words that answer each question.

1. What would you look under to find a country that was on the same side as the United States during the war?
   Allies   Axis countries   neutral countries

2. Which country helped the United States fight against Germany during World War II?
   Japan   Sweden   Great Britain

3. Soldiers from which country fought against German soldiers?
   Canada   Spain   Portugal

4. Which were two neutral countries?
   Switzerland and Sweden   Germany and Italy   Great Britain and France

5. Which was the largest group of nations?
   Axis countries   Allies   neutral countries

6. Which was the country of Turkey?
   one of the Axis countries   one of the Allies   one of the neutral countries

7. Which country did China fight against during the war?
   Japan   Mexico   Ireland

The End of World War II

Find Out

❶ How did American life change during World War II?

❷ How did General Eisenhower help the Allies win in Europe?

❸ Why did the United States drop atomic bombs on Japan?

NEW WORDS

ambulance
rationed
bullets
invaded
D-Day
admiral
atomic bomb

PEOPLE & PLACES

Japanese Americans
West Coast
Dwight D. Eisenhower
Italians
Douglas MacArthur
Chester W. Nimitz
Harry S Truman
Hiroshima
Nagasaki

Learning from Pictures Why do you think American soldiers raised an American flag on Iwo Jima during World War II? Iwo Jima is an island in the Pacific Ocean.

The Axis countries were fighting to conquer many countries during World War II. In December 1941 the United States began to fight in the war. Millions of American soldiers went to Europe, Africa, and Asia.

Life in the United States changed during the war. Millions of American men were soldiers in the war. Women also joined the United States Army and Navy. Many worked as nurses and **ambulance** drivers in the war. Millions of other women worked in factories to make the ships, airplanes, guns, tanks, and clothing that the soldiers needed. Because there were so many new jobs, the war ended the Great Depression.

Woman working in a factory during the war

PRIMARY SOURCE

"We were . . . entering the coast of France. . . . We saw hundreds and hundreds of ships below. . . . There was a tremendous [huge] wall of smoke all along the shore where the bombs and shells were exploding. . . . Our bombs went away at 6:30 a.m. . . ."

—*Allen W. Stephens,* American D-Day fighter pilot

Japanese Americans were forced to leave their homes to move to special camps.

American farmers worked hard to grow extra crops. The United States sent food to American and other Allied soldiers who were fighting the war. There was not enough food for people at home to have all they wanted. Some foods were **rationed**. Families could buy only small amounts of some foods, such as meat, sugar, and flour. Many people started their own gardens and grew food for their families.

The United States needed metal to make weapons. Many people collected old metal. Old metal was used to make ships, guns, tanks, and **bullets** for the war.

The United States government was unfair to Japanese Americans during the war. Most Japanese Americans lived in Hawaii, California, and other parts of the West Coast. But soon after Japan bombed Pearl Harbor, the government forced thousands of Japanese Americans to move to special camps. They had to live in small rooms. Guards watched the people in these camps day and night. But many Japanese American men decided they wanted to help the United States win the war. They fought for the United States even though they were not treated fairly. They were brave soldiers.

General Dwight D. Eisenhower led the American army in Europe. In 1944 he became the leader of all the Allied soldiers. Soldiers from Great Britain, France, Canada, the United States, and other countries were fighting for the Allies. General Eisenhower helped all these soldiers work together to fight against the Axis countries.

Thousands of Allied soldiers invaded France on June 6, 1944.

Dwight D. Eisenhower

General Eisenhower led the Allied soldiers against Italy. German soldiers went to Italy to help the Italians fight against the Allies. The Allies fought for many months in Italy. At last, in 1944 Italy surrendered.

Adolf Hitler still ruled France and most of Europe. On June 6, 1944, General Eisenhower **invaded** France with thousands of Allied soldiers. This day was called **D-Day**. After D-Day, more Allied soldiers invaded France. After two months the Allied soldiers captured Paris from the Germans. France soon became a free nation again.

The Germans were losing the war. But Adolf Hitler would not surrender. The Allies attacked Germany. American planes dropped bombs on German cities. The Soviet Union also bombed Germany. Much of Germany was destroyed. Finally, on May 7, 1945, the Germans surrendered to the Allies. Europe had peace again.

Thousands of Americans were fighting in Asia at the same time General Eisenhower and his soldiers were fighting in Europe. General Douglas MacArthur led American soldiers in Asia. Japan had captured the Philippines, Guam, and other islands in the Pacific Ocean. General MacArthur said that he would help Guam and the Philippines become free again.

American soldiers fought the Japanese on islands in the Pacific Ocean. **Admiral** Chester W. Nimitz also led

237

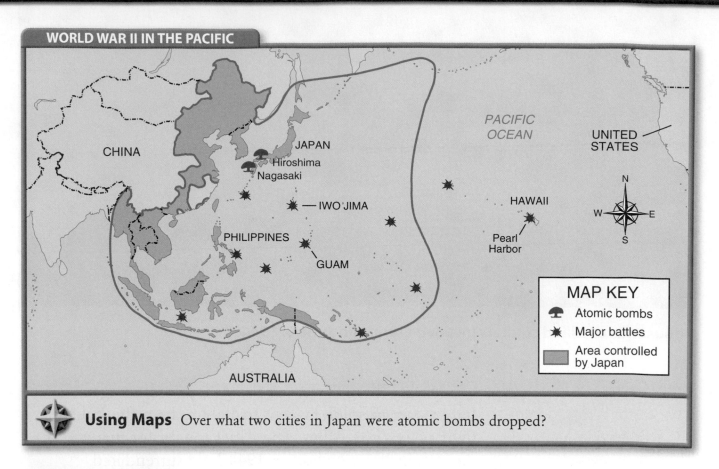

CHINA

JAPAN
Hiroshima
Nagasaki

— IWO JIMA

PHILIPPINES

GUAM

PACIFIC
OCEAN

UNITED
STATES

HAWAII

Pearl
Harbor

N
W   E
S

AUSTRALIA

MAP KEY

Atomic bombs

Major battles

Area controlled
by Japan

Using Maps Over what two cities in Japan were atomic bombs dropped?

Harry S Truman

**Atomic bomb
destroying Hiroshima**

Americans in the Pacific. American soldiers captured islands from Japan. They returned to Guam and the Philippines. In 1944 Guam and the Philippines became free. Then the United States attacked Japan. But they would not surrender.

The United States had a powerful new weapon called the **atomic bomb**. Harry S Truman had become the President of the United States. He wanted the war to end quickly. Every day more Americans were killed during the war. Japan would not stop fighting. President Truman decided to force Japan to surrender. He decided that an American plane would drop an atomic bomb on a Japanese city.

On August 6, 1945, the United States dropped the first atomic bomb. It destroyed most of the city of Hiroshima. Japan would still not surrender. A few days later, Americans dropped an atomic bomb on the city of Nagasaki. These powerful bombs killed thousands of Japanese. On August 14, 1945, Japanese leaders surrendered to the Allies. There was peace in Asia. World War II was finally over.

Using What You've Learned

Read and Remember

Choose a Word Choose the best word or words in blue print to finish each sentence. On your paper, write the word or words you choose.

Truman	World War II	rationed	tanks
MacArthur	Eisenhower	surrendered	metal

1. Foods such as sugar, flour, and meat were _____ in the United States during World War II.

2. Women worked in factories to make guns, _____ , ships, airplanes, and clothing.

3. Americans collected old _____ to use for ships and bullets.

4. On June 6, 1944, General _____ invaded France with thousands of Allied soldiers.

5. The Germans _____ on May 7, 1945.

6. General _____ helped Guam and the Philippines become free from Japan in 1944.

7. Harry S _____ was President at the end of World War II.

8. On August 14, 1945, _____ ended.

Think and Apply

Drawing Conclusions Read each pair of sentences. Then look in the box on page 240 for the conclusion you can make. On your paper, write the letter of the conclusion.

1. During the war millions of American men were in the United States Army.
   The factories needed workers to make airplanes and weapons.

2. Japanese Americans were forced to move to special camps.
   Guards watched the people in the camps all the time.

3. The Allies attacked Germany.
   Much of Germany was destroyed.

4 The United States dropped the first atomic bomb on a city in Japan. Japan still would not surrender.

5 General Eisenhower led Allied soldiers to free France from Germany. General MacArthur led American soldiers to capture islands from Japan.

6 Germany and Italy surrendered in Europe. Japan surrendered in the Pacific.

Conclusions

a. The United States dropped a second atomic bomb on Japan.

b. The United States government was unfair to Japanese Americans.

c. Many women worked in factories in the United States.

d. The Germans surrendered.

e. The Allies won World War II.

f. Generals Eisenhower and MacArthur were good leaders.

Skill Builder

Reading a Historical Map The historical map on page 238 shows Asia and the Pacific Ocean during World War II. Study the map and the map key. On your paper, write the answers to the questions below.

1 Which large country was partly controlled by Japan during World War II?

2 What are two places in the Pacific Ocean where major battles occurred?

3 Which two Japanese cities were destroyed by atomic bombs?

4 Where did a Pacific battle occur that was in an area Japan did not control?

5 How many major battles does the map show took place in the Pacific?

6 Which large country was south of the area that Japan controlled?

Journal Writing

At home in the United States, many Americans worked hard to help win World War II. Write a paragraph that tells what people did at home in the United States to help win World War II. Name at least three things.

Review

The chart on this page shows important events from 1914 to 1945. Study the chart. Then use the words and dates in blue print to finish the story. On your paper, write the words and dates you choose.

New Deal   1918   Japan
Central Powers   1939   stock market
Depression   vote   Constitution

World War I began in 1914 and ended in __(1)__ . During World War I, the United States, Great Britain, and France were three of the Allies. The Allies won against the __(2)__ .

In 1920 the Nineteenth Amendment was added to the __(3)__ . It gave women in every state the right to __(4)__ . The __(5)__ crashed in 1929. Millions of people lost their jobs during the Great __(6)__ . President Roosevelt's __(7)__ helped Americans get jobs.

World War II began in __(8)__ . In 1941 Japan attacked Pearl Harbor. Then the United States began to fight in World War II. In 1945 Germany, Italy, and __(9)__ surrendered.

Important Events from 1914 to 1945		
Event	Dates	What Happened?
World War I	1914–1918	The Allies and Central Powers fought. The Allies won.
Nineteenth Amendment Passed	1920	Women in every state were allowed to vote.
Great Depression	1929–1939	The stock market crashed. Millions of people lost their jobs. Roosevelt and the New Deal created jobs for Americans.
World War II	1939–1945	The United States and the Allies fought against Germany, Italy, and Japan. The Allies won.

Our Changing Nation

What was it like to be in the United States in August 1963? You could have been one of the 250,000 people who went to march on Washington, D.C. On that day you would have heard Martin Luther King, Jr., tell about his dream of a country where every person was treated fairly. Thousands of Americans wanted to change laws that were unfair.

The United States did change after World War II. The United States and the Soviet Union became enemies. Many Americans began moving from cities to suburbs. Americans learned to travel in space. The first union to help migrant farm workers was started. Thousands of Americans fought and died in the Vietnam War.

Read to Learn

> What would you have done if you had lived after World War II?

> Would you have marched with Martin Luther King, Jr., to change unfair laws?

> Would you have worked with other people to send rockets into space?

> How did the United States change after World War II?

North Korea invades South Korea.
1950

The Soviet Union builds the Berlin Wall.
1961

1950   1960

1953
Dwight D. Eisenhower becomes President. The Korean War ends.

American soldiers start fighting in Vietnam.
1963

César Chávez wins the first contract for migrant farm workers.
1970

The Berlin Wall is torn down.
1989

1970   **1980**   **1990**   **2000**

1963
Martin Luther King, Jr., leads the March on Washington.

1969
Apollo 11 goes to the moon.

1975
South Vietnam surrenders to North Vietnam.

1999
Eileen Collins commands a space shuttle flight.

243

Find Out

❶ What are differences between democracy and communism?

❷ What were two goals of the United States after World War II?

❸ How was the Cold War fought in different countries?

NEW WORDS

Cold War
democracy
organization
United Nations
spread of communism
NATO
missiles

PEOPLE & PLACES

Western Europe
Eastern Europe
East Germany
West Germany
Berlin
West Berlin
East Berlin
Korea
North Korea
South Korea

The Cold War

> **Learning from Pictures** Why do you think the Berlin Wall was built between West Berlin and Communist East Berlin?

The United States and the Soviet Union fought against Germany during World War II. Soon after the war, the United States and the Soviet Union became enemies. They began to fight against each other in a new kind of war. This new war was called the **Cold War**. The two countries did not attack each other. Instead each country tried to get other nations to join its side.

The Cold War began because the United States and the Soviet Union had different kinds of government. The government of the United States is a **democracy**. In a democracy people vote for their leaders. The people have a lot of freedom. The Soviet Union had a Communist government. In a Communist country, the government owns most of the land, stores, and businesses. People do not have freedom of speech or religion. During the Cold

Leaders from countries around the world work for world peace at the United Nations building in New York City. ➤

The United Nations building in New York City

The United Nations flag

War, dictators ruled the Soviet Union. The Soviet Union wanted to start Communist governments in other countries.

The United States had two goals after World War II. Its first goal was to start an **organization** that would work for world peace. The United States helped start the **United Nations**. This organization tries to help countries solve problems without fighting.

The United States' second goal was to help stop the **spread of communism** to other nations. The United States worked in two ways to help stop the spread of communism. First, the United States gave millions of dollars to the nations of Western Europe. The nations used this money to rebuild cities and farms that were destroyed during the war. The United States also helped the Japanese rebuild their nation. Japan and the nations of Western Europe became strong democracies. They did not become Communist nations.

Second, the United States helped start the North Atlantic Treaty Organization, or **NATO**. NATO was formed to prevent the Soviet Union from attacking Western Europe. Today, the United States, Canada, and many nations in Western and Eastern Europe belong to NATO. The armies of NATO nations would join together against an enemy during a war.

The Cold War began in Eastern Europe. When World War II ended, the Soviet army forced Poland and other nations to have Communist governments.

The Berlin Wall divided the city of Berlin.

The Cold War was fought in Germany, too. After World War II ended, Germany became two nations. East Germany became a Communist country. Soviet leaders told the East German government what to do. West Germany became a democracy. People had more freedom in West Germany. They also earned more money.

Berlin, the capital city of Germany, was in East Germany. The city of Berlin also was divided after the war. West Berlin became a democracy. East Berlin was a Communist city.

The Soviet Union wanted to win control of West Berlin. In June 1948 the Soviet Union blocked roads and railroads to West Berlin. The people of West Berlin could not get food from West Germany. So the United States, Great Britain, and France used airplanes to send food and other supplies to West Berlin. Finally in May 1949, the Soviet Union allowed West Berlin to receive supplies from West Germany again.

Thousands of people escaped from East Germany by going to West Berlin. From West Berlin they could move to West Germany. The Soviet Union wanted to stop people from leaving East Berlin. In 1961 the Soviets built a wall to separate East Berlin and West Berlin. Soldiers in East Berlin stood next to the wall. They stopped people who tried to leave. The Berlin Wall was not torn down until 1989.

The Soviet army forced nations of Eastern Europe to have Communist governments.

Many American soldiers fought for the United Nations in South Korea. ➤

NORTH AND SOUTH KOREA

CHINA

NORTH KOREA

SOUTH KOREA

Korea was divided after World War II.

John F. Kennedy

In 1949 Communists won control of China. Chinese leaders wanted to spread communism to Korea and to other countries in eastern Asia.

The Cold War became a real war in Korea. After World War II, Korea was divided into the nations of North Korea and South Korea. North Korea became a Communist country. In 1950 North Korean soldiers invaded South Korea. They wanted all of Korea to be one Communist nation.

The United Nations sent soldiers to South Korea. Most of the soldiers were Americans. Thousands of Chinese soldiers fought for North Korea. The Communists were forced to return to North Korea. The Korean War ended in 1953. North Korea and South Korea are still two separate countries today.

The Cold War almost became a real war in Cuba, too. Communists have ruled the island nation since 1959. In 1962 the Soviet Union gave Cuba dangerous weapons called **missiles**. Cuba could have used those missiles to destroy American cities. John F. Kennedy was President of the United States. He told the Soviet Union to remove the missiles. He said Americans would fight to remove the missiles. After a few days, the Soviet Union removed the missiles.

The Cold War lasted almost fifty years. During that time Americans feared the Cold War might become another world war. Read Chapter 43 to learn how the Cold War ended.

Using What You've Learned

Match Up Finish each sentence in Group A with words from Group B. On your paper, write the letter of the correct answer.

Group A

1. In a Communist country, the government owns _____

2. NATO was started to protect _____

3. In 1949 Communists won control of _____

4. The Cold War became a real war in _____

5. The Soviet Union sent dangerous missiles to _____

Group B

a. China.

b. Cuba.

c. the nations of Western Europe.

d. Korea.

e. most of the land, stores, and businesses.

Think and Apply

Understanding Different Points of View During the Cold War, Americans and Soviets had different points of view. Read the sentences below. On your paper, write **American** for each sentence that shows the American point of view. Write **Soviet** for each sentence that shows the Soviet point of view.

1. A dictator should rule the nation.

2. The people should have a lot of freedom.

3. The people should vote for their leaders.

4. The government should own the stores and businesses.

5. Other nations should have Communist governments.

6. NATO is needed to stop the spread of communism.

7. There should not be a wall between East Berlin and West Berlin.

8. People in East Berlin must not move to West Berlin.

Skill Builder

Reading a Historical Map The map below shows Europe in 1960. The map shows Communist nations and NATO nations. It also shows neutral nations that did not have Communist governments and did not belong to NATO. Study the map. On your paper, write the word or words that finish each sentence.

1 The largest Communist nation in 1960 was _____ .
Poland   East Germany   the Soviet Union

2 In 1960 two NATO nations were _____ .
France and Italy   Spain and Austria   Bulgaria and Romania

3 Switzerland was a _____ nation in 1960.
NATO   Communist   neutral

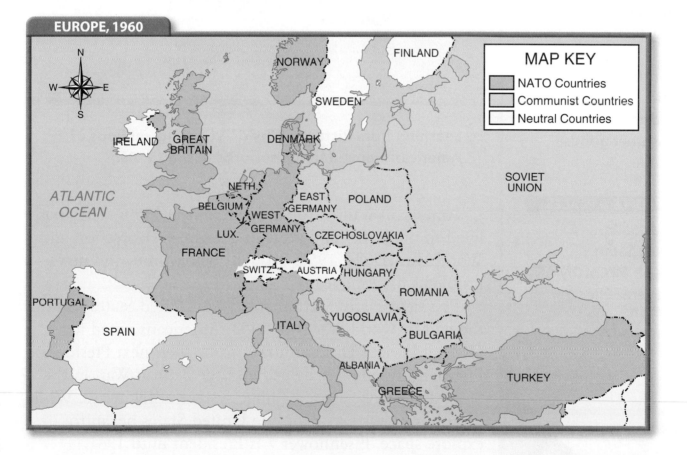

EUROPE, 1960

MAP KEY
- NATO Countries
- Communist Countries
- Neutral Countries

Journal Writing

Write a paragraph in your journal that tells how a Communist government is different from a democracy. Write at least four sentences.

America During the 1950s

Find Out

❶ How did American life improve during the 1950s?

❷ How did Senator Joseph McCarthy hurt the nation?

❸ What 1954 Supreme Court decision changed the United States?

NEW WORDS

veterans
baby boom
G.I. Bill of Rights
suburbs
polio
vaccine
consumer goods
decade

PEOPLE & PLACES

Jonas Salk
Albert Sabin
Joseph McCarthy
Margaret Chase Smith
Thurgood Marshall

 **Learning from Pictures Why do you think millions of Americans moved to the suburbs in the 1950s?**

Americans wanted to enjoy life in the 1950s. They had lived through the hard years of the Great Depression and World War II. The 1950s brought better times and new problems for Americans.

President Harry S Truman led the United States from the end of World War II to 1953. Americans voted for General Dwight D. Eisenhower to be their next President. President Eisenhower helped end the Korean War. In the United States, he started a huge system of highways. While Eisenhower was President, the United States began to explore space. Eisenhower was President until 1961.

After World War II, American soldiers returned home. People who have been soldiers are called **veterans**. Many veterans started families. The United States had a **baby boom** because millions of babies were born after the war.

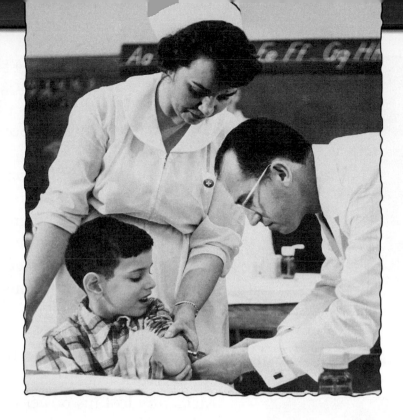

Jonas Salk made the first polio vaccine. ➤

Albert Sabin

Toward the end of World War II, Congress passed the **G.I. Bill of Rights** to help veterans. This law made it easy for veterans to get loans. The loans helped many veterans buy homes and go to college.

With the baby boom and the G.I. loans, families wanted new homes. Many homes were built in areas near cities. These areas were called **suburbs**. During the 1950s, millions of Americans moved to the suburbs. They worked in nearby cities. They often traveled on highways to get from the suburbs to the cities.

Before the 1950s many Americans got a terrible disease called **polio**. Some people never walked again after they had polio. Many people died. In the early 1950s, Dr. Jonas Salk made the first polio **vaccine**. People who took this medicine would not get polio. A few years later Dr. Albert Sabin made a different kind of polio vaccine. Today, doctors give polio vaccines to children around the world.

During the Great Depression, most Americans were too poor to buy goods. During World War II, most factories made weapons for the war. After the war factories began to make many **consumer goods**, or products people use. Americans bought new cars, refrigerators, and televisions. Television had been invented during the war.

Margaret Chase Smith

Thurgood Marshall

Many Americans had a great fear of communism during the 1950s. The fear grew during the Cold War. Americans knew the Soviet Union had built atomic bombs. They feared the Soviet Union might attack the United States.

A senator named Joseph McCarthy added to the fear of communism. He said many American Communists held important government jobs. McCarthy never proved that people were Communists. But most people were afraid to speak against McCarthy. They feared that they would be called Communists. They feared they would lose their jobs.

Senator Margaret Chase Smith spoke out against Senator McCarthy in the United States Senate. Later, Americans learned that McCarthy had told many lies. McCarthy lost his power in the Senate. But Americans continued to worry about communism for many years.

In 1954 the Supreme Court made a decision that changed the country. The decision was about a case called *Brown* v. *Board of Education of Topeka, Kansas*. The Court ruled that separate schools for African American children and white children were against the Constitution. This decision helped end segregation laws in the United States. Thurgood Marshall was an NAACP lawyer for this case. Marshall later became a Supreme Court justice.

The 1950s were a time when many Americans had good jobs and enjoyed a better life. The **decade** also brought many new problems and many changes to the United States.

Using What You've Learned

Read and Remember

Who Am I? Read each sentence. Then look at the names in blue print. Decide which person might have said the sentence. On your paper, write the name of the person you choose.

Thurgood Marshall	**Dwight D. Eisenhower**	**Jonas Salk**
Harry S Truman	**Margaret Chase Smith**	**Joseph McCarthy**

1. "I was President from 1945 to 1953."

2. "While I was President, a new system of highways was started."

3. "I made the first vaccine against polio."

4. "I said there were American Communists working in our government."

5. "As a senator, I spoke out against McCarthy."

6. "I was an NAACP lawyer for a case that helped end school segregation."

Think and Apply

Fact or Opinion Write **F** on your paper for each fact below. Write **O** for each opinion. You should find three sentences that are opinions.

1. Many new highways were built during the 1950s.

2. There was a baby boom after World War II.

3. The G.I. Bill of Rights helped many veterans buy homes.

4. Life in the suburbs was better than city life.

5. Albert Sabin made a polio vaccine.

6. Americans began to spend too much money on consumer goods.

7. Many Americans had a strong fear of communism in the 1950s.

8. In 1954 the Supreme Court ruled that separate schools for African American and white children were against the Constitution.

9. The 1950s were great years for Americans.

Skill Builder

Comparing Circle Graphs We can learn about population changes by comparing **circle graphs** about population. The two circle graphs below compare the population growth of Chicago and its suburbs in 1950 and 1960. Each graph adds up to 100 **percent**, or 100%. Study the two circle graphs.

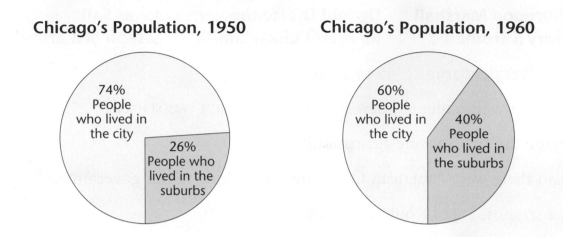

Chicago's Population, 1950

74% People who lived in the city

26% People who lived in the suburbs

Chicago's Population, 1960

60% People who lived in the city

40% People who lived in the suburbs

Choose a number or word in blue print to finish each sentence. On your paper, write the number or word you choose.

suburbs	26
faster	74

1. In 1950 people who lived in the city were _____ percent of Chicago's total population.

2. In 1950 people in the suburbs were _____ percent of the population.

3. In 1960 forty percent of the people in the Chicago area lived in the _____

4. The population in the suburbs grew _____ than the city population did from 1950 to 1960.

Journal Writing

The 1950s brought better times for many Americans. Read the chapter again. Choose two ways life improved during the 1950s. Write a paragraph in your journal that tells about these two good changes.

Martin Luther King, Jr.

Find Out

❶ What laws were unfair to African Americans?

❷ How did Martin Luther King, Jr., help change the bus law in Montgomery?

❸ How did the Civil Rights Act of 1964 help Americans?

NEW WORDS

minister
boycott
protest
march
civil rights
respect
Civil Rights Act of 1964
Nobel Peace Prize

PEOPLE & PLACES

Martin Luther King, Jr.
Coretta Scott
Montgomery
Rosa Parks
Birmingham

Martin Luther King, Jr., worked hard to change laws that were not fair.

After the Civil War, segregation laws were written in the South. These laws kept African Americans and white people apart. Other laws also were not fair to African Americans. In this chapter you will learn how Martin Luther King, Jr., worked to change unfair laws.

Martin Luther King, Jr., was born on January 15, 1929, in Georgia. King's father was a **minister**. During college King worked and studied hard. He became a minister. In 1953 King married a woman named Coretta Scott. They moved to Montgomery, Alabama. King became the minister of a church in Montgomery.

Martin Luther King, Jr., believed all segregation laws were wrong. Some laws made it hard for African Americans to vote. There was a law that said African Americans had to sit in the back seats of buses. Another law said that African American children

255

Montgomery

and white children had to go to separate schools. African Americans and white people could not use the same parks, pools, and beaches. They were not allowed to eat in the same restaurants.

In 1954 the Supreme Court ruled that separate schools for African American children and white children were against the Constitution. All school segregation laws had to be changed. Martin Luther King, Jr., believed that other segregation laws could be changed, too. King said he would find peaceful ways to change the laws.

One day in 1955, an African American woman named Rosa Parks got on a bus in Montgomery, Alabama. The bus driver told Parks to get up and let a white person have her seat. Parks refused to move. Two police officers took her to jail.

African American leaders in Montgomery learned what had happened to Rosa Parks. They wanted to change the city's unfair bus law. They started a **boycott** against the city's buses. During a boycott people stop buying a product or using a service. During this boycott African Americans stopped riding the city's buses. Martin Luther King, Jr., became one of the most important leaders of the boycott.

The boycott lasted for a year. Some African Americans went to work in cars and taxis. Many African Americans walked to work, even in cold, rainy weather. The city's buses lost a lot of money.

> **Learning from Pictures** Rosa Parks went to jail because she would not give up her seat on a bus. What do you think the policeman is doing?

Martin Luther King, Jr., helped lead the bus boycott. ➤

Newspaper reporters wrote about the Montgomery bus story in newspapers all over America. Martin Luther King, Jr., became a famous leader. In 1956 the Supreme Court ruled that bus segregation laws were against the Constitution. Soon after that the bus law was changed. The bus boycott ended. African Americans could sit anywhere on a bus.

King and other leaders tried to change more laws peacefully. African Americans were not allowed to eat in some restaurants. Only white people could eat in these restaurants. King told African Americans to sit down and ask for food in the restaurants. King also tried to help African Americans in northern cities get better houses and jobs.

In 1963 Martin Luther King, Jr., decided to lead a peaceful **protest** in Birmingham, Alabama. He wanted to change the city's unfair laws. The police and their dogs attacked King's group. Martin Luther King, Jr., was sent to jail. King wrote a letter to Americans from the Birmingham jail. He wrote that all Americans should have equal rights. People read King's letter. Many agreed that unfair laws should be changed.

Martin Luther King, Jr., worked with other leaders to plan a large **march** on Washington, D.C. The march would show all Americans that the nation needed new **civil rights** laws. In August 1963 more than 250,000

257

Learning from Pictures Why do you think so many people came to hear Martin Luther King, Jr., speak during the March on Washington in 1963? ➤

✒ PRIMARY SOURCE

"Now is the time to make real the promises of democracy."

—Martin Luther King, Jr.

Martin Luther King, Jr., with the Nobel Peace Prize

Americans joined the "March on Washington." African Americans and white Americans marched together.

During the march King made a famous speech. In the speech he said, "I have a dream." He said his dream was that all Americans would be treated fairly. He hoped all Americans would live together in peace. He wanted all people to **respect** one another. People in every state heard King's speech on television and radio.

The next year Congress passed the **Civil Rights Act of 1964**. The law said African Americans and white people could use the same schools, restaurants, parks, and buses. Today we do not have laws that keep African Americans and white people apart. In 1965 Congress passed a law that made it much easier for African Americans to vote.

Martin Luther King, Jr., was given the **Nobel Peace Prize** in 1964. This prize is given to a person who has worked hard for peace.

On April 4, 1968, Martin Luther King, Jr., was shot and killed. Martin Luther King, Jr., Day is now an American holiday in January. People in every state remember this great American. Many Americans continue to do the work started by Martin Luther King, Jr. They use peaceful ways to help all Americans live and work together in peace.

Using Primary Sources

Dear Mrs. Parks

Rosa Parks believed that segregation was wrong. On December 1, 1955, she was arrested because she would not give her seat on a Montgomery bus to a white person. Soon after that, African Americans decided to boycott the city's buses. Parks has worked for equal rights throughout her life. Thousands of students have written letters to her. She answered many of their letters in a book called *Dear Mrs. Parks: A Dialogue with Today's Youth*. Read parts of her letters below.

reenter
enter again

launched
started

justice
fairness

> *The custom of getting on the bus for black people in Montgomery in the 1950s was to pay at the front door, get off the bus, and then* **reenter** *through the back door to find a seat. Black people could not sit in the same rows with white people. . . .*
>
> *I did not get on the bus to get arrested; I got on the bus to go home. . . . Somehow, I felt that what I did was right by standing up to that bus driver. . . .*
>
> *It was not fair when I was put in jail for not giving up my seat on the bus to a white passenger. I was afraid because I could have been treated very badly by the police. . . . My arrest* **launched** *the Montgomery Bus Boycott, which helped to bring in the modern Civil Rights movement. . . .*
>
> *As the Montgomery Bus Boycott took place, the eyes of the world were upon us. . . . The strength of the message—equal* **justice** *for all citizens—rang across the globe. . . .*

On your paper, write the answer to each question.

1. How did African Americans get on buses in Montgomery?
2. Why did Rosa Parks get on the bus on the day she went to jail?
3. Why was Parks put in jail?
4. Why was Rosa Parks afraid?
5. **Think and Write** What was the message of the Montgomery Bus Boycott?

Using What You've Learned

Read and Remember

Choose a Word Choose the best word or words in blue print to finish each sentence. On your paper, write the word or words you choose.

northern	Rosa Parks	Civil Rights
Nobel	Birmingham	Washington, D.C.

1 In 1955 _____ refused to let a white person have her seat on a bus.

2 Martin Luther King, Jr., wrote a famous letter from a jail in _____ .

3 King helped African Americans in _____ cities get better jobs.

4 In 1963 King gave a speech during the March on _____ .

5 In 1964 Congress passed the _____ Act.

6 Martin Luther King, Jr., was given the _____ Peace Prize.

Using Graphic Organizers

Main Idea and Supporting Details Read each group of sentences below. One of the three sentences is a main idea. The other two sentences support the main idea. Copy the chart twice. Then complete one chart for each group of sentences.

1 King and other leaders tried to change laws peacefully.
The leaders planned a large march on Washington, D.C., in 1963.
King asked African Americans to sit in restaurants for white people.

2 The bus boycott lasted one year.
African Americans in Montgomery started a bus boycott to change an unfair bus law.
The city's buses lost a lot of money.

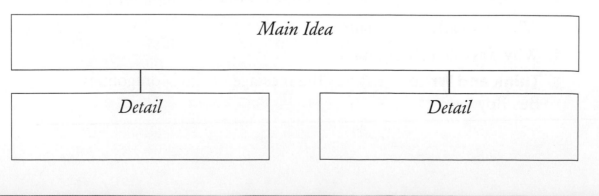

Americans Travel in Space

NEW WORDS

space race
satellite
astronauts
space shuttle
space station
rovers

PEOPLE & PLACES

Cape Kennedy
Neil Armstrong
Edwin Aldrin
Michael Collins
Eileen Collins
Ellen Ochoa
Hispanic American

> **Learning from Pictures** **The first person to walk on the moon was American Neil Armstrong. Why do you think the American flag was put on the moon?**

"Which country will be the first to send people to the moon?" Many people asked this question during the 1960s. Americans wanted to be the first to land a person on the moon.

In 1957 a **space race** began between the United States and the Soviet Union. The race began when the Soviet Union sent the world's first **satellite** into space. The next year Americans sent their first satellite into space.

The space race was part of the Cold War. Americans did not want the Soviets to reach the moon first. President John F. Kennedy promised that the United States would send people to the moon by 1970.

The United States sent the first people to the moon in 1969. The trip to the moon started at Cape Kennedy in

Neil Armstrong, Michael Collins, and Edwin Aldrin

FLORIDA

Cape Kennedy

A space shuttle takes off. ➤

Florida. The *Apollo 11* spaceship left from Cape Kennedy. Three **astronauts** were inside this spaceship. Neil Armstrong, Edwin Aldrin, and Michael Collins traveled to the moon in *Apollo 11*. After four days in space, they reached the moon.

On July 20, 1969, Neil Armstrong and Edwin Aldrin became the first people to walk on the moon. After 22 hours *Apollo 11* left the moon. The three astronauts returned to Earth in *Apollo 11*. They brought back rocks from the moon to Earth. After that, five more *Apollo* spaceships took Americans to the moon.

The *Apollo* spaceships could be used only once. So Americans invented a spaceship called the **space shuttle**. The space shuttle goes up into space like a rocket. It lands on Earth almost like an airplane.

Space travel has brought sad times to Americans. In 1986 the space shuttle *Challenger* went up in the sky. Suddenly it blew up and became a ball of fire. All seven Americans inside the *Challenger* died.

After the *Challenger* accident, Americans worked at building safer space shuttles. In 1988 Americans sent a new space shuttle safely into space.

On February 1, 2003, the space shuttle *Columbia* was returning from a two-week trip to space. Minutes away from landing, the shuttle broke apart. Six Americans and one Israeli were onboard. All seven astronauts died.

Astronauts can live for months in the International Space Station. ➤

Eileen Collins

A satellite

Since 1998 the United States and 15 countries have been building a large **space station**. It is called the International Space Station. While building it, astronauts live in the space station for months at a time. They also do many kinds of experiments. Satellites will be sent into space from the space station. The space station should be finished in 2007.

The year 1999 was an important year for women in space. Eileen Collins became the first woman to command a space shuttle flight. Earlier that year, Ellen Ochoa, a Hispanic American astronaut, traveled with a team on the space shuttle. Ochoa helped bring important supplies to the new space station.

In 2003 the United States sent **rovers** to the planet Mars. These rovers sent back photographs of Mars. They also collected rocks. Scientists hope to learn more about Mars from the photographs and the rocks.

Today hundreds of satellites are in space. Satellites help us learn about the weather. Television satellites bring us shows from countries around the world. Other satellites send news reports as soon as events happen.

The United States has explored space more often than any other nation. Space satellites help millions of people in many ways.

263

Using Geography Themes

Location: John F. Kennedy Space Center

The theme of location tells where a place is found. Sometimes people use directions to tell where a place is. People also can say what the place is near or what is around it.

Read the paragraphs about the John F. Kennedy Space Center. Study the photo below and the map on page 265.

In 1958 Americans needed the right location for sending their first satellite into space. Scientists wanted an area where few people lived. They wanted the location to be near the ocean. That would allow spaceships to land safely in the water. They also wanted a location that did not have snow in the winter. Snow would make it difficult to send rockets into space in cold weather. The eastern coast of Florida was a good location for building a space center.

At first all spaceships were sent into space at Cape Canaveral. Cape Canaveral also has been called Cape Kennedy. Cape Canaveral is part of a long island along the east coast of Florida. But the space center at Cape Canaveral was too small for sending large rockets into space. So the John F. Kennedy Space Center was built on nearby Merritt Island. It opened in 1962.

Merritt Island is west of Cape Canaveral. The Indian River separates Merritt Island from the Florida **mainland**. The 24-mile Canaveral National Seashore is north of Merritt Island. This is a place with very quiet beaches and lots of **wildlife**. Orlando is the closest large city. It is about 47 miles west of the space center.

Only part of Merritt Island is used for the Kennedy Space Center. Most of the island's land is used to protect more than 500 kinds of plants and animals. These plants and animals are part of the Merritt Island Wildlife Refuge.

All space flights that carry astronauts take off from the Kennedy Space Center. They also land at this space center. Spaceships that do not carry people still take off at Cape Canaveral. Nearby, many birds and other animals live in the peaceful wildlife refuge. The space center and wildlife refuge are open to visitors almost every day of the year.

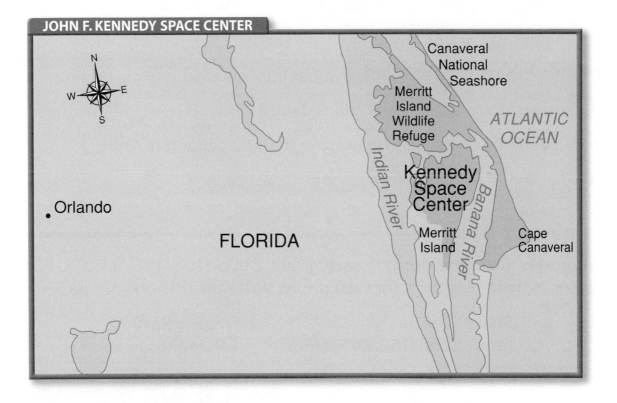

On your paper, write the answer to each question.

1. Why did Americans choose the eastern coast of Florida to build a space center?
2. On what island is the Kennedy Space Center?
3. How far is Orlando from the Kennedy Space Center?
4. Look at the map. What river separates the Kennedy Space Center from Cape Canaveral?
5. Is the wildlife refuge north or south of the space center?
6. What are two ways to describe where the space center is located?

Using What You've Learned

Read and Remember

Write the Answer On your paper, write a sentence to answer each question.

1. How did the Soviet Union start the space race in 1957?

2. By what year did President Kennedy say the United States would send people to the moon?

3. What was the name of the first spaceship that took Americans to the moon?

4. Who were the first three astronauts to fly to the moon?

5. Why did Americans invent the space shuttle?

6. What happened to the *Challenger* and the *Columbia*?

7. What did astronaut Eileen Collins do in 1999?

8. What did Ellen Ochoa help bring to the space station in 1999?

9. What did the rovers that were sent to Mars collect?

Think and Apply

Categories Read the words in each group. Decide how they are alike. Choose the best title in blue print for each group. Write the title on your paper.

Space Shuttle
International Space Station

Space Race
Satellite

1. part of the Cold War
   between the United States and
      the Soviet Union
   goal was to reach the moon first

2. first one sent into space in 1957
   helps people learn about events as
      soon as they happen
   helps people get weather reports

3. goes into space like a rocket
   lands like an airplane
   can be used many times

4. place to live in space
   built by 16 nations
   place for space experiments

Skill Builder

Reading a Line Graph The line graph below compares the amount of time four *Apollo* spaceships spent on the moon. Study the line graph.

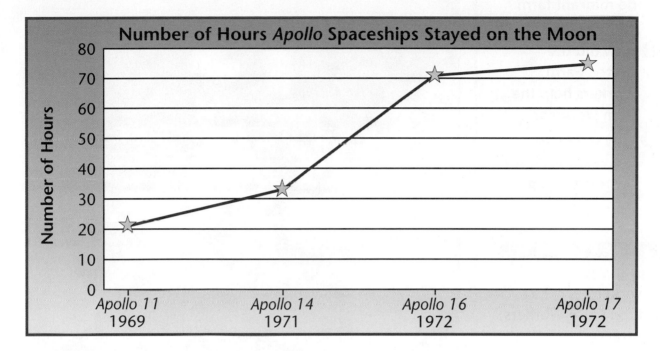

On your paper, write the answer that correctly answers each question.

1. How many hours did *Apollo 11* stay on the moon?
   22   33   75

2. How many hours did *Apollo 14* stay on the moon?
   22   33   75

3. Which spaceship stayed on the moon the most time?
   Apollo 11   *Apollo 16*   *Apollo 17*

4. What amount of time did each *Apollo* spaceship spend on the moon compared to the ones before?
   more   less   much less

Journal Writing

When Neil Armstrong stepped onto the moon for the first time, he spoke to all the people of Earth. He said, "That's one small step for (a) man; one giant leap for mankind." What do you think he meant when he said that? In your journal, write a paragraph that explains what Armstrong meant.

César Chávez and the Farm Workers

Find Out

❶ What problems do migrant farm workers have?

❷ How did the United Farm Workers help the farm workers?

❸ Why did César Chávez want farm owners to stop using pesticides?

NEW WORDS

migrant farm
  workers
United Farm Workers
contracts
grape growers
grape pickers
pesticides
fast
Teamsters

PEOPLE & PLACES

César Chávez
Dolores Huerta
Arturo Rodriguez

César Chávez was the leader of the United Farm Workers.

César Chávez was a Mexican American leader. He was born in Arizona in 1927. His parents came from Mexico. They owned a small farm in Arizona. During the Great Depression, they could not earn enough money to keep their farm. So the family moved to California when Chávez was ten years old. There they became **migrant farm workers**. Migrant farm workers work on one farm until there is no more work to do. Then they move to another farm.

Chávez and his family moved many times. Chávez went to 37 different schools because he moved so often. Most children of migrant farm workers go to many schools.

Migrant farm workers were paid very little money. Chávez decided to help the migrant farm workers.

**Learning from Pictures
What do you think
this migrant worker
is doing?** ➤

Dolores Huerta

**A poster asking people
to boycott grapes and
lettuce**

César Chávez liked the way Martin Luther King, Jr., used peaceful ways to change laws. Chávez said that he would find peaceful ways to help the farm workers, too.

In 1962 César Chávez started the first union for farm workers. Dolores Huerta, a Hispanic American, helped Chávez start the union. The union is called the **United Farm Workers**. Chávez wanted the union to get **contracts** for the farm workers. These papers would tell the farm owners how much money the farm workers had to be paid. The contracts would say how many hours each day the farm workers would work. The contracts also would say how the farm owners would keep the workers safe.

Most **grape growers** in California refused to give contracts and better salaries to the **grape pickers**. In 1965 Chávez told these farm workers to go on strike. During the strike the grape pickers did not work. They were not paid. Many Americans sent food and money to help the grape pickers. This strike lasted five years.

Chávez and Huerta also started a boycott against grape growers. Millions of people stopped buying California grapes that were not picked by union workers. The grape growers lost money. Finally, in 1970 most grape growers gave grape pickers their first contracts. The grape boycott ended. The grape pickers went back to work.

269

Arturo Rodriguez

César Chávez worked on another problem for the farm workers. Most grape growers spray **pesticides** on their grapes. The pesticides stop insects from eating the grapes. Doctors know that pesticides can make farm workers very sick. But grape growers would not stop using pesticides. So in 1988 Chávez stopped eating for 36 days. He drank only water. He used his **fast** to tell Americans about the pesticide problem. Some grape growers stopped spraying their grapes. But many grape growers continue to use pesticides.

Some farm workers have joined a different labor union called the **Teamsters**. The Teamsters union has helped some of the farm workers win new contracts.

César Chávez died in 1993. Arturo Rodriguez now leads the United Farm Workers. Dolores Huerta works with him. In 1997 Rodriguez and Huerta helped strawberry pickers get better pay and working conditions. In 2001 the United Farm Workers began to work to help improve United States immigration rules for all immigrant workers.

Many farm workers now have contracts from some of the fruit, flower, and vegetable growers. But other migrant workers still do not have contracts. They earn very little money. Thousands of migrant children are doing farm work each day. Many of these children do not go to school. Many farm workers continue to be sick because pesticides are sprayed on crops. The United Farm Workers continues to do Chávez's work.

PRIMARY SOURCE

"All workers deserve . . . respect, health care, housing and to make enough money to feed their family a decent [good] meal."

—*Arturo Rodriguez*

Pesticides are sprayed from a plane onto fields of crops. ➤

Using What You've Learned

Read and Remember

Choose the Answer Write the correct answers on your paper.

1. What do we call farm workers who move from farm to farm?
   migrant farm workers   union workers   striking workers

2. Who helped César Chávez start the United Farm Workers?
   Eileen Collins   Dolores Huerta   Rosa Parks

3. What did the California grape pickers do to get contracts?
   worked harder   called the President   went on strike

4. César Chávez started a boycott. What did he ask people not to buy?
   cotton   grapes   corn

5. What did most farm owners give the grape pickers in 1970?
   medicine   farms   contracts

Think and Apply

Sequencing Events Number your paper from 1 to 5. Write the sentences to show the correct order.

Arturo Rodriguez now leads the United Farm Workers.

In 1965 Chávez led a strike and a boycott against the grape growers.

César Chávez died in 1993.

César Chávez started the United Farm Workers in 1962.

As a child, César Chávez went to 37 different schools.

Journal Writing

Imagine you are a migrant farm worker in 1960. What are some things that need to be changed so you can have a better life? Write a paragraph in your journal that tells what needs to be changed.

Skill Builder

Using a Map Key to Read a Product Map A **product map** shows where different products are produced in an area. The **map key** explains what product symbols are used on the map. The product map below shows many important farm products of California. Study the map and the map key.

Write the correct answers on your paper.

1. What product is grown near Fresno?
   grapes   rice   lettuce

2. What product is grown near the Pacific Ocean?
   rice   lettuce   cotton

3. What is one product that is found in northern California?
   rice   cotton   cattle

4. Where is most of California's milk produced?
   near Sacramento   near Los Angeles   near Nevada

War in Vietnam

Find Out

❶ Why did the United States want to help South Vietnam?

❷ How did many Americans show they were against the war in Vietnam?

❸ What happened in Vietnam after all the American soldiers returned home?

NEW WORDS

protesters
cease-fire
memorial

PEOPLE & PLACES

Vietnam
Southeast Asia
North Vietnam
South Vietnam
Viet Cong
South Vietnamese
Lyndon B. Johnson
Richard Nixon
Maya Lin

Helicopters were used often during the fighting in Vietnam.

Vietnam is a country in Southeast Asia. In 1954 Vietnam was divided into two countries. The northern part was called North Vietnam. The southern part was called South Vietnam. Communists ruled North Vietnam. The leaders of South Vietnam did not want their country to be a Communist nation.

The two Vietnam nations agreed to hold elections in 1956. Their goal was to become one country. But South Vietnam's leaders decided not to hold elections. They said the Communists would prevent fair elections. So Vietnam remained two countries.

Many people in South Vietnam did not like the leaders of their government. The leaders were not honest. They did not work hard to help the nation's many poor people. Some people in South Vietnam began to fight against the government. They were called the Viet Cong. As time

A field in Vietnam

passed, many Viet Cong became Communists. They wanted South Vietnam to be a Communist nation. North Vietnam sent soldiers and weapons to help the Viet Cong in the war.

During the Cold War, Americans wanted to stop the spread of communism. Americans were worried because China, North Korea, and North Vietnam had become Communist nations. The Soviet Union and China sent many weapons to North Vietnam. The United States did not want the Communists to win in South Vietnam. From South Vietnam the Communists could win control of other countries in Southeast Asia.

In 1961 President John F. Kennedy began sending many weapons and planes to South Vietnam. American soldiers went to Vietnam to teach the South Vietnamese how to fight. But the Viet Cong were winning the war.

Lyndon B. Johnson became President in 1963. He sent more soldiers to Vietnam. In 1963 American soldiers began to fight the Viet Cong. Each year Johnson sent

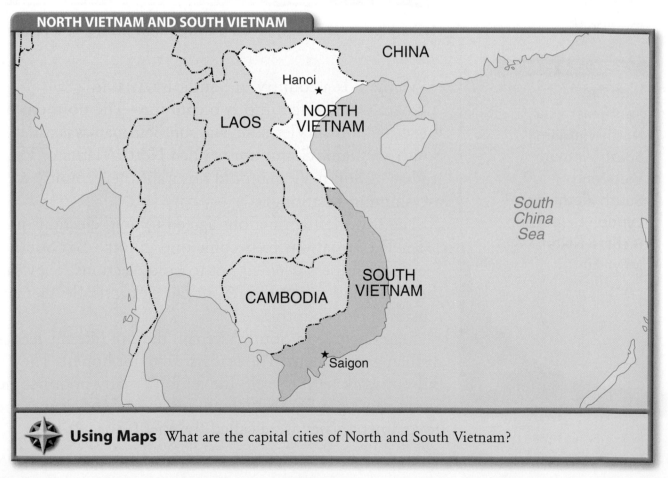

NORTH VIETNAM AND SOUTH VIETNAM

CHINA

Hanoi ★

LAOS

NORTH VIETNAM

South China Sea

CAMBODIA

SOUTH VIETNAM

★ Saigon

Using Maps What are the capital cities of North and South Vietnam?

Lyndon B. Johnson

Richard Nixon

more soldiers to fight in Vietnam. By 1968 there were 550,000 American soldiers fighting in Vietnam. The war lasted many years.

Every day Americans watched news reports about the war on television. They learned how hard it was to fight in Vietnam. Soldiers often fought in hot, dangerous jungles. Viet Cong soldiers hid in the jungles and attacked American soldiers. Communists from nearby countries helped the Viet Cong fight the Americans. Americans learned from news reports how many soldiers were killed each day.

During the Vietnam War, there were two groups of Americans. One group believed Americans must fight against communism in Vietnam. The other group was against sending Americans to fight in Vietnam. This group grew larger and larger during the war. These people said too many American soldiers were being killed. It cost millions of dollars for Americans to fight in Vietnam. Many Americans wanted this money to be spent in the United States.

By 1967 many Americans became **protesters** to show they were against the Vietnam War. Some protesters burned American flags. Others fought with police. There were fights and protests in every part of the country. A few protesters were killed.

In 1969 President Richard Nixon said that he would bring Americans home from Vietnam. Americans had

275

▶ **Learning from Pictures**
Maya Lin designed the Vietnam Memorial in Washington, D.C. Why do you think people visit the memorial? ▶

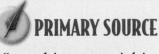

Many Vietnamese people now live in the United States.

taught the South Vietnamese how to fight the Viet Cong. The United States gave new weapons to South Vietnam.

On January 27, 1973, North Vietnam and South Vietnam promised to stop fighting. This was called a **cease-fire**. By 1975 most American soldiers were back home in the United States.

The fighting in Vietnam started again after American soldiers had returned home. By 1975 North Vietnam had captured most of South Vietnam. On April 30, 1975, South Vietnam surrendered. Vietnam became one Communist nation. Many people from South Vietnam left their country. Today, more than one million Vietnamese people are now American citizens.

The Vietnam War lasted longer than any other war Americans had fought in. Almost three million Americans fought in the Vietnam War. About 10,000 American women were in Vietnam. Many thousands of Americans were badly hurt in the war. About 58,000 Americans died.

Maya Lin designed a Vietnam **memorial**. It was built in Washington, D.C., to honor the Americans who died in Vietnam. The names of all the Americans who died are on the black walls of this memorial. Nearby, the Vietnam Women's Memorial honors the American women who were in the war. Millions of people visit these memorials each year.

276

Using What You've Learned

Read and Remember

Finish the Sentence On your paper, write the word or words that finish each sentence.

1. Vietnam is in _____ Asia.
   Northeast   Southeast   Northwest

2. In 1954 _____ was divided into two countries.
   Vietnam   the Soviet Union   China

3. The _____ in South Vietnam were Communists.
   protesters   Viet Cong   government leaders

4. In 1969 President _____ said he would bring Americans home from Vietnam.
   Kennedy   Johnson   Nixon

5. Almost 58 _____ Americans died in Vietnam.
   hundred   thousand   million

Think and Apply

Cause and Effect Match each cause on the left with an effect on the right. On your paper, write the letter of the effect.

Cause

1. North Vietnam wanted South Vietnam to be a Communist country, so _____

2. The United States did not want South Vietnam to be a Communist country, so _____

3. Many Americans wanted the United States to stop fighting in Vietnam, so _____

4. In 1975 North Vietnam won control of South Vietnam, so _____

Effect

a. American soldiers went to fight in South Vietnam.

b. all of Vietnam became one Communist nation.

c. they held protests against the war.

d. North Vietnam helped the Viet Cong fight in South Vietnam.

Skill Builder

Reading a Bar Graph The bar graph below shows the number of United States soldiers in Vietnam during the Vietnam War. Study the graph.

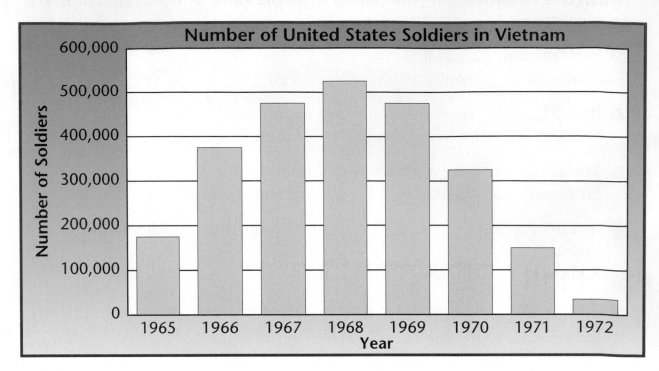

On your paper, write a sentence to answer each question.

1. In which year was the greatest number of United States soldiers in Vietnam?

2. In which years did the United States have more than 400,000 soldiers in Vietnam?

3. Did the United States have more soldiers in Vietnam during 1969 or during 1970?

4. In what year did the United States have less than 100,000 soldiers in Vietnam?

Journal Writing

Many protesters marched to show they were against the war in Vietnam. Why did they want soldiers from the United States to stop fighting in this war? Write a paragraph in your journal that tells what the protesters believed about the war.

Review

Study the time line on this page. Then use the words in blue print to finish the story. On your paper, write the words you choose.

Cuba	**Supreme Court**	**shuttle**
strike	**Berlin Wall**	**Cold War**
rovers	**South Vietnam**	**Communist**

After World War II, the __(1)__ began between the United States and the Soviet Union. The United States was very angry when the Soviet Union built the __(2)__ in 1961. In 1962 the Soviet Union sent missiles to __(3)__ . In 1963 Americans began to fight in __(4)__ . Vietnam became one __(5)__ country in 1975.

Many other events have occurred since World War II. In 1954 the __(6)__ ruled that there cannot be separate schools for African American children and white children. Grape pickers held a __(7)__ against grape growers in 1965. In 1999 Eileen Collins was the first woman to command a space __(8)__ flight. In 2003 the United States sent __(9)__ to Mars.

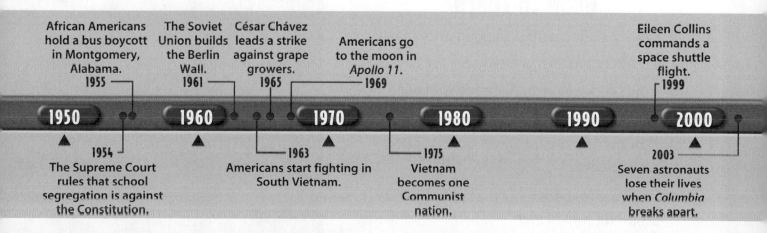

African Americans hold a bus boycott in Montgomery, Alabama.
1955

The Soviet Union builds the Berlin Wall.
1961

César Chávez leads a strike against grape growers.
1965

Americans go to the moon in *Apollo 11*.
1969

Eileen Collins commands a space shuttle flight.
1999

1950   1960   1970   1980   1990   2000

1954
The Supreme Court rules that school segregation is against the Constitution.

1963
Americans start fighting in South Vietnam.

1975
Vietnam becomes one Communist nation.

2003
Seven astronauts lose their lives when *Columbia* breaks apart.

Challenges in Today's World

The United States is a changing nation. As we start the 2000s, we must find new ways to solve problems. Pollution is a problem. We need clean air and clean water. We need new ways to keep peace in many parts of the world.

Americans are working to solve these problems. They are also working to improve their nation. They want more trade with other countries. They want to have enough energy for their cars and homes. People want better schools and better health care. They want to be safe both in the United States and when they travel to other parts of the world. During the 2000s, people will continue working to solve problems and to improve life for all Americans.

Congress passes the Clean Air Act and the Americans with Disabilities Act.
1990

1990

1991
The Cold War ends. United Nations soldiers attack Iraq during the Persian Gulf War.

Read to Learn

- How has our country changed since it first became a nation?

- How can we have better trade with our neighbors?

- How can the United States work toward world peace?

- What can you do to build a better United States for tomorrow?

The United States,
Mexico, and Canada
sign NAFTA.
1993

The United States helps
Palestinians and Israelis
sign a peace agreement.
1998

Terrorists attack
the United States
on September 11.
2001

The war with
Iraq begins.
2003

1995

2000

2005

1995
The United
States helps end
war in Bosnia.

1999
The United States
and NATO work for
peace in Kosovo.

2000
The United States
improves trade with
China.

2004
George W. Bush is
re-elected President
of the United States.

281

The United States and Its Neighbors

Find Out

❶ How have Canada and the United States worked together?

❷ How does selling oil help Mexico?

❸ How has NAFTA changed trade between Canada, Mexico, and the United States?

NEW WORDS

unguarded border
acid rain
chemicals
pollution
developing country
permission
illegal aliens
North American Free Trade Agreement (NAFTA)

PEOPLE & PLACES

Quebec
St. Lawrence Seaway
Great Lakes
Latin America
Brazil
Chile

President Bill Clinton signed the North American Free Trade Agreement in 1993.

Canada and Mexico are the closest neighbors of the United States. Each year millions of people from the United States visit Canada and Mexico. The map on page 283 shows the United States, Canada, and Mexico.

Canada is our northern neighbor. There is a strong friendship between the United States and Canada. The longest **unguarded border** in the world separates the two countries. The government of Canada is a democracy. Canada was settled by the French first. Later it was settled by the English. Both English and French are the languages of Canada.

Today most French people in Canada live in the area of Quebec. Many people in Quebec have wanted Quebec to be a separate nation. So far all of Canada has remained one nation.

Factory pollution

The United States and Canada built the St. Lawrence Seaway together. The seaway allows large ships to travel from the Atlantic Ocean all the way through the Great Lakes. Electricity is made by water power at the seaway. Both countries use this electricity.

Acid rain is a problem that both nations are trying to solve together. Factories and cars send smoke, dirt, and **chemicals** into the air. The smoke, dirt, and chemicals cause **pollution**. Pollution in the air causes acid rain. Acid rain harms forests, lakes, and farm soil.

American pollution causes nearly half the acid rain in Canada. In 1990 the United States Congress passed the Clean Air Act. This law said that Americans must cause less air pollution. People have found ways to help factories and cars send less pollution into the air. Today there is less acid rain in some areas of both countries.

The United States also has a strong friendship with Mexico. Mexico is our southern neighbor. The language

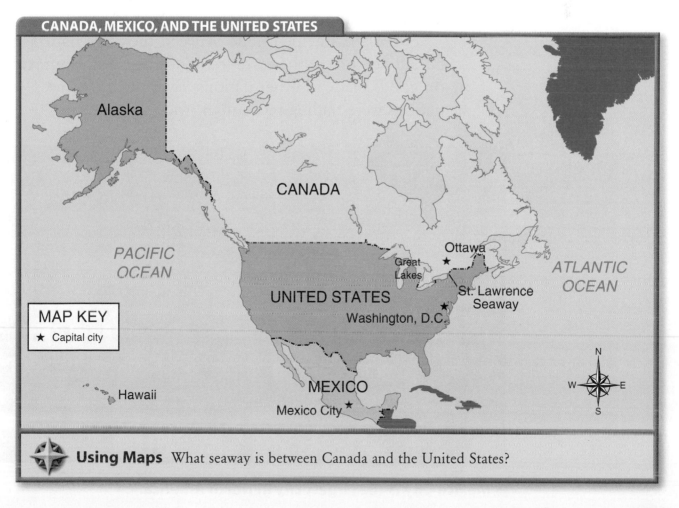

CANADA, MEXICO, AND THE UNITED STATES

Alaska

CANADA

PACIFIC OCEAN

Ottawa ★

Great Lakes

ATLANTIC OCEAN

St. Lawrence Seaway

UNITED STATES

Washington, D.C. ★

MAP KEY

★ Capital city

Hawaii

MEXICO

Mexico City ★

N
W · E
S

Using Maps What seaway is between Canada and the United States?

Border between Mexico and the United States

of Mexico is Spanish. Mexico has large amounts of oil. It earns about one third of its money by selling oil to other nations. Mexico City is the capital of Mexico.

Mexico is a **developing country**. A developing country does not have enough industries. Industries are the businesses and factories of an area. A developing country also has a very large number of poor people. Mexico is working hard to solve these problems. Life has improved for many Mexicans.

Each year thousands of Mexicans move to the United States. They hope to earn more money. Some Mexicans come to the United States without **permission**. People who come to the United States without permission are called **illegal aliens**. The United States is trying to stop illegal aliens from entering the country.

Trade is important between the United States, Canada, and Mexico. In 1993 the three nations signed an agreement to make trade easier with one another. This important agreement is called the **North American Free Trade Agreement**. It is often called NAFTA.

NAFTA has helped trade between the three nations because each year there are fewer tariffs. Tariffs are taxes on goods made in other nations. By 2003 the three nations were trading more than twice the amount of

▲ **Mexico City is the largest city in North America.**

❯ **Learning from Pictures** How do goods travel between the United States, Mexico, and Canada? ❯

PRIMARY SOURCE

"We fought for NAFTA, which created a free market with our neighbors."

—*President Bill Clinton*

The United States trades with countries in Latin America.

goods than before NAFTA began. By 2009 most goods from the three NAFTA nations will be bought and sold without tariffs.

NAFTA makes it easier for people in one country to get jobs in the other countries. It is also easier for people to own factories and businesses in the other countries. But the United States has been losing money because it buys more goods than it sells to its neighbors.

Americans have lost factory jobs because of NAFTA. This has happened because American businesses have built new factories in Mexico. Factory owners save money by paying low salaries to Mexican workers. Then the factory owners sell their goods in the United States.

The United States trades with other neighbors. These neighbors are the countries of Latin America. Brazil is the largest country in Latin America. It is becoming a leader in manufacturing. Americans buy many factory products from Brazil. Chile is another country in Latin America. It is the largest seller of copper in the world. The United States trades with Chile. Americans buy copper and fruit from Chile. There is friendship between the United States and its neighbors.

Using Geography Themes

Human/Environment Interaction: Acid Rain

The theme of human/environment interaction tells how people live in an area. People in cold areas wear coats. People near oceans might fish for their food. The theme also tells how people can change an area. People use the land to help them live and work. They cut down trees to build houses. Sometimes the ways people live and work can greatly harm the environment.

Read the paragraphs about acid rain. Study the photo below and the map on page 287.

Acid rain looks and tastes like plain rain. But acid rain causes terrible harm. It kills trees, farm crops, and other plants. Acid rain hurts fish and plants when it falls into lakes and rivers. Sometimes many fish die. When acid rain kills crops and fish, there is less food for people.

Acid rain is made when **fossil fuels** are burned. Coal, oil, and natural gas are fossil fuels. They were formed deep inside the earth very long ago. Power plants burn fossil fuels to make electricity. Gasoline is made from oil. Cars burn gasoline in order to move. Coal is the fuel that causes the most acid rain.

Power plants, factories, and cars send pollution into the air and sky when they burn fossil fuels. Rain becomes acid rain when it falls through clouds filled with air pollution. Acid rain also can fall as snow, fog, and icy rain.

Acid rain can hurt trees, farm crops, and other plants. ▷

The Northeast of the United States has many factories, cars, and power plants. It has a lot of acid rain. Winds blow the Northeast's air pollution into eastern Canada. It becomes acid rain there. American air pollution causes about half of Canada's acid rain.

The United States and Canada now have laws to control air pollution. By the year 2010, factories must make less pollution than they do today. Some car companies are making cars that need very little gasoline. Both countries are trying different ways to make **energy** without burning fossil fuel.

Many people are using less electricity so less fossil fuel is burned. They turn off electric lights and televisions when they do not need them. Some people get their electricity from energy made by wind or water. Others save gasoline by walking or riding a bike.

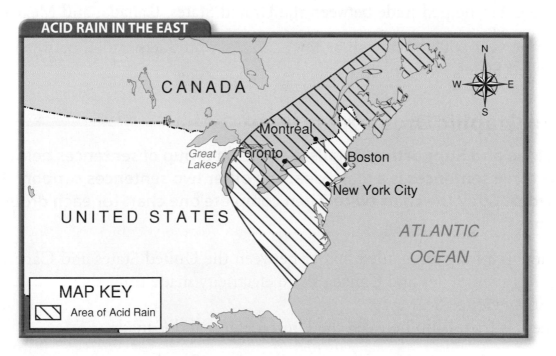

ACID RAIN IN THE EAST

CANADA

Montreal

Great Lakes · Toronto

Boston

New York City

UNITED STATES

ATLANTIC OCEAN

MAP KEY

Area of Acid Rain

On your paper, write the answer to each question.

1 How does acid rain hurt plants and fish?

2 What happens to the air when fossil fuels are burned?

3 How does American pollution in the Northeast hurt Canada?

4 What are the two nations doing to solve the acid rain problem?

5 How can people make less air pollution?

6 Look at the map. What are two cities in an area with acid rain?

Using What You've Learned

Read and Remember

Choose a Word Choose the best word or words in blue print to finish each sentence. On your paper, write the word or words you choose.

Quebec	**tariffs**	**oil**
Clean Air Act	**NAFTA**	

1. Most French people in Canada live in _____ .

2. Congress passed the _____ to control air pollution.

3. Mexico earns a lot of money by selling its _____ .

4. _____ has helped trade between the United States, Canada, and Mexico.

5. By the year 2009, there will be few _____ on products traded between the United States, Mexico, and Canada.

Using Graphic Organizers

Main Idea and Supporting Details Read each group of sentences below. One of the three sentences is a main idea. The other two sentences support the main idea. Copy the chart twice. Then complete one chart for each group of sentences.

1. There is a long unguarded border between the United States and Canada.
   The United States and Canada share electricity made from the
     St. Lawrence Seaway.
   There is friendship between the United States and Canada.

2. The United States buys factory products from Brazil.
   The United States trades with its neighbors in Latin America.
   The United States buys copper and fruit from Chile.

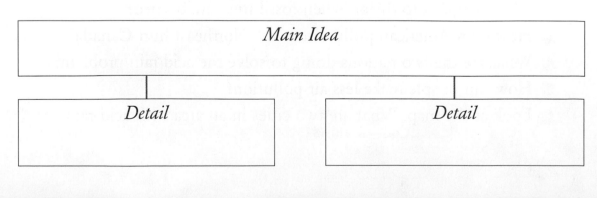

288

Skill Builder

Reading a Double Line Graph A **double line graph** compares facts by using two different lines. The graph below shows money the United States spent on **imports** from two NAFTA countries, Mexico and Canada, from 1994 to 2003. Imports are goods brought in from another country for sale or use. The United States also earns money from **exports** to Mexico and Canada. Exports are goods that are sold or traded to another country. The blue line shows how much money the United States spent on imports from Mexico. The red line shows how much money the United States spent on imports from Canada. Study the graph.

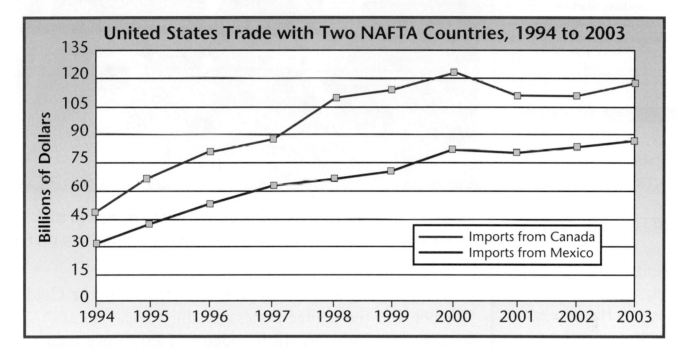

On your paper, write the date or words that answer each question.

1 In which year were American imports from Canada the least?
1994   1995   2001

2 In which year were American imports from Mexico the most?
1994   1999   2003

3 In 2002 the United States spent about how many billions of dollars on imports from Mexico?
113 billion   85 billion   55 billion

4 From 1994 to 2003, what happened to imports from Canada and Mexico?
grew smaller   grew larger   stayed the same

289

Find Out

❶ How did the Cold War end?

❷ How has the United States worked with the United Nations and NATO?

❸ How has the United States worked for peace in many parts of the world?

NEW WORDS

Persian Gulf War
relations
PNTR

PEOPLE & PLACES

Kuwait
Middle East
Iraq
Saddam Hussein
Israel
Arabs
Egypt
Bill Clinton
Jordan
Palestinians
Bosnia
Kosovo
Serbia

The United States As a World Leader

In 2003 the United States sent peacekeeping troops to the African nation of Liberia. There had been much fighting there.

You read about the Cold War in Chapter 36. The Cold War between the United States and the Soviet Union started after World War II. It ended in 1991. Since then the United States has been the strongest world leader.

The Cold War ended when the Soviet Union and the nations of Eastern Europe started new governments. These countries removed their Communist leaders. In 1989 the Berlin Wall in East Germany was torn down. A year later East Germany and West Germany became one nation again. Berlin became the capital of a united Germany.

The Soviet Union was made up of 15 smaller countries. One Communist government ruled these 15 countries. In 1991 the 15 countries became independent. They started their own governments. This was the end of the Soviet Union. Russia had been the largest country in the Soviet Union. Russia is trying to become a democracy.

The Berlin Wall was torn down in 1989.

Bill Clinton

Since the Cold War ended, the United Nations and the United States have worked to keep the peace in many parts of the world. Sometimes the United Nations sends soldiers to countries where there is fighting. Many of the soldiers are Americans. American soldiers also work with NATO to protect countries in Western and Eastern Europe.

The United States worked with the United Nations to help Kuwait. Kuwait is a small, oil-rich nation in the Middle East. In 1990 Iraq, Kuwait's neighbor, took control of Kuwait. Saddam Hussein, Iraq's leader, wanted Kuwait's oil. In 1991 the United States led many nations in a war against Iraq. The war was called the **Persian Gulf War**. Kuwait became a free country again.

Much fighting has also occurred between the nation of Israel and the Arab nations around it. These countries strongly disagree about who should own the land of Israel. The Arab nations think Israel should belong to the Arab people called Palestinians. The Jewish people want Israel to be their homeland.

In 1979 the United States helped Israel and Egypt sign a peace treaty. It was the first peace treaty between an Arab nation and Israel. In 1994 President Bill Clinton helped Israel and Jordan also sign a peace treaty.

The United States also has worked for peace between Israelis and Palestinians. In 1993 and 1998, the United States helped their leaders sign peace agreements. In 2000 their leaders met in the United States again, but they did

The Persian Gulf War was fought in the deserts of Kuwait and Iraq. ➤

not sign another peace agreement. That year there was more fighting between Israelis and Palestinians.

In 2003 the United States and many other countries helped make a plan for peace between Israelis and Palestinians. The plan is called a "roadmap" for peace. The goal of the plan was to end the Israeli-Palestinian conflict by 2005.

The United States has worked for peace in southern Europe. In 1992 a nation called Bosnia and Herzegovina became independent from Yugoslavia. Bosnia and Herzegovina is often called Bosnia. A war began between the three different groups of people who live in Bosnia. In 1995 their leaders met in the United States. They agreed to stop fighting. NATO soldiers, including Americans, went to Bosnia to help keep peace.

By 2004 only about 7,000 peacekeeping soldiers were needed because there was peace in Bosnia. The peacekeeping soldiers left. They had helped rebuild many towns in Bosnia which had been destroyed by the war.

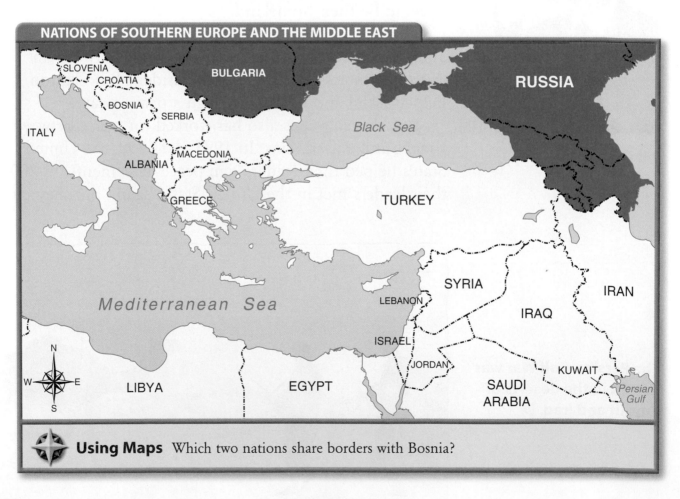

NATIONS OF SOUTHERN EUROPE AND THE MIDDLE EAST

Using Maps Which two nations share borders with Bosnia?

Learning from Pictures United States soldiers helped to rebuild Kosovo after the fighting stopped. How do you think these soldiers are helping the people of Kosovo?

The United States has worked for peace in Kosovo, another part of southern Europe. Kosovo is a state in a country called Serbia. Many people in Kosovo wanted to be independent from Serbia. In 1998 the Serbian army attacked Kosovo. The Serbians forced thousands of people to leave Kosovo. So in 1999 American pilots helped NATO bomb Serbia. After two months Serbia agreed to stop fighting. After the fighting stopped, many people returned to Kosovo. The United States and other countries helped rebuild Kosovo. They started to rebuild homes, hospitals, schools, and roads.

The United States has also helped African nations. There has been fighting in many parts of Africa. In 2004 the United States began to train 50,000 soldiers to help Africa. These African soldiers will try to keep peace between the people of different African nations.

Trade helps improve **relations** between the United States and other nations. The United States has given Permanent Normal Trade Relations, or **PNTR**, to many nations. This means that there are low tariffs on goods traded with these nations. In 2000 the United States gave PNTR to China. Since then there has been more trade each year between the United States and China. In 2003 the United States gave PNTR to Russia.

The United States continues to work for trade with many nations. It also helps bring peace to many nations.

293

Using What You've Learned

Read and Remember

True or False On your paper, write **T** for each sentence that is true. Write **F** for each sentence that is false.

1. The Berlin Wall was torn down.

2. Today the Soviet Union is the strongest world leader.

3. Since the Cold War, the United Nations has worked for world peace.

4. The United States helped Egypt and Jordan sign peace treaties with Israel.

5. There was a war between ten groups of people in Bosnia.

6. In 2000 the United States improved friendship with China when it gave PNTR to China.

Think and Apply

Cause and Effect Match each cause on the left with an effect on the right. On your paper, write the letter of the effect.

Cause	Effect
1. The Soviet Union and the nations of Eastern Europe removed their Communist governments, so _____	a. the United States led many nations in a war against Iraq.
2. Iraq would not leave Kuwait, so _____	b. the United States has tried to help Israelis and Palestinians sign peace agreements.
3. Israelis and Palestinians have been enemies, so _____	c. the United States began to train African soldiers to keep the peace.
4. Serbia would not stop fighting against Kosovo, so _____	d. the Cold War ended.
5. The United States wanted to help African nations in 2004, so _____	e. American pilots helped NATO bomb Serbia.

Skill Builder

Reading a Double Bar Graph A **double bar graph** compares facts by using two different colored bars. The double bar graph below shows imports and exports between the United States and China. Imports are goods brought in from another country for sale or use. Exports are goods that are sold or traded to another country. Study the graph.

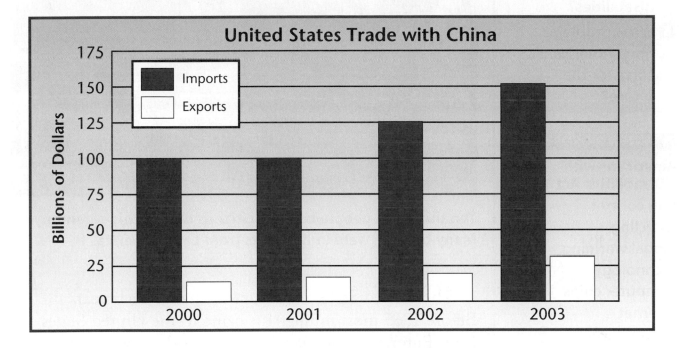

On your paper, write the number or date that answers each question.

1 How much did the United States buy from China in 2001?
  $20 billion $100 billion $140 billion

2 When did the United States buy the most goods from China?
  2001   2002   2003

3 How much more money did the United States spend on goods from China in 2002 than in 2001?
  $2 billion $25 billion $100 billion

4 When did China import almost $30 billion of American goods?
  2000   2002   2003

5 When did the United States have the least trade with China?
  2000   2001   2002

A Changing Nation

Find Out

❶ How is the United States changing?

❷ How have laws helped Americans who have disabilities?

❸ What problems must Americans solve for the future?

NEW WORDS

Americans with
  Disabilities Act
gun control
recycling
global warming
technology
computer chips
Internet
communicate
e-mail
cell phones
camera phones
genes
DNA

PEOPLE & PLACES

Ben Nighthorse
  Campbell

Ten thousand people became citizens during this ceremony. Many of them were immigrants from Latin America.

The United States continues to change each year. Before 1965 most immigrants came to the United States from Europe. A 1965 law has helped other people come to America. Thousands of Asians, Latin Americans, and people from other places become immigrants each year.

Two hundred years ago, all government leaders in the United States were white men. Now women are government leaders, too. African Americans, Asian Americans, and Hispanic Americans are in Congress. In 1992 Ben Nighthorse Campbell was elected the first Native American senator in more than sixty years.

American laws now say that all people should be treated fairly. The Civil Rights Act of 1964 said all people have equal rights. In 1990 Congress passed the **Americans with Disabilities Act**. This law said that Americans with disabilities have the same rights as other Americans.

Laws protect the rights of people with disabilities. ➤

Carleton Fiorina, Chief Executive Officer of a large computer company

Today American women work at every kind of job. Some women have become company presidents. But most women still earn less money than men do.

One problem in our country today is that 31 million Americans are poor. Many of these people are children.

Another problem in the United States is that each year thousands of people are killed by people with guns. The Constitution allows Americans to own guns. Most gun owners do not use guns to hurt people.

In 1994 Congress passed a **gun control** law. This law prevents store owners from selling guns to many people who were once in jail. Many Americans want the nation to have more laws to prevent dangerous people from buying guns. Other Americans are against more gun control laws. So far Congress has not passed more gun control laws.

The United States has many natural resources. Some of them are forests, metals, and coal. We must save our resources for tomorrow. Americans help save resources by **recycling**. Recycling means old products are reused and made into new products. Many people recycle plastic bottles, metal cans, newspapers, and glass bottles.

Countries burn oil, coal, and natural gas to make energy. These fossil fuels are being used up. In Chapter 42, you read that burning fossil fuel causes air pollution and acid rain.

Using wind power to make electricity

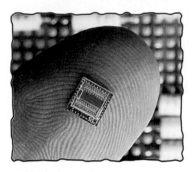

A computer chip

Air pollution causes another big problem called **global warming**. Global warming means Earth's air is becoming warmer. This is happening because factories and cars burn fossil fuels. Different gases become part of the air. These gases trap too much of the sun's heat near Earth. Global warming can cause snow and ice in cold areas to melt. It can cause dangerous weather changes in many parts of the world.

Americans buy large amounts of oil from other countries in order to make gasoline and electricity. But the United States is trying to find ways to make energy without using fossil fuels. Some people use energy from the sun to heat their homes. In California, wind power is used to make some of the state's electricity. Some cities have power plants that use garbage to make electricity.

Computers and other **technology** are changing America. **Computer chips** have made a lot of the new technology possible. Computer chips are tiny pieces of material that store large amounts of information. Computer chips are inside large and small computers. Today, many people use small computers that can fit in the palm of a hand. These hand-held computers do some of the same things as large computers.

The **Internet** is part of the new technology. It is a huge system that allows millions of computers to **communicate**

➤ **Learning from Pictures** What kind of technology are these students using? ➤

This scientist is using DNA information to help police learn if someone has done a crime. ➤

Person using a cell phone

Everyone can help save our natural resources by recycling.

with one another. **E-mail** allows people to send letters by computer to any part of the world in only a few seconds.

People have developed other ways to communicate with one another. Many people use **cell phones** that let them make calls from almost anywhere. The newest cell phones are **camera phones** that take pictures. The pictures can be sent to other camera phones or computers anywhere in the world.

Technology has also changed science. Scientists are studying the human **genes**. Genes are found in every cell of every living thing. Genes are made of material called **DNA**. All people have their own DNA pattern that is different from every other person's DNA. The DNA in your cells decides many things about you. It decides your hair color and eye color. The information in genes can help scientists understand why people get sick. It can also help scientists create medicines to cure diseases. Scientists have also used DNA information to learn which people have done crimes.

Science and technology are helping Americans create better medicine and other products. Americans are working to improve life for people everywhere.

Using What You've Learned

Read and Remember

Match Up Finish each sentence in Group A with words from Group B. On your paper, write the letter of the correct answer.

Group A

1. The Civil Rights Act of 1964 said _____

2. A 1990 law helped _____

3. In 1992 Ben Nighthorse Campbell was elected _____

4. Scientists study information in genes _____

Group B

a. people with disabilities.

b. all people have equal rights.

c. to create medicines to cure diseases.

d. the first Native American senator in more than sixty years.

Think and Apply

Categories Read the words in each group. Decide how they are alike. Choose the best title in blue print for each group. Write the title on your paper.

Recycling   Global Warming
Technology   Ways to Make Energy

1. wind power used to make electricity
   sun energy used to heat homes
   garbage used to make electricity

2. a way to save natural resources
   can reuse plastic and glass
   can reuse paper and metal

3. Internet
   cell phones
   camera phones

4. caused by burning of fossil fuels
   sun's heat is trapped near Earth
   can change the weather

Journal Writing

What problem in our nation do you think needs to be solved? Write a letter to your United States senator. Tell your senator about the problem. Tell the senator how you think the problem should be solved. Mail the letter to your senator in Washington, D.C.

Skill Builder

Writing an Outline An **outline** is a written plan that puts information in order. It groups a main idea with supporting details. Main ideas often have a Roman numeral in front of them. Supporting details often have a capital letter in front of them. Outlines can help you study or write a report. The outline below puts information from Chapter 44 in order. Read the outline and then answer the questions.

<table>
<tr><td></td><td colspan="2">A Changing Nation</td></tr>
<tr><td>I.</td><td colspan="2">Changing People</td></tr>
<tr><td></td><td>A.</td><td>New immigrants</td></tr>
<tr><td></td><td>B.</td><td>More jobs in government and business for women and minorities</td></tr>
<tr><td></td><td>C.</td><td>Fair treatment for the disabled</td></tr>
<tr><td>II.</td><td colspan="2">Problems in Our Nation</td></tr>
<tr><td></td><td>A.</td><td>Gun laws</td></tr>
<tr><td></td><td>B.</td><td>Recycling</td></tr>
<tr><td></td><td>C.</td><td>Global warming</td></tr>
<tr><td>III.</td><td colspan="2">New Technologies</td></tr>
<tr><td></td><td>A.</td><td>Computers and the Internet</td></tr>
<tr><td></td><td>B.</td><td>Camera phones</td></tr>
<tr><td></td><td>C.</td><td>Human genes and DNA</td></tr>
</table>

1) What is everything in the outline about?

2) What are the three main ideas of this outline?

3) What are the supporting details of main idea III?

4) Which main idea would you place the following detail under? *Saving our resources*

5) How can writing an outline help you when you read a chapter?

America Since the Year 2000

Find Out

❶ How was the 2000 election different from other elections?

❷ What did terrorists do on September 11, 2001?

❸ What happened during the Iraq War?

NEW WORDS

century
hijack
terrorism
passengers
al Qaeda
Patriot Act of 2001
Department of Homeland Security
weapons of mass destruction
Iraq War

PEOPLE & PLACES

George W. Bush
Al Gore
Rudolph Giuliani
World Trade Center
Pentagon
Osama bin Laden
Saudi Arabia
Afghanistan
Taliban

In the 2000 election, Al Gore and George W. Bush had almost the same number of votes. In the end, George W. Bush won the election.

On January 1, 2001, Americans entered the twenty-first **century**. The new century brought new problems.

Electing a new President became a problem in 2000. During the election, Al Gore and George W. Bush received almost the same number of votes. It took more than five weeks to decide who would be President. The United States Supreme Court made a decision that allowed George W. Bush to win the election. In January 2001, Bush became the nation's forty-third President.

Terrorism has been a very big problem since 2000. It is the use of force to scare and control people and nations. Terrorists are people who cause terrorism.

➤ **Learning from Pictures** The Twin Towers of the World Trade Center fell to the ground after a terrorist attack. What are the firemen doing? ➤

Rudy Giuliani, Mayor of New York City on September 11, 2001.

On the morning of September 11, 2001, nineteen Arab terrorists from the Middle East **hijacked** four airplanes. They crashed two of the planes into the tall Twin Towers of New York City's World Trade Center. Enormous fires filled the buildings and thousands of people were trapped. Later, the burning buildings fell to the ground. Nearly 3,000 people died. Rescue workers saved many others. Hundreds of brave firefighters and many police officers died as they tried to save people.

The terrorists crashed the third plane into the Pentagon. The Pentagon is a huge office building near Washington, D.C. Military offices are in the Pentagon. Almost 200 people were killed there.

Terrorists planned to crash the fourth plane inside Washington, D.C. But the plane's **passengers** had used cell phones and learned what happened to the Twin Towers and to the Pentagon. They decided to stop the terrorists from crashing into the capital. Instead, the plane crashed into a field in Pennsylvania. Forty people died.

The attacks of September 11 were the worst attacks ever on American land. All Americans were angry.

Some American soldiers traveled across the Afghan desert on horses. Afghan fighters traveled with them. ➤

Osama bin Laden

In 2002 Afghan girls were allowed to go to school for the first time in five years.

The nineteen terrorists who attacked America belonged to a large group called **al Qaeda**. Osama bin Laden leads al Qaeda. He believes in an extreme form of the Muslim religion. Most Muslims are against terrorism. But bin Laden and his followers hate freedom of religion, even for Muslims. They want to destroy America and its friends.

President George W. Bush said the United States would fight a War on Terrorism. The war began in the Asian country of Afghanistan where bin Laden was hiding. He had trained thousands of terrorists there. President Bush told Afghanistan's rulers, the Taliban, there would be war if they did not give bin Laden to the United States. The Taliban did not listen. So in October 2001, the American army attacked Afghanistan and defeated the Taliban. Americans helped start a new government that allowed more freedom. The soldiers did not find bin Laden. Still, in the next few years America and its friends captured terrorists in many countries. In 2004 Americans helped the people of Afghanistan have their first free election for a president.

Americans worked to stop terrorist attacks at home, too. Congress passed a law called the **Patriot Act of 2001**. This law gave the government more power to search for people who might be terrorists. Some Americans think this law takes too many rights away from the people.

In 2003 Congress also created the **Department of Homeland Security**. Its job is to stop terrorism in the United States.

After September 11, President George W. Bush was worried that terrorists might get dangerous weapons from Iraq. In Chapter 43 you read that the United States fought Iraq during the Persian Gulf War in 1991. At the war's end, Kuwait became free. However, Iraq's dictator, Saddam Hussein, continued to rule his country. Anyone who tried to go against him was put in jail or killed.

At the end of the Persian Gulf War, Iraq promised to destroy its **weapons of mass destruction**. These are weapons that can kill thousands of people at a time. President George W. Bush did not want terrorists to get these dangerous weapons. He also did not want Iraq to use them against other countries. He said Iraq must prove to United Nations workers that it had destroyed the weapons. Saddam refused to tell what had happened to all of the weapons.

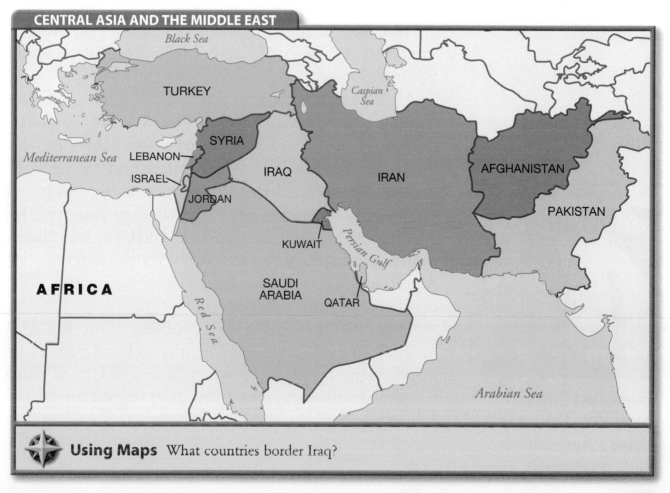

CENTRAL ASIA AND THE MIDDLE EAST

Using Maps What countries border Iraq?

In 2004 Iraq's new leaders took office.

During the Iraq War, American soldiers took down a statue of Saddam Hussein.

In March 2003 the United States attacked Iraq. Britain, Spain, Italy, and other nations joined the United States in the **Iraq War**. United States soldiers quickly forced Saddam from power. He went into hiding, but American soldiers captured him in December 2003.

After Saddam's capture, fighting still continued. There were many attacks against both American soldiers and many citizens of Iraq. The United States helped to rebuild the country's schools, roads, hospitals, and oil fields. The United States wanted Iraq to rule itself again. On June 28, 2004, new Iraqi leaders began to rule their country. Three days later the American soldiers handed Saddam Hussein over to the Iraqis to be put on trial for his crimes. American soldiers did not find weapons of mass destruction after the war ended.

Terrorism continues to be a problem in the world today. Terrorists attacks have happened in all parts of the world. Many people have been killed. The United States has joined with many other countries to find terrorists and stop them.

Using What You've Learned

Read and Remember

Write the Answer On your paper write one or more sentences to answer each question.

1. How was the 2000 election different from other elections?

2. Where did the four planes crash on September 11, 2001?

3. Who is Osama bin Laden?

4. Why did bin Laden and the al Qaeda terrorists hate the United States?

5. What did the United States do in Afghanistan?

6. How does the Department of Homeland Security protect the United States?

7. Who is Saddam Hussein?

8. Why did the United States go to war against Iraq in 2003?

Think and Apply

Sequencing Events Number your paper from 1 to 5. Write the sentences to show the correct order.

In January 2001 George W. Bush became the forty-third President of the United States.

Terrorists hijacked four planes and attacked the United States on September 11, 2001.

Iraqi leaders took control of their government on June 28, 2004.

Congress passed the Patriot Act in 2001.

Saddam Hussein ruled Iraq after the Persian Gulf War ended in 1991.

Journal Writing

Write a paragraph that tells what happened in the United States on September 11, 2001. Tell how you feel about what happened that day.

Skill Builder

Reading a Newspaper A **newspaper** reports the news that happens each day. It reports events in the United States and in other countries. It also has news stories about sports, science, cooking, and many other topics. Newspapers have a table of contents on the first or second page that tells you where to find information. The first page of a newspaper is called the front page. The title of the story on the front page is called the headline.

Read the front page of this newspaper:

CHICAGO DAILY REPORT

Partly Cloudy

JUNE 28, 2004

Iraqi Leaders in Control of Government

Baghdad, Iraq, June 28, 2004– The United States gave a group of Iraqi leaders short-term control of Iraq's new government. President Ghazi Al-Yawer leads the new government. Ayad Allawi is the new Prime Minister.

Some Iraqis think the event does not mean anything. Others say it is a step in the right direction. United States soldiers will stay in Iraq for now, but the new government will help to run the country. It will also help to plan national elections.

(See page 2)

TABLE OF CONTENTS

News	1	Food	40
Editorial	28	Business	42
Science	34	Weather	44
Sports	37	Movies	46
TV	48		

On your paper, write the answer to each question.

1 What is the date on the front page?

2 What is the headline?

3 What page has the news story for the front page?

4 Where can you find an article about baseball?

5 What information would you find on page 44?

CHAPTER
46

Find Out

❶ How is America's population changing?

❷ Why are Americans worried about Social Security?

❸ What is the No Child Left Behind law?

NEW WORDS

diverse
baby boomers
retire
Social Security
Medicare
medical
health insurance

PEOPLE & PLACES

George W. Bush
Edward Kennedy

Working for a Better Tomorrow

The population of the United States is growing more diverse.

The population of the United States is changing. First, the population continues to grow larger. Almost 300 million people now live in the United States. Almost 70 million more people lived in the United States in 2000 than in 1980.

America's population is also growing more **diverse**. Immigrants from many countries continue coming to America. Today more than one out of ten Americans was born in a different country. As you read in Chapter 44, many Americans now come from countries in Asia and Latin America. People from other countries bring new art and music to the United States. They also bring delicious new foods. Tacos, egg rolls, sushi, and bagels are popular foods. Immigrants brought these foods to the United States.

309

Many baby boomers will soon retire from their jobs. Some will enjoy spending more time with their families. >

Social Security card

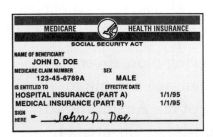

Medicare card

America's population is also growing older. In Chapter 37 you read about the baby boom that happened after World War II. That was when millions of babies were born in about 15 years. The people born during that time are called **baby boomers**. Most baby boomers are now in their 50s. They will soon **retire** from their jobs. When they do they will have less money to pay for the things they need.

Social Security helps people who retire pay for the things they need. Social Security is money that people get from the government each month. The money comes from taxes that people pay when they are working. Retired workers can begin receiving Social Security money when they are 62 years old. **Medicare** is another government service for older people. It helps people who are 65 and older pay for **medical** care.

Today, many Americans worry that there will not be enough Social Security and Medicare money for all the baby boomers when they retire. Government leaders are looking at ways to protect Social Security. One way is to raise the age at which people can start to receive Social Security money. Another way is to raise the Social Security taxes that workers pay. The government may also decide to pay less money to retired people.

Another problem facing our country is that many Americans do not get the health care they need. Today, millions of working people do not have enough money to pay for **health insurance** for themselves and their families. Without health insurance, they may not have the money to pay for doctors and hospitals when they are sick. They also find it hard to pay for the medicines they need. In 2003 Congress passed a law to help Americans who are 65 and older pay for their medicines. More work must be done to help all Americans get good health care.

Our country also needs people to be well educated. Soon after becoming president, George W. Bush asked Congress to pass a law to help education. In 2001 Congress passed a law called "No Child Left Behind." The new law says that all children in all states must take reading and math tests in grades three through eight each year. Schools must give extra help to children who do not do well on the tests. The law also gives more government money to schools. The money must be used to help children improve their reading and math.

The children in schools today will be the voters of tomorrow. Every vote is important in an election. Education will help future voters make good decisions for America.

Learning from Pictures A good education is important for all students. What do you think these students are doing?

In 2004 George W. Bush was re-elected President of the United States. ➤

In 2004 Americans voted for a President again. Americans had to decide whether George W. Bush or John F. Kerry would be the best leader. On Election Day 2004, George W. Bush received the most votes. In January 2005, George W. Bush promised to lead the nation for four more years.

Americans are proud of their country. They are proud that people from many countries live together in peace. They are also proud that their country has always been a democracy. For more than 200 years, Americans have voted for their leaders.

America's story is not yet finished. In the years ahead, we must protect Social Security for all Americans. We must work for better health care. We must also save energy and natural resources so we have them for tomorrow. Many people will be working for America. You can work with them. You can save energy and resources for our country. You can write letters to government leaders. Tell them how you think they should solve our problems. As an adult, you can vote for the best leaders for our nation. You will be building a better America for tomorrow.

Using Primary Sources

The Debate for President on October 12, 2004

Before the 2004 election for President, there were three debates on TV between President George W. Bush and Senator John Kerry. Each man answered questions about America's problems. Each man tried to prove that he would be the better President. Read parts of what George W. Bush told Americans at the end of the final debate. He wanted them to believe that he should be President for four more years.

economy
the way a country earns and uses money

optimistic
hopeful

pursue
chase

transform
change

prosperous
to be comfortable because there is enough money

> ...We've been through a lot together during the last three-and-three-quarters years...We've come through ... an attack on our country. And yet because of the hard work of the American people and good policies this *economy* is growing.... We reformed our school system...Over the next four years we'll continue to insist on excellence in every classroom in America so that our children have a chance to realize the great promise of America.
>
> Over the next four years we'll continue to work to make sure health care is available and affordable. Over the next four years we'll continue to... help heal the hurt that exists in some of our country's neighborhoods.
>
> I'm *optimistic* that we'll win the war on terror.... And as we *pursue* the enemy wherever it exists we'll also spread freedom and liberty. We've got great faith in the ability of liberty to *transform* societies.... My hope for America is a *prosperous* America, a hopeful America and a safer world....

On a separate sheet of paper, write the answer to each question.

1. What was one big problem that President Bush had to take care of soon after becoming President?

2. What is happening to the economy?

3. What did President Bush do for America's schools?

4. What are two goals that President Bush has for the next four years?

5. **Think and Write** What are President Bush's hopes for America, and how are your hopes the same or different?

Using What You've Learned

Read and Remember

Choose a Word Choose the best word or words in blue print to finish each sentence. On your paper, write the word or words you choose.

diverse	**baby boomers**	**Social Security**
retire	**health insurance**	

1. The United States is becoming more _____ .

2. The large group of people who were born after World War II are called _____ .

3. People who _____ may have less money to pay for the things they need.

4. _____ is money people get from the government each month when they retire.

5. Many Americans cannot get good health care because they do not have _____ .

Think and Apply

Categories Read the words in each group. Decide how they are alike. Find the best title in blue print for each group. Write the title on your paper.

Protecting Social Security
No Child Left Behind Law

Changing Population
Working for a Better America

1. save energy and natural resources
   write to government leaders
   vote in elections

2. almost 300 million people
   more retired people
   more Asians and Latin Americans

3. a law passed in 2001
   reading and math tests each year
   more government money
    for education

4. raise the age people can retire
   raise the taxes working people pay
   pay less to retired people

Journal Writing

Every person can help the United States. Write a paragraph that tells three or more ways that you can work for a better America.

Review

The chart on this page shows important events from 1990 to 2004. Study the chart. Then use the words in blue print to finish the story. On your paper, write the words you choose.

Pentagon   Cold War   NAFTA   George W. Bush
Disabilities   medicine   China   Saddam Hussein

There have been many important events since 1990. In that year Congress helped many Americans by passing the Americans with __(1)__ Act. The __(2)__ ended in 1991. In 1993 Canada, Mexico, and the United States signed __(3)__ . The United States gave PNTR to __(4)__ in 2000, and the two nations have more trade.

On September 11, 2001, terrorists attacked the World Trade Center and the __(5)__ . In 2003 the United States went to war against Iraq and captured __(6)__ . That same year Congress passed a law to help older Americans pay for __(7)__ . __(8)__ won the election for President in 2004.

Important Events from 1990 to 2004		
Date	Event	Results
1990	Congress passes the Americans with Disabilities Act.	Americans with disabilities have the same rights as other Americans.
1991	The Cold War ends.	The United States is the strongest world leader.
1993	NAFTA is signed by the United States, Canada, and Mexico.	There are fewer tariffs between the three nations.
2000	United States gives PNTR to China.	There is more trade between the two nations.
2001	Terrorists attack the World Trade Center and Pentagon.	The United States starts a War on Terrorism.
2003	The United States goes to war against Iraq.	Saddam Hussein is no longer Iraq's dictator.
2003	Congress passes a law to help older Americans pay for medicine.	It is easier for older people to buy medicine.
2004	Americans vote for a new President.	George W. Bush wins the election.

THE UNITED STATES

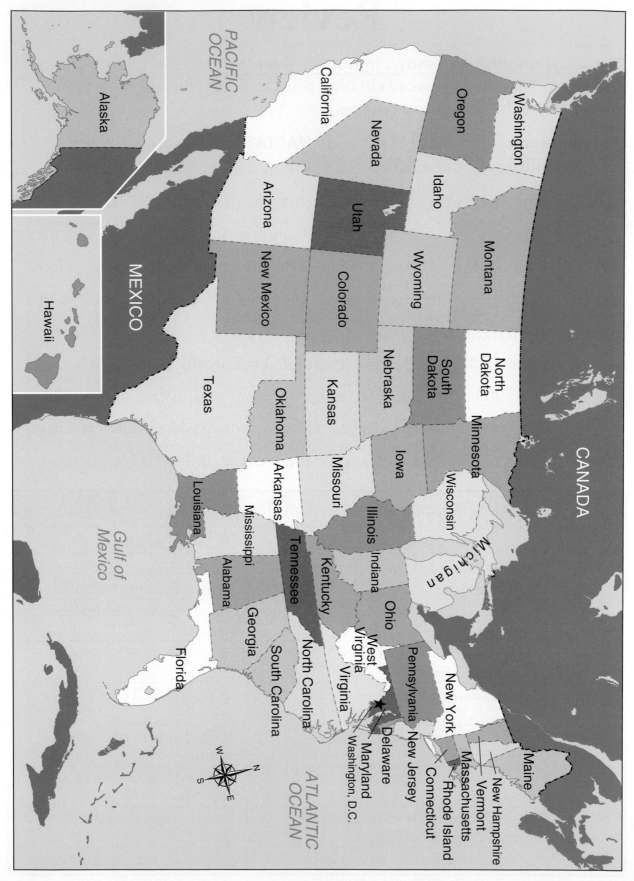

THE UNITED STATES: LANDFORMS

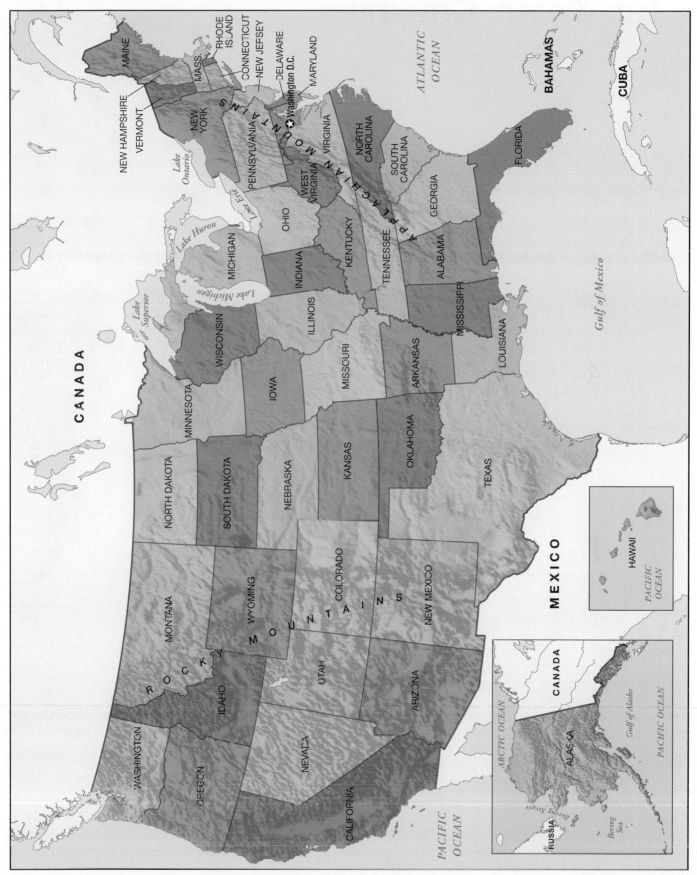

The World: Countries

Alaska
(U.S.)

CANADA

**NORTH
AMERICA**

UNITED STATES

*ATLANTIC
OCEAN*

*PACIFIC
OCEAN*

See inset below

Hawaii
(U.S.)

MEXICO

VENEZUELA

COLOMBIA

GUYANA
SURINAME
FRENCH GUIANA

GALAPAGOS IS.
(ECUADOR)

ECUADOR

**SOUTH
AMERICA**

PERU

BRAZIL

BOLIVIA

PARAGUAY

*PACIFIC
OCEAN*

SAMOA
ISLANDS

FRENCH POLYNESIA
(FRANCE)

URUGUAY

CHILE

ARGENTINA

FALKLAND IS.
(U.K.)

Gulf of Mexico

U.S.

BAHAMAS

*ATLANTIC
OCEAN*

Turks & Caicos
Islands (U.K.)

CUBA

MEXICO

*Cayman
Islands
(U.K.)*

HAITI

DOMINICAN
REPUBLIC

*Virgin
Islands
(U.S.)*

*Virgin
Islands
(U.K.)*

ANTIGUA &
BARBUDA

GUATEMALA

BELIZE

JAMAICA

*Puerto Rico
(U.S.)*

ST. KITTS AND NEVIS

Guadeloupe
(France)

DOMINICA

Martinique
(France)

ST. LUCIA

HONDURAS

Caribbean Sea

NETHERLANDS
ANTILLES
(Neth.)

ST. VINCENT AND
THE GRENADINES

BARBADOS

NICARAGUA

*ARUBA
(Neth.)*

GRENADA

EL
SALVADOR

COSTA
RICA

*Panama
Canal*

TRINIDAD
& TOBAGO

*PACIFIC
OCEAN*

PANAMA

COLOMBIA

VENEZUELA

GUYANA

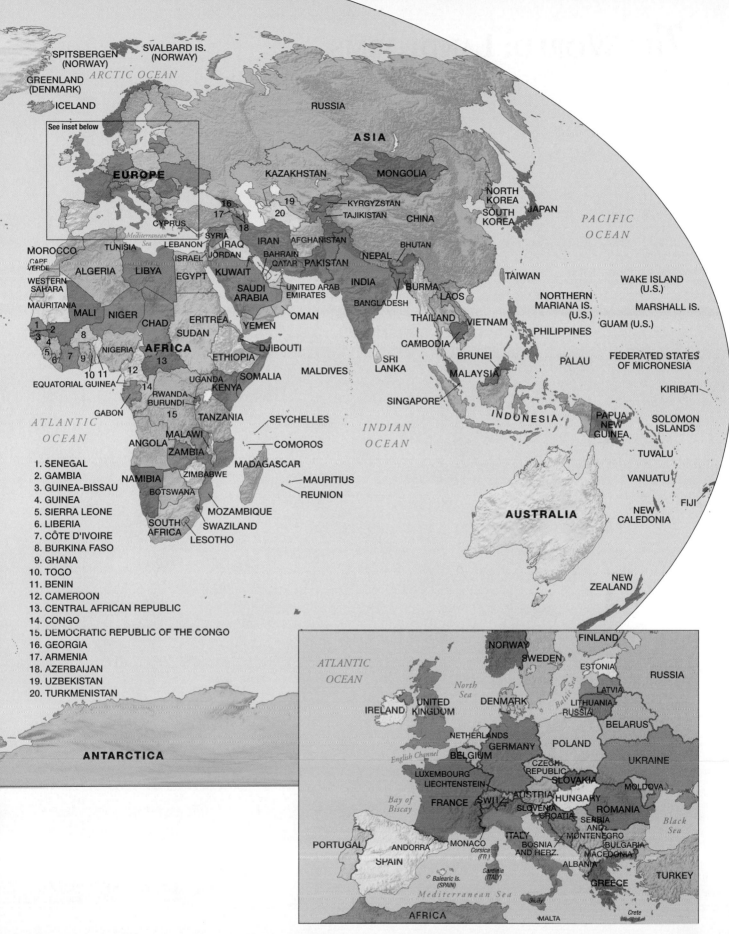

SPITSBERGEN
(NORWAY)

SVALBARD IS.
(NORWAY)

ARCTIC OCEAN

GREENLAND
(DENMARK)

ICELAND

See inset below

EUROPE

RUSSIA

ASIA

KAZAKHSTAN

MONGOLIA

NORTH
KOREA

JAPAN

KYRGYZSTAN

TAJIKISTAN

CHINA

SOUTH
KOREA

*PACIFIC
OCEAN*

16

17

18

CYPRUS

19

20

*Mediterranean
Sea*

SYRIA

LEBANON

IRAQ

IRAN

AFGHANISTAN

MOROCCO

TUNISIA

ISRAEL

JORDAN

BHUTAN

NEPAL

TAIWAN

WAKE ISLAND
(U.S.)

CAPE
VERDE

ALGERIA

LIBYA

EGYPT

KUWAIT

BAHRAIN
QATAR

PAKISTAN

INDIA

BURMA

NORTHERN
MARIANA IS.
(U.S.)

MARSHALL IS.

WESTERN
SAHARA

SAUDI
ARABIA

UNITED ARAB
EMIRATES

BANGLADESH

LAOS

GUAM (U.S.)

MAURITANIA

MALI

NIGER

CHAD

SUDAN

ERITREA

OMAN

YEMEN

THAILAND

VIETNAM

PHILIPPINES

FEDERATED STATES
OF MICRONESIA

1

2

3

4

5

6

8

7

9

NIGERIA

AFRICA

13

DJIBOUTI

ETHIOPIA

CAMBODIA

SRI
LANKA

BRUNEI

PALAU

MALDIVES

10 11

12

EQUATORIAL GUINEA

14

UGANDA

SOMALIA

KENYA

MALAYSIA

KIRIBATI

RWANDA
BURUNDI

15

TANZANIA

SEYCHELLES

*INDIAN
OCEAN*

SINGAPORE

INDONESIA

PAPUA
NEW
GUINEA

SOLOMON
ISLANDS

GABON

*ATLANTIC
OCEAN*

ANGOLA

MALAWI

ZAMBIA

COMOROS

MADAGASCAR

TUVALU

NAMIBIA

ZIMBABWE

BOTSWANA

MAURITIUS

REUNION

VANUATU

NEW
CALEDONIA

FIJI

1. SENEGAL
2. GAMBIA
3. GUINEA-BISSAU
4. GUINEA
5. SIERRA LEONE
6. LIBERIA
7. CÔTE D'IVOIRE
8. BURKINA FASO
9. GHANA
10. TOGO
11. BENIN
12. CAMEROON
13. CENTRAL AFRICAN REPUBLIC
14. CONGO
15. DEMOCRATIC REPUBLIC OF THE CONGO
16. GEORGIA
17. ARMENIA
18. AZERBAIJAN
19. UZBEKISTAN
20. TURKMENISTAN

MOZAMBIQUE

SWAZILAND

SOUTH
AFRICA

LESOTHO

AUSTRALIA

NEW
ZEALAND

ANTARCTICA

*ATLANTIC
OCEAN*

NORWAY

SWEDEN

FINLAND

IRELAND

UNITED
KINGDOM

*North
Sea*

DENMARK

ESTONIA

Baltic Sea

RUSSIA

LATVIA

LITHUANIA

RUSSIA

BELARUS

NETHERLANDS

English Channel

BELGIUM

GERMANY

POLAND

LUXEMBOURG

LIECHTENSTEIN

CZECH
REPUBLIC

SLOVAKIA

UKRAINE

MOLDOVA

*Bay of
Biscay*

FRANCE

AUSTRIA

SWI.

SLOVENIA

HUNGARY

CROATIA

ROMANIA

SERBIA
AND
MONTENEGRO

PORTUGAL

ANDORRA

MONACO

*Corsica
(FR.)*

ITALY

BOSNIA
AND HERZ.

BULGARIA

MACEDONIA

*Black
Sea*

SPAIN

*Balearic Is.
(SPAIN)*

*Sardinia
(ITALY)*

ALBANIA

TURKEY

GREECE

Mediterranean Sea

Sicily

Crete

AFRICA

MALTA

319

THE WORLD: LANDFORMS

ARCTIC OCEAN

Bering
Sea

**NORTH
AMERICA**

R O C K Y   M O U N T A I N S

Mississippi River

APPALACHIAN MTNS.

Gulf of
Mexico

ATLANTIC
OCEAN

Caribbean Sea

PACIFIC
OCEAN

Amazon River

**SOUTH
AMERICA**

A
N
D
E
S

ARCTIC OCEAN

EUROPE

URAL MOUNTAINS

ASIA

Danube River

ALPS

Mediterranean Sea

Hwang He

Chang Jiang

Indus River

HIMALAYAS

Ganges River

PACIFIC OCEAN

Niger River

Nile River

AFRICA

Arabian Sea

INDIAN OCEAN

AUSTRALIA

Darling River

ANTARCTICA

Declaration of Independence

When in the course of human events, it becomes necessary for one people to dissolve the political bands which have connected them with another, and to assume among the powers of the earth the separate and equal station to which the laws of nature and of nature's God entitle them, a decent respect to the opinions of mankind requires that they should declare the causes which impel them to the separation.

Sometimes in history one group of people may want to be free from the country that rules it. The group must tell the world why. That is the reason for the Declaration of Independence.

We hold these truths to be self-evident: that all men are created equal, that they are endowed by their Creator with certain unalienable rights, that among these are life, liberty, and the pursuit of happiness.

We believe some things are always true. All people are equal. God gave all people rights that other people should not be able to take away. These rights include life, freedom, and the chance to be happy.

That to secure these rights, governments are instituted among men, deriving their just powers from the consent of the governed; that whenever any form of government becomes destructive of these ends, it is the right of the people to alter or to abolish it, and to institute new government, laying its foundation on such principles and organizing its powers in such form as to them shall seem most likely to effect their safety and happiness. Prudence, indeed, will dictate that governments long established should not be changed for light and transient causes; and accordingly all experience hath shown, that mankind are more disposed to suffer while evils are sufferable, than to right themselves by abolishing the forms to which they are accustomed. But when a long train of abuses and usurpations, pursuing invariably the same object, evinces a design to reduce them under absolute despotism, it is their right, it is their duty, to throw off such government, and to provide new guards for their future security.

People make governments to keep their rights safe. People agree to give governments power. If the governments do a poor job, the people can change or end the government. Governments should not be changed for small reasons. But when a government treats its people very badly, the people must put an end to the government. The people can start a new government.

Such has been the patient sufferance of these colonies; and such is now the necessity which constrains them to alter their former systems of government. The history of the present king of Great Britain is a history of repeated injuries and usurpations, all having in direct object the establishment of an absolute tyranny over these states. To prove this, let facts be submitted to a candid world.

For a long time, the colonies have been treated badly by the king's government. This is why they need to change their government. King George has hurt the colonies again and again. His goal is to control the colonies. We want the world to know these facts:

He has refused his assent to laws, the most wholesome and necessary for the public good.

The king does not make laws that are good for the colonies.

He has forbidden his governors to pass laws of immediate and pressing importance, unless suspended in their operation till his assent should be obtained, and when so suspended, he has utterly neglected to attend to them.

The king will not let us make our own laws. He takes too much time to agree to the ones he thinks are good.

He has refused to pass other laws for the accommodation of large districts of people, unless those people would relinquish the right of representation in the legislature, a right inestimable to them and formidable to tyrants only.

He has not let us have our leaders speak for us.

He has called together legislative bodies at places unusual, uncomfortable, and distant from the depository of their public records, for the sole purpose of fatiguing them into compliance with his measures.

He has made leaders meet in strange, uncomfortable, and far away places. He hopes leaders will become tired and obey his orders.

He has dissolved Representative Houses repeatedly, for opposing with manly firmness his invasions on the rights of the people.

He has closed meetings of leaders in the colonies when they say the king has treated the people badly.

He has refused for a long time, after such dissolutions, to cause others to be elected; whereby the legislative powers, incapable of annihilation, have returned to the people at large for their exercise; the state remaining, in the mean time, exposed to all the dangers of invasion from without, and convulsions within.

He has taken a long time to allow elections. The colonists were in danger because they could not make laws to keep them safe.

He has endeavored to prevent the population of these states; for that purpose obstructing the laws of naturalization of foreigners, refusing to pass others to encourage their migration hither, and raising the conditions of new appropriations of lands.

King George has tried to stop the colonies from growing. He would not allow other Europeans to settle in the colonies. He has made it hard to buy land in America.

He has obstructed the administration of justice, by refusing his assent to laws for establishing judiciary powers.

He would not let us set up courts.

He has made judges dependent on his will alone, for the tenure of their offices, and the amount and payment of their salaries.

The king pays the judges. They make unfair decisions to keep their jobs.

He has erected a multitude of new offices, and sent hither swarms of officers to harass our people, and eat out their substance.

The king has sent many government people. They bother us and use up our supplies.

He has kept among us, in times of peace, standing armies without the consent of our legislatures.

The king has kept his armies here and we do not want them.

He has affected to render the military independent of and superior to the civil power.

He has tried to make his armies more powerful than our government.

He has combined with others to subject us to a jurisdiction foreign to our constitution, and unacknowledged by our laws; giving his assent to their acts of pretended legislation:

King George has worked with Parliament to make unfair laws that we did not help write.

For quartering large bodies of armed troops among us;

They made us let British soldiers stay in our homes.

For protecting them, by a mock trial, from punishment for any murders which they should commit on the inhabitants of these states;

British soldiers who killed our colonists went free without real trials.

For cutting off our trade with all parts of the world;

They stopped us from trading with other countries.

For imposing taxes on us without our consent;

They made unfair tax laws for us.

For depriving us, in many cases, of the benefits of trial by jury;

They often took away our right to have a fair trial.

For transporting us beyond seas to be tried for pretended offenses;

They made some of us go to Great Britain to go on trial for made-up crimes.

For abolishing the free system of English laws in a neighboring province, establishing therein an arbitrary government, and enlarging its boundaries so as to render it at once an example and fit instrument for introducing the same absolute rule into these colonies;

They took away the fair government of an area that is our neighbor. They gave them an unfair government. This was to show us how Great Britain can have complete rule over the colonies.

For taking away our charters, abolishing our most valuable laws, and altering fundamentally the forms of our governments;

They took away our land agreements. They changed our most important laws. They changed our government.

For suspending our own legislatures, and declaring themselves invested with power to legislate for us in all cases whatsoever.

They have stopped our leaders from making laws. They say they have the power to make all our laws.

He has abdicated government here, by declaring us out of his protection and waging war against us.

King George has given up his power to rule us because he does not keep us safe. He says he is fighting a war against us.

He has plundered our seas, ravaged our coasts, burnt our towns, and destroyed the lives of our people.

The king has attacked our ships and destroyed our ports. He has burned our towns and destroyed our lives.

He is at this time transporting large armies of foreign mercenaries to complete the works of death, desolation, and tyranny, already begun with circumstances of cruelty and perfidy scarcely paralleled in the most barbarous ages, and totally unworthy the head of a civilized nation.

He is bringing soldiers from other countries to destroy the colonies. A modern king should not allow soldiers to be so horrible.

He has constrained our fellow citizens taken captive on the high seas to bear arms against their country, to become the executioners of their friends and brethren, or to fall themselves by their hands.

He has taken Americans off our ships at sea. He has made them fight against other Americans.

He has excited domestic insurrections amongst us, and has endeavored to bring on the inhabitants of our frontiers, the merciless Indian savages, whose known rule of warfare, is an undistinguished destruction of all ages, sexes and conditions.

He has told those who work for us to fight against us. He has tried to get Native Americans to attack us.

In every stage of these oppressions we have petitioned for redress in the most humble terms; our repeated petitions have been answered only by repeated injury. A prince whose character is thus marked by every act which may define a tyrant is unfit to be the ruler of a free people.

We have asked the king to stop treating us unfairly. But he has only made things harder for us. A king who acts so unfairly is not good enough to rule a free people.

Nor have we been wanting in attentions to our British brethren. We have warned them from time to time of attempts by their legislature to extend an unwarrantable jurisdiction over us. We have reminded them of the circumstances of our emigration and settlement here. We have appealed to their native justice and magnanimity, and we have conjured them by the ties of our common kindred to disavow these usurpations, which would inevitably interrupt our connections and correspondence. They too have been deaf to the voice of justice and of consanguinity. We must, therefore, acquiesce in the necessity which denounces our separation, and hold them, as we hold the rest of mankind, enemies in war, in peace friends.

We have told the British people many times how poorly Parliament has treated us. We hoped they would help us. But they did not listen to us. Now we must say that we are a separate nation. We will treat Great Britain as we treat all other nations.

We, therefore, the representatives of the United States of America, in General Congress assembled, appealing to the Supreme Judge of the world for the rectitude of our intentions, do, in the name, and by authority of the good people of these colonies, solemnly publish and declare, that these united colonies are, and of right ought to be, free and independent states; that they are absolved from all allegiance to the British crown, and that all political connection between them and the state of Great Britain is, and ought to be, totally dissolved; and that as free and

independent states, they have full power to levy war, conclude peace, contract alliances, establish commerce, and to do all other acts and things which independent states may of right do.

As leaders of the people of the United States, we say that these colonies are united as an independent nation. We have no more ties to Great Britain. As an independent nation, we have the right to make war. We have the right to make peace treaties. We have the right to trade with all nations. We have the right to do all the things a nation does.

And for the support of this declaration, with a firm reliance on the protection of Divine Providence, we mutually pledge to each other our lives, our fortunes and our sacred honor.

We now trust that God will keep us safe. We promise our lives, our money, and our honor for this Declaration.

John Hancock
(President,
Massachusetts)

Georgia
Button Gwinnett
Lyman Hall
George Walton

North Carolina
William Hooper
Joseph Hewes
John Penn

South Carolina
Edward Rutledge
Thomas Heyward, Jr.
Thomas Lynch, Jr.
Arthur Middleton

Maryland
Samuel Chase

William Paca
Thomas Stone
Charles Carroll of
Carrollton

Virginia
George Wythe
Richard Henry Lee
Thomas Jefferson
Benjamin Harrison
Thomas Nelson, Jr.
Francis Lightfoot Lee
Carter Braxton

Pennsylvania
Robert Morris
Benjamin Rush
Benjamin Franklin
John Morton
George Clymer
James Smith

George Taylor
James Wilson
George Ross

Delaware
Caesar Rodney
George Read
Thomas McKean

New York
William Floyd
Philip Livingston
Francis Lewis
Lewis Morris

New Jersey
Richard Stockton
John Witherspoon
Francis Hopkinson
John Hart
Abraham Clark

New Hampshire
Josiah Bartlett
William Whipple
Matthew Thornton

Massachusetts
John Adams
Samuel Adams
Robert Treat Paine
Elbridge Gerry

Rhode Island
Stephen Hopkins
William Ellery

Connecticut
Roger Sherman
Samuel Huntington
William Williams
Oliver Wolcott

The Constitution
of the United States of America

PREAMBLE

We, the People of the United States, in order to form a more perfect Union, establish justice, insure domestic tranquility, provide for the common defense, promote the general welfare, and secure the blessings of liberty to ourselves and our posterity, do ordain and establish this Constitution for the United States of America.

The Constitution is a set of laws for the United States. The first part of the Constitution is called the Preamble. It starts with the words "We the people of the United States." This means the laws were made by the American people and not by a king. It also means the laws are for all the states. The states form one nation. The Preamble tells us the goals of the Constitution. The goals are to create a strong government that will help people have peace and freedom.

ARTICLE I. THE LEGISLATIVE BRANCH

Section 1. The Congress

All legislative powers herein granted shall be vested in a Congress of the United States, which shall consist of a Senate and House of Representatives.

The Constitution separates the government's powers into three branches. This is called the **separation of powers**. The writers of the Constitution did not want any person or any part of government to have too much power. With too much power, a leader could take away freedom from the people. The writers remembered how King George had used his power to take away American freedom. They did not want Americans to have that kind of problem again. So they gave Congress the power to make laws. Article 1 tells about the powers of Congress. Congress is the **legislative** [lawmaking] branch of the government. Only Congress can write laws for the United States. Congress gets its power from the American people. Americans vote for the people who will represent them in Congress.

Congress has two parts. Each part is called a house. The Senate and the House of Representatives are the two houses of Congress.

Section 2. The House of Representatives

The House of Representatives shall be composed of members chosen every second year by the people of the several states, and the electors in each state shall have the qualifications requisite for electors of the most numerous branch of the state legislature.

Once in two years, Americans vote for people in their state to be members of the House of Representatives. Members serve two-year terms.

No person shall be a Representative who shall not have attained the age of 25 years, and been seven years a citizen of the United States, and who shall not, when elected, be an inhabitant of that state in which he shall be chosen.

To work in the House, a person must be 25 years old. A person must be an American citizen for seven years. All members of the House must live in the state that they represent.

~~Representatives and direct taxes shall be apportioned among the several states which may be included within this Union, according to their respective numbers, which shall be determined by adding to the whole number of free persons, including those bound to service for a term of years, and excluding Indians not taxed, three fifths of all other persons.~~ The actual enumeration shall be made within three years after the first meeting of the Congress of the United States, and within every subsequent term of ten years, in such manner as they shall by law direct. The number of Representatives shall not exceed one for every 30,000, but each state shall have at least one Representative; and until such enumeration shall be made, the state of New Hampshire shall be entitled to choose three, Massachusetts eight, Rhode Island and Providence Plantations one, Connecticut five, New York six, New Jersey four, Pennsylvania eight, Delaware one, Maryland six, Virginia ten, North Carolina five, South Carolina five, and Georgia three.

States with large populations send more people to work in the House of Representatives. States with smaller populations send fewer people to work in the House. Every ten years there must be a **census** [a counting of all people in the country by government workers]. When a state's population changes, the number of representatives that a state sends to Congress changes.

When vacancies happen in the representation from any state, the executive authority thereof shall issue writs of election to fill such vacancies.

The House of Representatives shall choose their Speaker and other officers; and shall have the sole power of impeachment.

The members of the House of Representatives must vote for a leader. The leader is called the Speaker of the House. The House of Representatives is the only part of the government that can **impeach** [accuse] a government leader for doing things wrongly. Only two presidents, Andrew Johnson and Bill Clinton, were impeached.

Section 3. The Senate

The Senate of the United States shall be composed of two Senators from each state, ~~chosen by the legislature thereof,~~ for six years; and each Senator shall have one vote.

Every state, large or small, sends two senators to make laws in the United States Senate. Senators serve six-year terms. In 1913, the Seventeenth Amendment was passed. It gave Americans the right to vote for their United States Senators.

Immediately after they shall be assembled in consequence of the first election, they shall be divided as equally as may be into three classes. The seats of the Senators of the first class shall be vacated at the expiration of the second year, of the second class at the expiration of the fourth year, and of the third class at the expiration of the sixth year, so that one third may be chosen every second year; ~~and if vacancies happen by resignation, or otherwise, during the recess of the legislature of any state, the executive thereof may make temporary appointments until the next meeting of the legislature, which shall then fill such vacancies.~~

No person shall be a Senator who shall not have attained the age of thirty years, and been nine years a citizen of the United States, and who shall not, when elected, be an inhabitant of that state for which he shall be chosen.

To become a senator, a person must be 30 years old. The person must be a citizen for at least nine years. All senators must live in the states that they represent.

The Vice President of the United States shall be President of the Senate, but shall have no vote, unless they be equally divided.

The Vice President of the United States works as President of the Senate. He can vote only to break a **tie vote** [an equal number of votes that are for and against a law the Senate is working on]. Senators must vote for people to be leaders of the Senate.

The Senate shall choose their other officers, and also a President *pro tempore*, in the absence of the Vice President, or when he shall exercise the office of President of the United States.

The Senate shall have the sole power to try all impeachments. When sitting for that purpose, they shall be on oath or affirmation. When the President of the United States is tried, the Chief Justice shall preside: and no person shall be convicted without the concurrence of two thirds of the members present.

Judgment in cases of impeachment shall not extend further than to removal from office, and disqualification to hold and enjoy any office of honor, trust, or profit, under the United States: but the party convicted shall nevertheless be liable and subject to indictment, trial, judgment, and punishment, according to law.

If the House of Representatives impeaches a government leader, there must be a trial in the Senate to decide if a government leader is guilty of doing things wrongly. The **Chief Justice** [leader] of the Supreme Court is the judge at trials in the Senate. If a government leader is found guilty during a Senate trial, the leader loses his job. Since 1789, only seven people have been found guilty during Senate trials. The seven guilty people were judges.

Section 4. Elections

The times, places, and manner of holding elections for Senators and

Representatives, shall be prescribed in each state by the legislature thereof; but the Congress may at any time by law make or alter such regulations, except as to the places of choosing Senators.

States can make their own rules about voting for members of Congress. Congress has the power to change state voting laws.

Elections for Congress must be on a Tuesday in early November in every state.

The Congress shall assemble at least once in every year, ~~and such meeting shall be on the first Monday in December, unless they shall by law appoint a different day~~.

Congress must meet at least once a year.

Section 5. Meetings of Congress

Each House shall be the judge of the elections, returns, and qualifications of its own members, and a majority of each shall constitute a quorum to do business; but a smaller number may adjourn from day to day, and may be authorized to compel the attendance of absent members, in such manner, and under such penalties as each House may provide.

The House of Representatives and the Senate write their own rules. They make rules about how many members must be at meetings when there will be voting on **bills** [the ideas for new laws]. Members can be punished if they miss too many meetings.

Each House may determine the rules of its proceedings, punish its members for disorderly behavior, and, with the concurrence of two thirds, expel a member.

Each house has its own rules about **debate** [talking about problems]. Senators are allowed to talk for a long time. Members of the House of Representatives can talk for only a short time.

Each House shall keep a journal of its proceedings, and from time to time publish the same, excepting such parts as may in their judgment require secrecy; and the yeas and nays of the members of either House on any question, shall, at the desire of one fifth of those present, be entered on the journal.

Both the Senate and the House of Representatives must keep journals. The journals tell what happened at meetings. They show how members voted for different bills. The journals of Congress are called *The Congressional Record*. Everyone can read these journals in public libraries. These journals help Americans decide if members of Congress are doing a good job.

Neither House, during the session of Congress, shall, without the consent of the other, adjourn for more than three days, nor to any other place than that in which the two Houses shall be sitting.

Section 6. Salaries and Rules

The Senators and Representatives shall receive a compensation for their services, to be ascertained by law, and paid out of the Treasury of the United States. They shall in all cases, except treason, felony, and breach of the peace, be privileged from arrest during their attendance at the session of their respective Houses, and in going to and returning from the same; and for any speech or debate in either House, they shall not be questioned in any other place.

Members of the Senate and the House of Representatives must be paid salaries. The writers of the Constitution wanted members of Congress to be paid so that poor people as well as rich people would have enough money to be members.

No Senator or Representative shall, during the time for which he was elected, be appointed to any civil office under the authority of the United States, which shall have been created, or the emoluments whereof shall have been increased during such time; and no person holding any office under the United States, shall be a member of either House during his continuance in office.

Members of Congress cannot hold other government jobs while serving in Congress. This rule was written so that there would be a separation of powers between the three branches of government. This rule stops members of Congress from working for the other branches.

Section 7. Bills

All bills for raising revenue shall originate in the House of Representatives; but the Senate may propose or concur with amendments as on other bills.

All tax bills must be written and then passed by the House of Representatives. Then the tax bills are sent to the Senate. The Senate must pass the tax bills in order for them to become laws.

Every bill which shall have passed the House of Representatives and the Senate, shall, before it become a law, be presented to the President of the United States; if he approve he shall sign it, but if not he shall return it, with his objections, to that House in which it shall have originated, who shall enter the objections at large on their journal, and proceed to reconsider it. If after such reconsideration two thirds of that House shall agree to pass the bill, it shall be sent, together with the objections, to the other House, by which it shall likewise be reconsidered, and if approved by two thirds of that House, it shall become a law. But in all such cases the votes of both Houses shall be determined by yeas and nays, and the names of the persons voting for and against the bill shall be entered on the journal of each House respectively. If any bill shall not be returned by the President within ten days (Sundays excepted) after it shall have been presented to him, the same shall be a law, in like manner as if he had signed it, unless the Congress by their adjournment prevent its return, in which case it shall not be a law.

Congress must obey rules when writing new laws. The first step when writing laws is for the House or Senate to write a bill that has the ideas for the new law. Then both the House and the Senate must vote to **pass** [approve] the bill. After that the bill must be sent to the President. The bill becomes a law if the President signs it. Sometimes a President feels the new law will hurt the country. He may not want the bill to become a law. So the President can **veto** [refuse to sign] the bill. But that bill can still become a law. The bill must be sent back to Congress. It can become a law if two thirds of the members of both houses vote for it.

Every order, resolution, or vote, to which the concurrence of the Senate and House of Representatives may be necessary (except on a question of adjournment), shall be presented to the President of the United States; and before the same shall take effect, shall be approved by him, or being disapproved by him, shall be repassed by two thirds of the Senate and House of Representatives, according to the rules and limitations prescribed in the case of a bill.

Section 8. Powers of Congress

The Congress shall have power:

To lay and collect taxes, duties, imposts, and excises, to pay the debts and provide for the common defense and general welfare of the United States; but all duties, imposts, and excises shall be uniform throughout the United States;

To borrow money on the credit of the United States;

To regulate commerce with foreign nations, and among the several states, and with the Indian tribes;

To establish a uniform rule of naturalization, and uniform laws on the subject of bankruptcies throughout the United States;

To coin money, regulate the value thereof, and of foreign coin, and fix the standard of weights and measures;

To provide for the punishment of counterfeiting the securities and current coin of the United States;

To establish post offices and post roads;

To promote the progress of science and useful arts, by securing for limited times to authors and inventors the exclusive right to their respective writings and discoveries;

To constitute tribunals inferior to the Supreme Court;

To define and punish piracies and felonies committed on the high seas, and offenses against the law of nations;

To declare war, grant letters of marque and reprisal, and make rules concerning captures on land and water;

To raise and support armies; but no appropriation of money to that use shall be for a longer term than two years;

To provide and maintain a navy;

To make rules for the government and regulation of the land and naval forces;

To provide for calling forth the militia to execute the laws of the Union, suppress insurrections and repel invasions;

To provide for organizing, arming, and disciplining the militia, and for governing such part of them as may be employed in the service of the United States, reserving to the states respectively, the appointment of the officers, and the authority of training the militia according to the discipline prescribed by Congress;

To exercise exclusive legislation, in all cases whatsoever, over such district (not exceeding ten miles square) as may, by cession of particular states, and the acceptance of Congress, become the seat of the government of the United States, and to exercise like authority over all places purchased by the consent of the legislature of the state in which the same shall be, for the erection of forts, magazines, arsenals, dockyards, and other needful buildings. And,

To make all laws which shall be necessary and proper for carrying into execution the foregoing powers, and all other powers vested by this Constitution in the government of the United States, or in any department or officer thereof.

Congress has all of these powers:

1. Congress makes tax laws. Congress can collect taxes. Taxes pay for highways, national parks, the army, and many other things.

2. Congress can borrow money. One of the ways it borrows money is by selling savings bonds.

3. Congress writes laws about trade between the states. It writes laws about trade with other nations.

4. Congress writes laws about how people from other countries can become American citizens.

5. Congress writes laws about printing money and making coins.

6. Congress sets up different kinds of courts.

7. Congress approves treaties with other countries.

8. Congress can **declare war** [decide that the United States will go to war] against another country.

9. Congress can form an army and a navy. Congress decides how much money to give the army and navy.

10. Congress can form a **National Guard** [soldiers to protect Americans in the United States].

Congress can write all the laws it needs to carry out its powers. This is a very important rule in the Constitution. This rule allows Congress to write laws that help the United States as the country grows and changes. The Constitution has been the law of the United States for more than 225 years because Congress has the power to always write the new laws the nation needs.

Section 9. Powers Not Given to Congress

The migration or importation of such persons as any of the states now existing shall think proper to admit, shall not be prohibited by the Congress prior to the year 1808; but a tax or duty may be imposed on such importation, not exceeding ten dollars for each person.

The privilege of the writ of *habeas corpus* shall not be suspended, unless when in cases of rebellion or invasion the public safety may require it.

No bill of attainder or *ex post facto* law shall be passed.

No capitation, or other direct tax, shall be laid, unless in proportion to the census or enumeration herein before directed to be taken.

No tax or duty shall be laid on articles exported from any state.

No preference shall be given by any regulation of commerce or revenue to the ports of one state over those of another: nor shall vessels bound to, or from, one state be obliged to enter, clear, or pay duties in another.

No money shall be drawn from the treasury, but in consequence of appropriations made by law; and a regular statement and account of the receipts and expenditures of all public money shall be published from time to time.

No title of nobility shall be granted by the United States; and no person holding any office of profit or trust under them, shall, without the consent of the Congress, accept of any present, emolument, office, or title, of any kind what-ever, from any king, prince, or foreign state.

Congress does <u>not</u> have these powers:

1. Congress cannot send people to jail without a fair trial.

2. Congress cannot tax goods that are shipped between states.

3. Congress cannot spend government money unless it has passed laws that tell Congress how to spend money. For example, Congress can pass a law that tells how much money to spend for the army. Congress must publish information about how it spends government money. This is important because Americans have the right to know how their tax money is used.

4. Congress cannot give any American a special title such as king, queen, or prince. The writers of the Constitution wanted all Americans to be equal before the law. Special titles like king and queen make some people more important than others.

Section 10. Powers Not Given to the States

No state shall enter into any treaty, alliance, or confederation; grant letters of marque and reprisal; coin money; emit bills of credit; make any thing but gold and silver coin a tender in payment of debts; pass any bill of attainder, *ex post facto* law, or law impairing the obligation of contracts, or grant any title of nobility.

No state shall, without the consent of the Congress, lay any imposts or duties on imports or exports, except what may be absolutely necessary for executing its inspection laws: and the net produce of all duties and imposts, laid by any state on imports or exports, shall be for the use of the Treasury of the United States; and all such laws shall be subject to the revision and control of the Congress.

No state shall, without the consent of Congress, lay any duty of tonnage, keep troops, or ships of war in time of peace, enter into any agreement or compact with another state, or with a foreign power, or engage in war, unless actually invaded, or in such imminent danger as will not admit of delay.

The Constitution gives different powers to the **federal** [national government in Washington, D.C.] and state governments. The federal government has all of the powers for working with other countries. States cannot make treaties with other countries. States cannot go to war against other countries. States cannot have their own army and navy. However, states can send soldiers to be part of the National Guard. States cannot make their own money or their own stamps. The federal government makes the same money for all states.

ARTICLE II. THE EXECUTIVE BRANCH

Section 1. President and Vice President

The executive power shall be vested in a President of the United States of America. He shall hold his office during the term of four years, and, together with the Vice President, chosen for the same term, be elected, as follows:

The writers of the Constitution gave the government an executive branch. The job of the executive branch is to carry out the laws that Congress makes. The President is the leader of the executive branch. The writers wanted the President to have less power than a king. They decided to limit his power so he could not take away freedom from Americans the way King George did. They gave the President enough power to be a strong leader. The Vice President helps the President. Both leaders serve four-year terms.

The executive branch helps the government have **checks and balances**. This means that each branch stops the other branches from having too much power. You read in Article 1 that checks and balances allow a President to veto a bill. Only Congress can write and pass laws. But the President can use the veto to stop a bill from becoming a law.

Each state shall appoint, in such manner as the legislature thereof may direct, a number of electors equal to the whole number of Senators and Representatives to which the state may be entitled in the Congress: but no Senator or Representative, or person holding an office of trust or profit under the United States, shall be appointed an elector.

The electors shall meet in their respective states, and vote by ballot for two persons, of whom one at least shall not be an inhabitant of the same state with themselves. And they shall make a list of all the persons voted for, and of the number of votes for each; which list they shall sign and certify, and transmit sealed to the seat of the government of the United States, directed to the President of the Senate. The President of the Senate shall, in the presence of the Senate and House of Representatives, open all the certificates, and the votes shall then be counted. The person having the greatest number of votes shall be the President, if such number be a majority of the whole number of electors appointed; and if there be more than one who have such majority, and have an equal number of votes, then the House of Representatives shall immediately choose by ballot one of them for President; and if no person have a majority, then from the five highest on the list the said House shall in like manner choose the President. But in choosing the President, the votes shall be taken by states, the representation from each state having one vote; a quorum for this purpose shall consist of a member or members from two thirds of the states, and a majority of all the states shall be necessary to a choice. In every case, after the choice of the President, the person having the greatest number of votes of the electors shall be the Vice President. But if there should remain two or more who have equal votes, the Senate shall choose from them by ballot the Vice President.

The Congress may determine the time of choosing the electors, and the day on which they shall give their votes; which day shall be the same throughout the United States.

The Constitution has rules about how to elect the President and Vice President. These rules were changed by the 12th Amendment in 1804.

The Constitution said people should vote for people called **electors**. The number of electors for each state is the same as the number of senators and representatives a state has in Congress. The electors vote for the President and Vice President. The person who wins the most **electoral votes** [votes from electors] becomes the next President. Elections for President are held on a Tuesday in early November.

No person except a natural-born citizen, or a citizen of the United States, at the time of the adoption of this Constitution, shall be eligible to the office of President; neither shall any person be eligible to that office who shall not have attained the age of 35 years, and been 14 years a resident within the United States.

The President must be a person who was born in the United States. He must be at least 35 years old. He must have lived in the United States for at least 14 years. The writers did not say the President must be a man. But all American Presidents have been men.

In case of the removal of the President from office, or of his death, resignation, or inability to discharge the powers and duties of the said office, the same shall devolve on the Vice President, and the Congress may by law provide for the case of removal, death, resignation, or inability, both of the President and Vice President, declaring what officer shall then act as President, and such officer shall act accordingly until the disability be removed, or a President shall be elected.

The Vice President becomes the President if the President dies, leaves the job, or cannot work. If the country does not have a Vice President, Congress must decide who will become President.

The President shall, at stated times, receive for his services a compensation, which shall neither be increased nor diminished during the period for which he shall have been elected, and he shall not receive within that period any other emolument from the United States, or any of them.

The President must be paid a salary. Congress decides how much the President will be paid. The writers of the Constitution wanted poor people and rich people to be able to be President. Since the President earns a salary, a poor person would be able to have this job.

George Washington, the first President, was paid $25,000. In 2001, Congress voted to pay President George W. Bush $400,000. Today, most famous baseball players earn much more money than the President.

Before he enter on the execution of his office, he shall take the following oath or affirmation:

"I do solemnly swear (or affirm) that I will faithfully execute the office of President of the United States, and will to the best of my ability, preserve, protect, and defend the Constitution of the United States."

On the day a person becomes President, he must make a promise to the American people. That promise is called the **Presidential Oath**. The President promises to carry out the duties of his new job. He also promises to protect the Constitution and carry out its laws.

Section 2. President's Powers

The President shall be Commander in Chief of the Army and Navy of the United States, and of the militia of the several states, when called into the actual service of the United States; he may require the opinion, in writing, of the principal officer in each of the executive departments, upon any subject relating to the duties of their respective offices, and he shall have power to grant reprieves and pardons for offenses against the United States, except in cases of impeachment.

He shall have power, by and with the advice and consent of the Senate, to make treaties, provided two thirds of the Senators present concur; and he shall nominate, and by and with the advice and consent of the Senate, shall appoint ambassadors, other public ministers and consuls, judges of the Supreme Court, and all other officers of the United States, whose appointments are not herein otherwise provided for, and which shall be established by law: but the Congress may by law vest the appointment of such inferior officers, as they think proper, in the President alone, in the courts of law, or in the heads of departments.

The President shall have power to fill up all vacancies that may happen during the recess of the Senate, by granting commissions which shall expire at the end of their next session.

The President has these important powers:

1. The President is commander-in-chief of the Army, Navy, and National Guard.
2. The President can **pardon** [forgive] people who have done crimes against the federal government. People who are pardoned by the President cannot be put on trial. They cannot be sent to jail.
3. The President can make treaties with other countries. But the Senate must vote to approve these treaties. The President can **appoint** [give jobs to] people to work as ambassadors [representatives] to other countries. The President appoints new judges for the Supreme Court. The Senate must vote to approve the people who are given these jobs. These are more examples of checks and balances in the Constitution. The President can have a **cabinet**, a group of department leaders who work with him. One important executive department is the Department of State. Department leaders are called secretaries.

Section 3. Other Powers

He shall from time to time give to the Congress information of the state of the Union, and recommend to their consideration such measures as he shall judge necessary and expedient; he may, on extraordinary occasions, convene both Houses, or either of them, and in case of disagreement between them, with respect to the time of adjournment, he may adjourn them to such time as he shall think proper; he shall receive ambassadors and other public ministers; he shall take care that the laws be faithfully executed, and shall commission all the officers of the United States.

The President has other jobs that must be done:

1. The President must give a speech to both houses of Congress. Most of the time the President does this in January. The speech is called the **State of the Union address**.

2. The President can ask Congress to meet if there are emergencies that must be worked on.

3. The President can ask Congress to write new laws.

4. The President must meet with ambassadors from other countries. He can decide how the United States will work with other countries.

5. The President must carry out all laws made by Congress.

Section 4. Impeachment

The President, Vice President, and all civil officers of the United States, shall be removed from office on impeachment for, and conviction of, treason, bribery, or other high crimes and misdemeanors.

The President, Vice President and other government leaders can be impeached. They can be impeached for helping enemies of the United States. They can also be impeached for doing crimes.

ARTICLE III. THE JUDICIAL BRANCH

Section 1. Judges

The judicial power of the United States, shall be vested in one Supreme Court, and in such inferior courts as the Congress may from time to time ordain and establish. The judges, both of the Supreme and inferior courts, shall hold their offices during good behavior, and shall, at stated times, receive for their services, a compensation, which shall not be diminished during their continuance in office.

The judicial branch is the third branch of government. The Supreme Court has the power to judge if laws and actions obey the Constitution. It is the highest court in the United States. Congress has the power to make lower courts.

The judges of the Supreme Court can keep their jobs for as long as they live. Lower federal court judges also keep their jobs for as long as they live.

The writers of the Constitution did not want judges to be afraid of Congress or the President when making decisions. Congress or the President might not like their decisions. So the writers gave the judges lifetime jobs so they would make honest decisions and not lose their jobs.

Section 2. Federal Courts

The judicial power shall extend to all cases, in law and equity, arising under this Constitution, the laws of the United States, and treaties made, or which shall be made, under their authority; to all cases affecting ambassadors, other public ministers and consuls; to all cases of admiralty and maritime jurisdiction; to controversies to which the United States shall be a party; to controversies between two or more states, ~~between a state and citizens of another state;~~ between citizens of different states; between citizens of the same state claiming lands under grants of different states, and ~~between a state, or the citizens thereof, and foreign states, citizens or subjects~~.

Federal courts can hear many kinds of cases. Cases may be about the laws of Congress, problems between two states, and other kinds of problems.

The Supreme Court has a very important power. It is the power of **judicial review**. This means the Supreme Court can decide if any law in the nation is **unconstitutional**. An unconstitutional law does not obey the Constitution. Unconstitutional laws must be changed. This is another example of checks and balances. The Supreme Court can force both the states and Congress to change laws that are against the Constitution. It can also force the President to change actions that are against the Constitution.

In all cases affecting ambassadors, other public ministers and consuls, and those in which a state shall be party, the Supreme Court shall have original jurisdiction. In all the other cases before mentioned, the Supreme Court shall have appellate jurisdiction, both as to law and fact, with such exceptions, and under such regulations, as the Congress shall make.

The Supreme Court is sometimes the first court to hear a case. Most of the time the Supreme Court hears cases that were already heard in a lower court. The Supreme Court can change a decision that was made by a lower court. But Supreme Court decisions are final. They cannot be changed by any other court.

The trial of all crimes, except in cases of impeachment, shall be by jury; and such trial shall be held in the state where the said crimes shall have been committed; but when not committed within any state, the trial shall be at such place or places as the Congress may by law have directed.

All people accused of federal crimes can have a jury trial.

The writers of the Constitution believed that every person must have the right to a fair jury trial.

Section 3. Treason

Treason against the United States, shall consist only in levying war against them, or in adhering to their enemies, giving them aid and comfort. No person shall be convicted of treason unless on the testimony of two witnesses to the same overt act, or on confession in open court.

The Congress shall have power to declare the punishment of treason, but no attainder of treason shall work corruption of blood, or forfeiture except during the life of the person attainted.

Treason means helping the enemies of the United States. A court can find a person guilty of treason only if two people tell a judge that they saw the same act of treason. Guilty people may also tell a judge that they did acts of treason.

Congress can make laws to punish people who are guilty of treason. The guilty person's family and friends cannot be punished.

ARTICLE IV. RELATIONS BETWEEN STATES

Section 1. Laws

Full faith and credit shall be given in each state to the public acts, records, and judicial proceedings of every other state. And the Congress may by general laws prescribe the manner in which such acts, records, and proceedings shall be proved, and the effect thereof.

Every state must respect the laws of every other state. For example, each state has its own marriage laws. People can get married in one state and then move to another state. The new state must accept that the people are married.

Section 2. Citizens

The citizens of each state shall be entitled to all privileges and immunities of citizens in the several states.

People from one state can visit other states. They have the same rights as the citizens of the state.

A person charged in any state with treason, felony, or other crimes, who shall flee from justice, and be found in another state, shall, on demand of the executive authority of the state from which he fled, be delivered up, to be removed to the state having jurisdiction of the crime.

People may do crimes and escape to other states. When those people are found, they must be returned to the state they came from.

No person held to service or labor in one state, under the laws thereof, escaping into another, shall, in consequence of any laws or regulation therein, be discharged from such service or labor, but shall be delivered up on claim of the party to whom such service or labor may be due.

Section 3. States and Territories

New states may be admitted by the Congress into this Union; but no new state shall be formed or erected within the jurisdiction of any other state; nor any state be formed by the junction of two or more states, or parts of states, without the consent of the legislatures of the states concerned, as well as of the Congress.

The Congress shall have power to dispose of and make all needful rules and regulations respecting the territory or other property belonging to the United States; and nothing in this Constitution shall be so construed as to prejudice any claims of the United States, or of any particular state.

Congress has the power to allow new states to become part of the United Stages. Since 1787, 37 states have become part of the United States.

The United States also owns public land and territories such as the island of Guam. Only Congress can make rules about selling or controlling public land and territories.

Section 4. Protecting the States

The United States shall guarantee to every state in this Union a republican form of government, and shall protect each of them against invasion; and on application of the legislature, or of the executive (when the legislature cannot be convened) against domestic violence.

Every state of the United States must have a government that has three branches. It must have a lawmaking branch, an executive branch, and a judicial branch. A state cannot have a king as a leader. If fighting starts in a state, the National Guard can be called in to end the fighting in the state.

ARTICLE V. ADDING AMENDMENTS

The Congress, whenever two thirds of both Houses shall deem it necessary, shall propose amendments to this Constitution, or, on the application of the legislatures of two thirds of the several states, shall call a convention for proposing amendments, which, in either case, shall be valid to all intents and purposes, as part of this Constitution, when ratified by the legislatures of three fourths of the several states, or by conventions in three fourths thereof, as the one or the other mode of ratification may be proposed by the Congress; provided that no amendment which may be made prior to the year 1808 shall in any manner affect the first and fourth clauses in the ninth section of the first article; and that no state, without its consent, shall be deprived of its equal suffrage in the Senate.

Amendments, or new laws, can be added to the Constitution. This article of the Constitution tells how new amendments can be added. It is difficult to add new amendments. Since 1787, only 27 amendments have been added to the Constitution.

ARTICLE VI. THE SUPREME LAW OF THE LAND

All debts contracted and engagements entered into, before the adoption of this Constitution, shall be as valid against the United States, under this Constitution, as under the Confederation.

The United States borrowed money to pay for the American Revolution. It also borrowed money after the war. The writers of the Constitution decided that the United States must repay all of the money it had borrowed. Other nations would trust the United States because it paid its debts.

This Constitution, and the laws of the United States which shall be made in pursuance thereof; and all treaties made, or which shall be made, under the authority of the United States, shall be the supreme law of the land; and the judges, in every state, shall be bound thereby, anything in the constitution or laws of any state to the contrary notwithstanding.

The Senators and Representatives before mentioned, and the members of the several state legislatures, and all executive and judicial officers, both of the United States and of the several states, shall be bound, by oath or affirmation, to support this Constitution; but no religious test shall ever be required as a qualification to any office or public trust under the United States.

The Constitution is the highest law in the land. All the laws of Congress and all state laws must agree with the Constitution.

All members of Congress must take an oath and promise to obey the Constitution. All members of state governments must take the same oath. Members of the executive and judicial branches must also make the same promise.

Freedom of religion is important in the United States. People never have to be part of a religious group to get a government job.

ARTICLE VII. RATIFICATION

The ratification of the conventions of nine states, shall be sufficient for the establishment of this Constitution between the states so ratifying the same.

Done in convention by the unanimous consent of the states present the 17th day of September in the year of our Lord 1787 and of the independence of the United States of America the 12th. IN WITNESS whereof we have hereunto subscribed our names,

The Constitution will become the nation's law when nine states **ratify** [approve] it. Each state must hold a special meeting to ratify the Constitution.

The Constitution was signed by leaders from 12 states at the end of the Constitutional Convention. It was signed on September 17, 1787. Here are the names of the leaders who signed and the states they came from:

George Washington
President and deputy from Virginia
attest: William Jackson, Secretary

New Hampshire
John Langdon
Nicholas Gilman

Massachusetts
Nathaniel Gorham
Rufus King

Connecticut
William Samuel Johnson
Roger Sherman

New York
Alexander Hamilton

New Jersey
William Livingston
David Brearley
William Paterson
Jonathan Dayton

Pennsylvania
Benjamin Franklin
Thomas Mifflin
Robert Morris
George Clymer
Thomas FitzSimons
Jared Ingersoll
James Wilson
Gouverneur Morris

Delaware
George Read
Gunning Bedford, Jr.
John Dickinson
Richard Bassett
Jacob Broom

Maryland
James McHenry

Daniel of St. Thomas Jenifer
Daniel Carroll

Virginia
John Blair
James Madison, Jr.

North Carolina
William Blount
Richard Dobbs Spaight
Hugh Williamson

South Carolina
John Rutledge
Charles Cotesworth Pinckney
Charles Pinckney
Pierce Butler

Georgia
William Few
Abraham Baldwin

The Constitution was ratified in 1788. In 1789 Congress met for the first time. That year George Washington became the first President of the United States.

AMENDMENTS

In 1791 the first ten amendments became part of the Constitution. These amendments are called the Bill of Rights. The Bill of Rights protects the freedom of all Americans.

AMENDMENT 1. Freedom of Religion, Speech, Press, Assembly, and Petition

Congress shall make no law respecting an establishment of religion, or prohibiting the free exercise thereof, or abridging the freedom of speech, or of the press; or the right of the people peaceably to assemble, and to petition the government for a redress of grievances.

The First Amendment is very important because it protects five kinds of freedom. It protects freedom of religion. It protects freedom of speech. This allows people to speak against the government and not be sent to jail. This amendment protects freedom of the press. This allows people to write stories that may be against the government in books and newspapers. The First Amendment protects the right to **assemble** [to stand with a large group of people and protest peacefully against government actions]. It also protects your right to **petition** [ask the government to correct problems].

Freedom of religion was very important to the people who wrote the Constitution. They remembered that the Pilgrims and other groups first came to America because they did not want to pray in the Church of England. The writers of the Constitution wanted America to be different than England. They believed the government should not force people to belong to any religion. So the First Amendment also says that Congress cannot write laws that make one religion the main religion of the nation. The First Amendment also says there must be **separation of church and state**. This means that religion must be completely separate from the government. Tax money cannot be used to build churches or other religious buildings. Tax money cannot be used to pay church leaders. Classes in public schools cannot teach about religion.

AMENDMENT II. The Right to Bear Arms

A well regulated militia, being necessary to the security of a free state, the right of the people to keep and bear arms shall not be infringed.

Every state needs soldiers to protect its people. Today soldiers of the National Guard protect people in the United States. The government cannot stop people from owning guns. The federal and state governments can pass laws to control how guns are sold.

AMENDMENT III. The Housing of Soldiers

No soldier shall, in time of peace, be quartered in any house, without the consent of the owner, nor in time of war, but in a manner to be prescribed by law.

Before the American Revolution, the British forced Americans to have British soldiers in their homes. The writers did not want Americans to have this problem again. So this amendment says people cannot be forced to have soldiers eat and sleep in their homes when the United States has peace with other countries. During a war, Congress can pass a law that says soldiers must be allowed to sleep in the homes of Americans.

AMENDMENT IV. Search and Arrest

The right of the people to be secure in their persons, houses, papers, and effects, against unreasonable searches and seizures, shall not be violated, and no warrants shall issue, but upon probable cause, supported by oath or affirmation, and particularly describing the place to be searched, and the persons or things to be seized.

People have the right to be safe in their own homes. The police cannot search a person's home without a **warrant** [a search paper from a judge]. Judges must have very good reasons to give the police search warrants.

AMENDMENT V. The Rights of Accused Persons

No person shall be held to answer for a capital, or otherwise infamous crime, unless on a presentment or indictment of a grand jury, except in cases arising in the land or naval forces, or in the militia, when in actual service, in time of war or public danger; nor shall any person be subject for the same offenses to be twice put in jeopardy of life or limb; nor shall be compelled in any criminal case to be a witness against himself, nor be deprived of life, liberty, or property, without due process of law; nor shall private property be taken for public use without just compensation.

The Fifth Amendment protects people who may have done crimes. A **grand jury**, a jury of about 25 people, must listen to information about the accused person. Then the grand jury decides if the person should have a jury trial because the person may be guilty. The grand jury may decide that the accused person does not need a trial because there is not enough information to prove the person may be guilty. Then the accused person is allowed to remain free.

Accused people cannot be forced to speak against themselves during a trial. Instead, during a trial they can say, "I take the Fifth Amendment." Every accused person has the right to **due process** [fair treatment that obeys the law].

AMENDMENT VI. The Right to a Fair Trial

In all criminal prosecutions, the accused shall enjoy the right to a speedy and public trial, by an impartial jury of the state and district wherein the crime shall have been committed, which district shall have been previously ascertained by law, and to be informed of the nature and cause of the accusation; to be confronted with the witnesses against him; to have compulsory process for obtaining witnesses in his favor; and to have the assistance of counsel for his defense.

The writers of the Constitution wanted the United States to be different from Great Britain. In Great Britain, accused people sometimes stayed in jail for years before they had a trial. Sometimes the trials were held secretly. The writers wanted to be fair to accused people. In the United States, every person who is accused of a crime has the right to a fair jury. The trials cannot be held secretly. Every accused person also has the right to have a lawyer help with the trial. A person may not have enough money to pay for a lawyer. Then a government lawyer will help the accused person both before and during the trial.

AMENDMENT VII. Civil Cases

In suits at common law, where the value in controversy shall exceed twenty dollars, the right of trial by jury shall be preserved, and no fact tried by a jury, shall be otherwise re-examined in any court of the United States, than according to the rules of the common law.

This amendment says people have the right to a jury trial in **civil cases**. Civil cases are not about crimes. They are often about money, property, or divorce. Today people can have jury trials for civil cases in both federal and state courts.

AMENDMENT VIII. Bail and Punishment

Excessive bail shall not be required, nor excessive fines imposed, nor cruel and unusual punishments inflicted.

People who are accused of crimes can often stay out of jail until their trial if they pay **bail** money. Bail is money that an accused person gives the court. When people pay bail, they promise to be in court for their trial. They promise not to run away. The bail money is returned when accused people go to their trials. People who do not have enough money to pay bail must wait in jail until their trial. This amendment helps accused people because it says courts cannot ask people to pay unfair amounts of bail money.

This amendment also protects people who have been found guilty during their trial. Guilty people cannot be punished in ways that are not fair and cruel. For example, a person may be found guilty of stealing a small amount of money. It would not be fair to keep this person in jail for many years.

AMENDMENT IX. Other Rights

The enumeration in the Constitution, of certain rights, shall not be construed to deny or disparage others retained by the people.

The Constitution explains certain rights like freedom of religion and speech. But people have many other rights such as the right to go to school or to work. Many rights are not explained in the Constitution. The government must protect all rights that people have even if they are not in the Constitution.

AMENDMENT X. Powers Belonging to States

The powers not delegated to the United States by the Constitution, nor prohibited by it to the states, are reserved to the states respectively, or to the people.

This is the last amendment in the Bill of Rights. The writers of the Constitution wanted to be sure the federal government would not become too powerful. Many people feared that the states would not have enough power. This amendment says that powers not given to the federal government belong to state governments and their people. For example, the Constitution did not give the federal government the power to make laws about marriage and divorce. So the states have the power to make marriage and divorce laws.

AMENDMENT XI. Cases Against States (1795)

The judicial power of the United States shall not be construed to extend to any suit in law or equity, commenced or prosecuted against one of the United States by citizens of any state, or by citizens or subjects of any foreign state.

A person from one state cannot have a trial against another state in a federal court. A person from a different country cannot do this either.

AMENDMENT XII. Election of the President and Vice President (1804)

The electors shall meet in their respective states and vote by ballot for President and Vice President, one of whom, at least, shall not be an inhabitant of the same state with themselves; they shall name in their ballots the person voted for as President, and in distinct ballots the person voted for as Vice President, and they shall make distinct lists of all persons voted for as President, and of all persons voted for as Vice President, and of the number of votes for each, which lists they shall sign and certify, and transmit sealed to the seat of the government of the United States, directed to the President of the Senate; the President of the Senate shall, in the presence of the Senate and House of Representatives, open all the certificates and the votes shall then be counted. The person having the greatest number of votes for President shall be the President, if such number be a majority of the whole number of electors appointed; and if no person have such majority, then from the persons having the highest numbers, not exceeding three on the list of those voted for as President, the House of Representatives shall choose immediately, by ballot, the President. But in choosing the President, the votes shall be taken by states, the representation from each state having one vote; a quorum for this purpose shall consist of a member or members from two-thirds of the states, and a majority of all the states shall be necessary to a choice. ~~And if the House of Representatives shall not choose a President whenever the right of choice shall devolve upon them, before the fourth day of March next following, then the Vice President shall act as President, as in the case of the death or other constitutional disability of the President.~~ The person having the greatest number of votes as Vice President, shall be the Vice President, if such number be a majority of the whole number of electors appointed, and if no person have a majority, then from the two highest numbers on the list, the Senate shall choose the Vice President; a quorum for the purpose shall consist of two-thirds of the whole number of Senators, and a majority of the whole number shall be necessary to a choice. But no person constitutionally ineligible to the office of President shall be eligible to that of Vice President of the United States.

Article II of the Constitution changed the way Americans elect a President. Until 1800, people voted for electors. The electors then voted for the President. They had two **candidates** [people who want to be elected] to vote for. The candidate who received the most electoral votes became President. The other candidate became the Vice President. In 1800, both Thomas Jefferson and Aaron Burr wanted to be President. Both men received the same number of votes. So members of the House of Representatives had to vote for one of the men to be President. The House chose Jefferson but many people were unhappy about the election.

The Twelfth Amendment was written to improve the way Americans choose a President. The new amendment said electors must vote separately for President and Vice President. The candidate for President must win the **majority** [more than half] of electoral votes to become President. The candidate for Vice President must also win the majority of votes. The House of Representatives votes for a President if a candidate does not receive a majority of electoral votes. The Senate elects the Vice President if no candidate receives a majority of votes.

AMENDMENT XIII. Slavery (1865)

Section 1. Neither slavery nor involuntary servitude, except as a punishment for a crime whereof the party shall have been duly convicted, shall exist within the United States, or any place subject to their jurisdiction.

Section 2. Congress shall have power to enforce this article by appropriate legislation.

This amendment ended slavery in the United States. Congress has the power to carry out this amendment.

AMENDMENT XIV. Rights of Citizens (1868)

Section 1. All persons born or naturalized in the United States, and subject to the jurisdiction thereof, are citizens of the United States and of the state wherein they reside. No state shall make or enforce any law which shall abridge the privileges or immunities of citizens of the United States; nor shall any state deprive any person of life, liberty, or property, without due process of law; nor deny to any person within its jurisdiction the equal protection of the laws.

Section 2. Representatives shall be apportioned among the several states according to their respective numbers, counting the whole number of persons in each state, excluding Indians not taxed. But when the right to vote at any election for the choice of electors for President and Vice President of the United States, representatives in Congress, the executive and judicial officers of a state, or the members of the legislature thereof, is denied to any of the male inhabitants of such state, being 21 years of age, and citizens of the United States, or in anyway abridged, except for participation in rebellion or other crime, the basis of representation therein shall be reduced in the proportion which the number of such male citizens shall bear to the whole number of male citizens 21 years of age in such state.

Section 3. No person shall be a Senator or Representative in Congress, or elector of President and Vice President, or hold any office, civil or military, under the United States, or under any state, who, having previously taken an oath, as a member of Congress, or as an officer of the United States, or as a member of any state legislature, or as an executive or judicial officer of any state, to support the Constitution of the United States, shall

have engaged in insurrection or rebellion against the same, or given aid or comfort to the enemies thereof. But Congress may, by a vote of two-thirds of each house, remove such disability.

Section 4. The validity of the public debt of the United States, authorized by law, including debts incurred for payment of pensions and bounties for services in suppressing insurrection or rebellion, shall not be questioned. But neither the United States nor any state shall assume or pay any debt or obligation incurred in aid of insurrection or rebellion against the United States, or any claim for the loss or emancipation of any slave; but all such debts, obligations and claims shall be held illegal and void.

The Fourteenth Amendment is one of the most important. It has these laws:

1. All people who are born in the United States are citizens. People from other nations can follow certain laws to become citizens. Before this amendment was written, African Americans could not be citizens. The Fourteenth Amendment said African Americans were citizens of both their state and the United States. All people must have equal rights. States must protect the rights of all people.

2. The number of members a state sends to the House of Representatives depends on the state's population. African Americans must be counted as part of a state's population. States must allow all men who are more than 21 years old to vote.

3. People who have worked against the United States cannot be in Congress.

They cannot be part of the federal government. This law punished people who fought for the South during the Civil War.

4. The United States borrowed a lot of money to pay for the Civil War. The government must repay the money.

5. Congress can make laws to carry out the Fourteenth Amendment.

Section 5. The Congress shall have power to enforce, by appropriate legislation, the provisions of this article.

AMENDMENT XV. Right to Vote (1870)

Section 1. The right of citizens of the United States to vote shall not be denied or abridged by the United States or by any state on account of race, color, or previous condition of servitude.

Section 2. The Congress shall have power to enforce this article by appropriate legislation.

All citizens who are men can vote. This amendment gave African Americans the right to vote. Congress can make laws to carry out this amendment.

AMENDMENT XVI. Income Tax (1913)

The Congress shall have power to lay and collect taxes on incomes, from whatever source derived, without apportionment among the several states, and without regard to any census or enumeration.

Congress can write laws about **income taxes** and collect income taxes. Income tax is a tax on the money people earn.

AMENDMENT XVII. Election of Senators (1913)

The Senate of the United States shall be composed of two Senators from each state, elected by the people thereof, for six years; and each Senator shall have one vote. The electors in each state shall have the qualifications requisite for electors of the most numerous branch of the state legislatures.

When vacancies happen in the representation of any state in the Senate, the executive authority of such state shall issue writs of election to fill such vacancies: *Provided*, That the legislature of any state may empower the executive thereof to make temporary appointments until the people fill the vacancies by election as the legislature may direct.

This amendment shall not be so construed as to effect the election or term of any Senator chosen before it becomes valid as part of the Constitution.

This amendment changed the way Americans elect United States senators. The people of each state vote for senators in November elections. They vote for senators the same way they vote for members of the House of Representatives. This method continues to be the one that is used today.

AMENDMENT XVIII. Prohibition of Liquor (1919)

Section 1. After one year from the ratification of this article the manufacture, sale, or transportation of intoxicating liquors within, the importation thereof into, or the exportation thereof from the United States and all territory subject to

~~the jurisdiction thereof for beverage purposes is hereby prohibited.~~

~~**Section 2.** The Congress and the several states shall have concurrent power to enforce this article by appropriate legislation.~~

~~**Section 3.** This article shall be inoperative unless it shall have been ratified as an amendment to the Constitution by the legislatures of the several states, as provided in the Constitution, within seven years from the date of the submission hereof to the states by the Congress.~~

This amendment said that **liquor** [drinks like wine, beer, and whiskey] could not be made, bought, or sold in the United States. Millions of people did not agree with this law. A lot of liquor was bought and sold in ways that were against the law.

AMENDMENT XIX. Woman Suffrage (1920)

The right of citizens of the United States to vote shall not be denied or abridged by the United States or by any state on account of sex.

Congress shall have power to enforce this article by appropriate legislation.

All women who are citizens have the right to vote in all elections. Congress has the power to pass laws to carry out this amendment.

AMENDMENT XX. Lame Duck Amendment (1933)

Section 1. The terms of the President and Vice President shall end at noon on the 20th day of January, and the terms of Senators and Representatives at noon on the third day of January, of the years in which such terms would have ended if this article had not been ratified; and the terms of their successors shall then begin.

Section 2. The Congress shall assemble at least once in every year, and such meeting shall begin at noon on the third day of January, unless they shall by law appoint a different day.

Section 3. If, at the time fixed for the beginning of the term of the President, the President elect shall have died, the Vice President elect shall become President. If a President shall not have been chosen before the time fixed for the beginning of his term, or if the President elect shall have failed to qualify, then the Vice President elect shall act as President until a President shall have qualified; and the Congress may by law provide for the case wherein neither a President elect nor a Vice President elect shall have qualified, declaring who shall then act as President, or the manner in which one who is to act shall be selected, and such person shall act accordingly until a President or Vice President shall have qualified.

Section 4. The Congress may by law provide for the case of the death of any of the persons from whom the House of Representatives may choose a President whenever the right of choice shall have devolved upon them, and for the case of the death of any of the persons from whom the Senate may choose a Vice President whenever the right of choice shall have devolved upon them.

Section 5. Sections 1 and 2 shall take effect on the 15th day of October following the ratification of this article.

Section 6. This article shall be inoperative unless it shall have been ratified as an amendment to the Constitution by the legislatures of three-fourths of the several states within seven years from the date of its submission.

Each new President and Vice President begin their term on January 20. The terms for senators and members of the House begin on January 3. Before this amendment was passed, people who won elections in November did not begin their terms until March.

Congress must meet at least once a year. The meetings should begin on January 3 at noon.

If the President dies, the Vice President becomes the next President.

AMENDMENT XXI. Repeal of the Eighteenth Amendment (1933)

Section 1. The Eighteenth article of amendment to the Constitution of the United States is hereby repealed.

Section 2. The transportation or importation into any state, territory, or possession of the United States for delivery or use therein of intoxicating liquors, in violation of the laws thereof, is hereby prohibited.

Section 3. This article shall be inoperative unless it shall have been ratified as an amendment to the Constitution by conventions in the several states, as provided in the Constitution, within seven years from the date of the submission hereof to the states by the Congress.

The Eighteenth Amendment on prohibition is no longer a law of the United States. States can pass their own laws about buying and selling liquor.

AMENDMENT XXII. Terms of the Presidency (1951)

Section 1. No person shall be elected to the office of the President more than twice, and no person who has held the office of President, or acted as President, for more than two years of a term to which some other person was elected President shall be elected to the office of the President more than once. But this article shall not apply to any person holding the office of President when this article was proposed by the Congress, and shall not prevent any person who may be holding the office of President, or acting as President, during the term within which this article becomes operative from holding the office of President or acting as President during the remainder of such term.

Section 2. This article shall be inoperative unless it shall have been ratified as an amendment to the Constitution by the legislatures of three fourths of the several States within seven years from the date of its submission to the States by Congress.

A person cannot be elected President for more than two terms. A person cannot be President for more than ten years.

George Washington was President for two terms. Every President served only one or two terms until Franklin D. Roosevelt became President. He was elected to four terms. Many people feared that a President could become too powerful if he served for so many years. This amendment was added to the Constitution to prevent that problem.

AMENDMENT XXIII. Voting in the District of Columbia (1961)

Section 1. The district constituting the seat of government of the United States shall appoint in such manner as the Congress may direct: A number of electors of President and Vice President equal to the whole number of Senators and Representatives in Congress to which the district would be entitled if it were a state, but in no event more than the least populous state; they shall be in addition to those appointed by the states, but they shall be considered, for the purposes of the election of the President and Vice President, to be electors appointed by a state; and they shall meet in the district and perform such duties as provided by the Twelfth article of amendment.

This amendment allows the citizens of Washington, D.C., to vote in elections for President. Washington, D.C., has three electoral votes. Congress has the power to write laws to carry out this amendment.

Washington, D.C., the capital of the United States, is in the District of Columbia. The capital city is between the states of Maryland and Virginia but it is not part of any state. People who lived in the nation's capital city were never allowed to vote in elections for President. This amendment changed that problem. Washington, D.C., has about the same population as some of the smallest states. So the capital city has three electoral votes that is the same number of votes given to states with the smallest populations.

The people of Washington D.C., cannot vote for members of Congress. Many Americans believe it is not fair that citizens of the capital are not represented in Congress. They hope that some day another amendment will be added to the Constitution to solve this problem.

Section 2. The Congress shall have power to enforce this article by appropriate legislation.

AMENDMENT XXIV. Poll Taxes (1964)

Section 1. The right of citizens of the United States to vote in any primary or other election for President or Vice President, for electors for President or Vice President, or for Senator or Representative in Congress, shall not be denied or abridged by the United States or any state by reason of failure to pay any poll tax or other tax.

Section 2. The Congress shall have the power to enforce this article by appropriate legislation.

A **poll tax** is a tax that people had to pay in order to vote. After 1889 many states had poll taxes. Poll taxes made it difficult for poor African Americans to vote. This amendment said people could not lose their right to vote in national elections because they could not pay a poll tax. Congress has the power to make laws to carry out this amendment. Today all poll taxes are unconstitutional.

AMENDMENT XXV. Presidential Succession (1967)

Section 1. In case of the removal of the President from office or his death or resignation, the Vice President shall become President.

Section 2. Whenever there is a vacancy in the office of the Vice President, the President shall nominate a Vice President who shall take office upon confirmation by a majority vote of both houses of Congress.

Section 3. Whenever the President transmits to the president *pro tempore* of the Senate and the Speaker of the House of Representatives his written declaration that he is unable to discharge the powers and duties of his office, and until he transmits to them a written declaration to the contrary, such powers and duties shall be discharged by the Vice President as Acting President.

Section 4. Whenever the Vice President and a majority of either the principal officers of the executive departments or of such other body as Congress may by law provide, transmit to the President pro tempore of the Senate and the Speaker of the House of Representatives their written declaration that the President is unable to discharge the powers and duties of his office, the Vice President shall immediately assume the powers and duties of the office as Acting President.

Thereafter, when the President transmits to the President pro tempore of the Senate and the Speaker of the House of Representatives his written declaration that no inability exists, he shall resume the powers and duties of his office unless the Vice President and a majority of either the principal officers of the executive department or of such other body as Congress may by law provide, transmit within four days to the President pro tempore of the Senate and the Speaker of the House of Representatives their written declaration that the President is unable to discharge the powers and duties of his office. Thereupon Congress shall decide the issue, assembling within 48 hours for that purpose if not in session. If the Congress, within 21 days after receipt of the latter written declaration, or, if Congress is not in session, within 21 days after Congress is required to assemble, determines by two-thirds vote of both houses that the President is unable to discharge the powers and duties of his office, the Vice President shall continue to discharge the same as Acting President; otherwise, the President shall resume the powers and duties of his office.

This amendment tries to solve the problem of what to do if the President dies or cannot work. If the President dies or **resigns** [leaves his job], then the Vice President becomes President.

If the Vice President dies or leaves his job, the nation needs a new Vice President. The President can choose a person to be Vice President. Both houses of Congress must vote to approve the person chosen for Vice President.

If a President is sick or not able to do his job, the Vice President will do the job until the President can work again. Once the President is able to work, the Vice President will return to his job of being Vice President.

AMENDMENT XXVI. Voting Age of 18 (1971)

Section 1. The right of citizens of the United States, who are 18 years of age or older, to vote shall not be denied or abridged by the United States or by any state on account of age.

Section 2. The Congress shall have power to enforce this article by appropriate legislation.

All citizens who are at least 18 years old can vote in state and national elections. Congress can make laws to carry out this amendment.

In 1787, only white men could vote. As time passed, new amendments allowed more and more people to vote. Today all citizens who are at least eighteen years old can vote.

AMENDMENT XXVII. Congressional Pay (1992)

No law varying the compensation for the services of the Senators and Representatives shall take effect, until an election of Representatives shall have intervened.

This amendment allows Congress to raise salaries for members of the House and Senate. However, this amendment was written so that members of Congress cannot pay themselves more money. But the higher salaries will be paid after the next election for Senators and Representatives. The new members of Congress will receive the higher salaries. In 2004, the salary for members of Congress was $158,100.

The Fifty States

Alabama

Date of Statehood 1819, order 22nd
Area in Square Miles 51,718, **rank** 29th
Population 4,500,752, **rank** 23rd

State Symbols
State tree Southern pine
State flower Camellia
State bird Yellowhammer

Alaska

Date of Statehood 1959, order 49th
Area in Square Miles 589,878, **rank** 1st
Population 648,818, **rank** 46th

State Symbols
State tree Sitka spruce
State flower Forget-me-not
State bird Willow ptarmigan

Arizona

Date of Statehood 1912, order 48th
Area in Square Miles 114,007, **rank** 6th
Population 5,580,811, **rank** 18th

State Symbols
State tree Paloverde
State flower Saguaro cactus blossom
State bird Cactus wren

Arkansas

Date of Statehood 1836, order 25th
Area in Square Miles 53,183, **rank** 27th
Population 2,725,714, **rank** 32nd

State Symbols
State tree Pine tree
State flower Apple blossom
State bird Mockingbird

California

Date of Statehood 1850, order 31st
Area in Square Miles 158,648, **rank** 3rd
Population 35,484,453, **rank** 1st

State Symbols
State tree California redwood
State flower Golden poppy
State bird California valley quail

Colorado

Date of Statehood 1876, order 38th
Area in Square Miles 104,091, **rank** 8th
Population 4,550,688, **rank** 22nd

State Symbols
State tree Blue spruce
State flower Rocky Mountain columbine
State bird Lark bunting

Population estimates are based on 2003 information from the United States Census Bureau.

Connecticut

Date of Statehood 1788,
    order 5th
Area in Square Miles 5,006, **rank** 48th
Population 3,483,372, **rank** 29th

State Symbols

State tree White oak
State flower Mountain laurel
State bird Robin

Georgia

Date of Statehood 1788,
    order 4th
Area in Square Miles 58,930, **rank** 21st
Population 8,684,715, **rank** 9th

State Symbols
State tree Live oak
State flower Cherokee rose
State bird Brown thrasher

Delaware

Date of Statehood 1787,
    order 1st
Area in Square Miles 2,026, **rank** 49th
Population 817,491, **rank** 45th

State Symbols
State tree American holly
State flower Peach blossom
State bird Blue hen chicken

Hawaii

Date of Statehood 1959,
    order 50th
Area in Square Miles 6,459, **rank** 47th
Population 1,257,608, **rank** 42nd

State Symbols
State tree Kukui
State flower Yellow hibiscus
State bird Nene (Hawaiian goose)

Florida

Date of Statehood 1845,
    order 27th
Area in Square Miles 58,681, **rank** 22nd
Population 17,019,068, **rank** 4th

State Symbols
State tree Sabal palmetto palm
State flower Orange blossom
State bird Mockingbird

Idaho

Date of Statehood 1890,
    order 43rd
Area in Square Miles 83,574, **rank** 13th
Population 1,366,332, **rank** 39th

State Symbols
State tree White pine
State flower Syringa
State bird Mountain bluebird

Illinois

Date of Statehood 1818,
   order 21st
Area in Square Miles 56,343, **rank** 24th
Population 12,653,544, **rank** 5th

State Symbols
State tree White oak
State flower Native violet
State bird Cardinal

Indiana

Date of Statehood 1816,
   order 19th
Area in Square Miles 36,185, **rank** 38th
Population 6,195,643, **rank** 14th

State Symbols
State tree Tulip tree
State flower Peony
State bird Cardinal

Iowa

Date of Statehood 1846,
   order 29th
Area in Square Miles 56,276, **rank** 25th
Population 2,944,062, **rank** 30th

State Symbols
State tree Oak
State flower Wild rose
State bird Eastern goldfinch

Kansas

Date of Statehood 1861,
   order 34th
Area in Square Miles 82,282, **rank** 14th
Population 2,723,507, **rank** 33rd

State Symbols
State tree Cottonwood
State flower Sunflower
State bird Western meadowlark

Kentucky

Date of Statehood 1792,
   order 15th
Area in Square Miles 40,395, **rank** 37th
Population 4,117,827, **rank** 26th

State Symbols
State tree Kentucky coffee tree
State flower Goldenrod
State bird Kentucky cardinal

Louisiana

Date of Statehood 1812,
   order 18th
Area in Square Miles 47,752, **rank** 31st
Population 4,496,334, **rank** 24th

State Symbols
State tree Bald cypress
State flower Magnolia
State bird Brown pelican

Maine

Date of Statehood 1820,
　　order 23rd
Area in Square Miles 33,128, **rank** 39th
Population 1,305,728, **rank** 40th

State Symbols
State tree White pine
State flower White pine cone
　　& tassel
State bird Chickadee

Michigan

Date of Statehood 1837,
　　order 26th
Area in Square Miles 58,513, **rank** 23rd
Population 10,079,985, **rank** 8th

State Symbols
State tree White pine
State flower Apple blossom
State bird Robin

Maryland

Date of Statehood 1788,
　　order 7th
Area in Square Miles 10,455, **rank** 42nd
Population 5,508,909, **rank** 19th

State Symbols
State tree White oak
State flower Black-eyed Susan
State bird Baltimore oriole

Minnesota

Date of Statehood 1858,
　　order 32nd
Area in Square Miles 84,397, **rank** 12th
Population 5,059,375, **rank** 21st

State Symbols
State tree Norway pine
State flower Pink and white lady's
　　slipper
State bird Common loon

Massachusetts

Date of Statehood 1788,
　　order 6th
Area in Square Miles 8,257, **rank** 45th
Population 6,433,422, **rank** 13th

State Symbols
State tree American elm
State flower Mayflower
　　(trailing arbutus)
State bird Chickadee

Mississippi

Date of Statehood 1817,
　　order 20th
Area in Square Miles 47,716, **rank** 32nd
Population 2,881,281, **rank** 31st

State Symbols
State tree Magnolia
State flower Magnolia
State bird Mockingbird

Missouri

Date of Statehood 1821, order 24th
Area in Square Miles 69,686, **rank** 19th
Population 5,704,484, **rank** 17th

State Symbols
State tree Flowering dogwood
State flower Hawthorn
State bird Bluebird

Montana

Date of Statehood 1889, order 41st
Area in Square Miles 147,047, **rank** 4th
Population 917,621, **rank** 44th

State Symbols
State tree Ponderosa pine
State flower Bitterroot
State bird Western meadowlark

Nebraska

Date of Statehood 1867, order 37th
Area in Square Miles 77,359, **rank** 15th
Population 1,739,291, **rank** 38th

State Symbols
State tree Cottonwood
State flower Goldenrod
State bird Western meadowlark

Nevada

Date of Statehood 1864, order 36th
Area in Square Miles 110,561, **rank** 7th
Population 2,241,154, **rank** 35th

State Symbols
State tree Single-leaf piñon & bristlecone pine
State flower Sagebrush
State bird Mountain bluebird

New Hampshire

Date of Statehood 1788, order 9th
Area in Square Miles 9,283, **rank** 44th
Population 1,287,687, **rank** 41st

State Symbols
State tree White birch
State flower Purple lilac
State bird Purple finch

New Jersey

Date of Statehood 1787, order 3rd
Area in Square Miles 7,790, **rank** 46th
Population 8,638,396, **rank** 10th

State Symbols
State tree Red oak
State flower Purple violet
State bird Eastern goldfinch

New Mexico

Date of Statehood 1912,
  order 47th
Area in Square Miles 121,593, **rank** 5th
Population 1,874,614, **rank** 36th

State Symbols
State tree Piñon
State flower Yucca
State bird Roadrunner

North Dakota

Date of Statehood 1889,
  order 39th
Area in Square Miles 70,704, **rank** 17th
Population 633,837, **rank** 48th

State Symbols
State tree American elm
State flower Wild prairie rose
State bird Western meadowlark

New York

Date of Statehood 1788,
  order 11th
Area in Square Miles 49,112, **rank** 30th
Population 19,190,115, **rank** 3rd

State Symbols
State tree Sugar maple
State flower Rose
State bird Bluebird

Ohio

Date of Statehood 1803,
  order 17th
Area in Square Miles 41,328, **rank** 35th
Population 11,435,798, **rank** 7th

State Symbols
State tree Buckeye
State flower Scarlet carnation
State bird Cardinal

North Carolina

Date of Statehood 1789,
  order 12th
Area in Square Miles 52,672, **rank** 28th
Population 8,407,248, **rank** 11th

State Symbols
State tree Pine
State flower Flowering dogwood
State bird Cardinal

Oklahoma

Date of Statehood 1907,
  order 46th
Area in Square Miles 69,919, **rank** 18th
Population 3,511,532, **rank** 28th

State Symbols
State tree Redbud
State flower Mistletoe
State bird Scissortailed flycatcher

Oregon

Date of Statehood 1859,
  order 33rd
Area in Square Miles 97,052, **rank** 10th
Population 3,559,596, **rank** 27th

State Symbols
State tree Douglas fir
State flower Oregon grape
State bird Western meadowlark

South Carolina

Date of Statehood 1788,
  order 8th
Area in Square Miles 31,113, **rank** 40th
Population 4,147,152, **rank** 25th

State Symbols
State tree Palmetto
State flower Yellow jessamine
State bird Carolina wren

Pennsylvania

Date of Statehood 1787,
  order 2nd
Area in Square Miles 45,308, **rank** 33rd
Population 12,365,455, **rank** 6th

State Symbols
State tree Hemlock
State flower Mountain laurel
State bird Ruffed grouse

South Dakota

Date of Statehood 1889,
  order 40th
Area in Square Miles 77,122, **rank** 16th
Population 764,309, **rank** 46th

State Symbols
State tree Black Hills spruce
State flower American pasqueflower
State bird Ring-necked pheasant

Rhode Island

Date of Statehood 1790,
  order 13th
Area in Square Miles 1,213, **rank** 50th
Population 1,076,164, **rank** 43rd

State Symbols
State tree Red maple
State flower Violet
State bird Rhode Island Red

Tennessee

Date of Statehood 1796,
  order 16th
Area in Square Miles 42,146, **rank** 34th
Population 5,841,748, **rank** 16th

State Symbols
State tree Tulip poplar
State flower Iris
State bird Mockingbird

Texas

Date of Statehood 1845,
    order 28th
Area in Square Miles 266,874, **rank** 2nd
Population 22,118,509, **rank** 2nd

State Symbols
State tree Pecan
State flower Bluebonnet
State bird Mockingbird

Utah

Date of Statehood 1896,
    order 45th
Area in Square Miles 84,905, **rank** 11th
Population 2,351,467, **rank** 34th

State Symbols
State tree Blue spruce
State flower Sego lily
State bird Seagull

Vermont

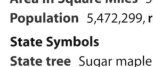

Date of Statehood 1791,
    order 14th
Area in Square Miles 9,615, **rank** 43rd
Population 619,107, **rank** 49th

State Symbols
State tree Sugar maple
State flower Red clover
State bird Hermit thrush

Virginia

Date of Statehood 1788,
    order 10th
Area in Square Miles 40,598, **rank** 36th
Population 7,386,330, **rank** 12th

State Symbols
State tree Flowering dogwood
State flower Flowering dogwood
State bird Cardinal

Washington

Date of Statehood 1889,
    order 42nd
Area in Square Miles 68,126, **rank** 20th
Population 6,131,445, **rank** 15th

State Symbols
State tree Western hemlock
State flower Coast rhododendron
State bird Willow goldfinch or wild canary

West Virginia

Date of Statehood 1863,
    order 35th
Area in Square Miles 24,231, **rank** 41st
Population 1,810,354, **rank** 37th

State Symbols
State tree Sugar maple
State flower Rhododendron
State bird Cardinal

Wisconsin

Date of Statehood 1848,
    order 30th
Area in Square Miles 56,145, **rank** 26th
Population 5,472,299, **rank** 20th

State Symbols
State tree Sugar maple
State flower Wood violet
State bird Robin

Wyoming

Date of Statehood 1890,
    order 44th
Area in Square Miles 97,914, **rank** 9th
Population 501,242, **rank** 50th

State Symbols
State tree Cottonwood
State flower Indian paintbrush
State bird Western meadowlark

Territories and Possessions of the United States of America

District of Columbia

Status federal district
Area in Square Miles 68
Population 563,384

Symbols
Tree Scarlet oak
Flower American beauty rose
Bird Wood thrush

American Virgin Islands

Status territory
Area in Square Miles 151
Population 124,778

Symbols
Tree n.a.
Flower Yellow elder
Bird Yellow breast

Puerto Rico

Status commonwealth
Area in Square Miles 3,515
Population 3,878,532

Symbols
Tree Ceiba
Flower Maga
Bird Reinita

Guam

Status territory
Area in Square Miles 209
Population 163,941

Symbols
Tree Ifit (Intsiabijuga)
Flower Puti Tai Nobio (Bougainvillea)
Bird Toto (Fruit dove)

Northern Marianas

Status commonwealth
Area in Square Miles 184
Population 78,252

Symbols
Tree n.a.
Flower n.a.
Bird n.a.

American Samoa

Status territory
Area in Square Miles 77
Population 57,902

Symbols
Tree Ava
Flower Paogo
Bird n.a.

n.a. = not applicable/not available

Presidents of the United States

1

George Washington
Years in Office: 1789–1797

6

John Quincy Adams
Years in Office: 1825–1829

11

James K. Polk
Years in Office: 1845–1849

2

John Adams
Years in Office: 1797–1801

7

Andrew Jackson
Years in Office: 1829–1837

12

Zachary Taylor
Years in Office: 1849–1850

3

Thomas Jefferson
Years in Office: 1801–1809

8

Martin Van Buren
Years in Office: 1837–1841

13

Millard Fillmore
Years in Office: 1850–1853

4

James Madison
Years in Office: 1809–1817

9

William Henry Harrison
Years in Office: 1841

14

Franklin Pierce
Years in Office: 1853–1857

5

James Monroe
Years in Office: 1817–1825

10

John Tyler
Years in Office: 1841–1845

15

James Buchanan
Years in Office: 1857–1861

Abraham Lincoln
Years in Office: 1861–1865

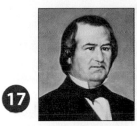

Andrew Johnson
Years in Office: 1865–1869

Ulysses S. Grant
Years in Office: 1869–1877

Rutherford B. Hayes
Years in Office: 1877–1881

James A. Garfield
Years in Office: 1881

Chester A. Arthur
Years in Office: 1881–1885

Grover Cleveland
Years in Office: 1885–1889

Benjamin Harrison
Years in Office: 1889–1893

Grover Cleveland
Years in Office: 1893–1897

William McKinley
Years in Office: 1897–1901

Theodore Roosevelt
Years in Office: 1901–1909

William Howard Taft
Years in Office: 1909–1913

Woodrow Wilson
Years in Office: 1913–1921

Warren G. Harding
Years in Office: 1921–1923

Calvin Coolidge
Years in Office: 1923–1929

31

Herbert Hoover
Years in Office: 1929–1933

32

Franklin D. Roosevelt
Years in Office: 1933–1945

33

Harry S Truman
Years in Office: 1945–1953

34

Dwight D. Eisenhower
Years in Office: 1953–1961

35

John F. Kennedy
Years in Office: 1961–1963

36

Lyndon B. Johnson
Years in Office: 1963–1969

37

Richard M. Nixon
Years in Office: 1969–1974

38

Gerald R. Ford
Years in Office: 1974–1977

39

Jimmy Carter
Years in Office: 1977–1981

40

Ronald Reagan
Years in Office: 1981–1989

41

George Bush
Years in Office: 1989–1993

42

William J. Clinton
Years in Office: 1993–2001

43

George W. Bush
Years in Office: 2001–

GLOSSARY

abolitionists page 103
Abolitionists were people who worked to end slavery in the United States.

acid rain page 283
Acid rain forms when pollution in the air becomes part of the rain.

acres page 202
Acres are units of land. One acre equals 4,840 square yards.

admiral page 237
An admiral is a very important officer in the United States Navy.

airmail page 218
Airmail is mail carried by airplane.

Allies page 208
The nations that fought the Central Powers during World War I were the Allies. During World War II, the Allies fought the Axis countries.

al Qaeda page 304
Al Qaeda is a terrorist group.

ambulance page 235
An ambulance is a special car or truck used to take hurt people to a hospital.

amendments page 68
Amendments are laws that are added to the Constitution.

American Federation of Labor (AFL) page 190
The American Federation of Labor was started to help workers. Many unions are part of the AFL.

American Revolution page 43
The American Revolution was the war that the American colonies fought against Great Britain from 1775 to 1781.

Americans with Disabilities Act page 296
The Americans with Disabilities Act is a law that protects the rights of people with disabilities. It was passed in 1990.

appeasement page 229
Appeasement means giving in to keep peace.

arrested page 194
To be arrested means to be held by the police.

assembly line page 170
In an assembly line, a product moves from worker to worker until it is put together.

assured page 50
Assured means made sure or certain.

astronauts page 262
Astronauts are people who travel in space.

atomic bomb page 238
An atomic bomb is a very powerful bomb.

Axis countries page 229
Germany, Italy, and Japan were the main Axis countries that fought against the Allies during World War II.

baby boom page 250
A baby boom is a large number of babies born during a period of time.

baby boomers page 310
People born soon after World War II are called baby boomers.

battlefields page 140
Battlefields are areas of land on which battles are fought.

battleship page 163
A battleship is a ship that is used for fighting wars at sea.

bear page 197
To bear is to put up with.

367

big business page 183
Big business means one person or one business controls many other businesses.

Bill of Rights page 68
The Bill of Rights is the first ten amendments added to the Constitution.

body of water page 32
A body of water is a large area of water. Lakes, rivers, and oceans are bodies of water.

bombs page 228
Bombs are weapons that destroy things when they are made to explode.

border page 93
A border is a line that separates one state from another. A border can also separate cities, towns, and countries.

boroughs page 180
Boroughs are towns or parts of cities.

Boston Tea Party page 42
During the Boston Tea Party, Americans went on three British tea ships. They threw all the tea into the ocean because they did not want to pay a tea tax.

boundaries page 61
Boundaries are the lines around a city, state, or country. Rivers, oceans, and mountains can be boundaries. Boundaries are often shown as lines drawn on maps.

boycott page 256
During a boycott, people stop buying or using a product or a service.

branches of government page 67
The three branches of government in the United States are Congress, the President, and the Supreme Court, as well as the people who work for them.

buffalo page 5
Buffalo are oxen. They are large animals with horns and fur.

building armies page 208
Nations that are building armies are making many weapons and are teaching many people to be soldiers.

bullets page 236
Bullets are small pieces of metal that are shot out of guns.

camera phones page 299
Camera phones are cell phones that can take pictures.

canals page 90
Canals are waterways that connect bodies of water, such as rivers.

capital page 17
The capital of a country or a state is the city where the government meets.

captured page 80
Captured means took and held a person, place, or thing by using force.

cease-fire page 276
A cease-fire happens when countries agree to stop fighting during a war.

cell phones page 299
Cell phones are phones that send signals through the air.

Central Powers page 209
The Central Powers were the nations that fought against the Allies during World War I.

century page 302
A century is one hundred years.

chemicals page 283
Chemicals are dry or liquid materials that can make things change.

child labor page 197
Child labor is working children. Laws have been passed to end child labor.

Church of England page 20
The Church of England is all the churches in England that accept the ruler of England as the head of the church.

citizens page 118
Citizens are members of a country.

civil rights page 257
Civil rights are the rights that the Constitution gives all American citizens.

Civil Rights Act of 1964 page 258
The Civil Rights Act of 1964 is a law passed by Congress to protect the rights of all American citizens.

Civil War page 139
The Civil War was the war fought between the North and the South from 1861 to 1865.

claimed page 11
When a country claimed land, it meant it would own and rule that land.

climate page 134
Climate is the usual weather in an area.

coast page 123
A coast is land along an ocean.

Cold War page 244
The Cold War was a struggle between the United States and the Soviet Union over the spread of communism.

colony page 21
A colony is land ruled by another nation.

commander in chief page 59
The commander in chief is the most important leader of the American army.

communicate page 298
To communicate is to give information to others by writing or speaking.

communism page 217
Communism is a type of government. In communism, the government owns most land and businesses.

computer chips page 298
Computer chips are tiny pieces of material that store large amounts of information. They are used in computers and cell phones.

concentration camps page 230
Concentration camps were places where German soldiers sent many people during World War II.

Congress page 66
Congress is the United States Senate and House of Representatives. Men and women in Congress write laws for the United States.

conquer page 228
To conquer means to win control of a country during a war.

conservation page 201
Conservation is the act of protecting natural resources.

Constitution page 55
A constitution is a set of laws. The United States Constitution is a set of laws for the United States.

Constitutional Convention page 60
The Constitutional Convention was a set of important meetings in 1787. During the meetings, American leaders wrote a set of new laws for the United States.

consumer goods page 251
Consumer goods are products that people use, such as cars or telephones.

contracts page 269
Contracts are agreements between two or more people to do something.

conveyor belt page 170
A conveyor belt is a long, moving belt that carries parts past factory workers.

cotton page 5
Cotton is a plant used to make cloth. You can wear clothes made of cotton.

cotton gin page 88
A cotton gin is a machine that removes seeds from cotton plants.

crashed page 223
When the stock market crashed, the price of stocks became low.

credit page 215
Credit is a way to buy goods by paying for them over time.

crops page 75
Crops are plants grown by farmers. Corn, potatoes, and cotton are three kinds of crops.

dams page 126
Dams are strong walls built to hold back water in rivers.

D-Day page 237
D-Day was June 6, 1944. On that day, thousands of Allied soldiers attacked German soldiers in France.

decade page 252
A decade is ten years.

Declaration of Independence page 46
The Declaration of Independence was an important paper that said the American colonies were a free nation.

declared war page 209
If a country says that it is going to fight in a war against another country, it has declared war on that country.

democracy page 244
A democracy is a government that allows people to choose their own leaders.

Department of Homeland Security page 305
The Department of Homeland Security helps government groups stop terrorism.

departure page 82
Departure means leaving.

depression page 222
A depression is a time when most businesses lose money and many people lose their jobs.

destroyed page 140
Destroyed means ruined. A war can destroy homes, farms, and cities.

developing country page 284
A developing country is a country that does not have enough industries. Many people in the country work on farms.

dictator page 228
A dictator is a ruler who has full control over the government of a country.

discrimination page 202
Discrimination is the act of treating a person unfairly because of his or her race, religion, or physical disability.

diverse page 309
When a country is diverse it has a large variety of people.

DNA page 299
DNA is found in all living things. DNA controls many things about a person, such as hair color.

doubled page 76
When the United States doubled in size, it became twice as large as it had been.

drilled page 184
Drilled means used a special machine to make a deep hole in the earth.

drought page 224
A drought is a long time without rain.

Dust Bowl page 224
When winds blew thick dust across the Great Plains in the 1930s, the area became known as the Dust Bowl. One cause of the dust was a long drought.

economy page 313
The economy of a country is the way it earns and uses money.

education page 102
Education is the learning a person gets from school, people, and places.

elected page 224
If Americans gave a person enough votes to become President, they elected that person.

election page 194
People vote for their leaders during an election.

electric sparks page 54
Electric sparks are tiny bits of electricity that give off small amounts of light for a few seconds.

e-mail page 299
E-mail is a way for people to send letters by computer.

Emancipation Proclamation page 140
The Emancipation Proclamation was a paper that said all slaves in the Confederate States were free. It went into effect in 1863.

employed page 197
Employed means used. Workers are employed by business owners.

employers page 189
Employers are people who hire other people to work for them.

energy page 287
Energy gives things power. Heat, light, and electricity are three forms of energy.

environment page 126
The environment is the land, water, and climate of an area.

equal page 46
People who are equal have the same importance.

equal rights page 149
People who have equal rights have the same rights that other people have.

escape page 132
To escape means to get free.

exports page 289
Exports are goods that are sold or traded to another country.

fare page 151
A fare is money paid for a ride or trip.

fast page 270
A fast is a long time without food.

First Lady page 61
The wife of the President of the United States is called the First Lady.

fort page 112
A fort is a building from which an army can fight its enemies.

fossil fuels page 286
Fossil fuels are materials used for energy. They are found deep inside the earth and were made long ago. Coal, oil, and natural gas are fossil fuels.

freedom of religion page 20
Freedom of religion means one can pray the way he or she wants to pray.

freedom of the press page 68
Freedom of the press means a person can write what he or she wants to write in newspapers and books.

freedom of the seas page 80
Freedom of the seas means that people can sail ships wherever they want.

Fugitive Slave Act page 132
The Fugitive Slave Act was a law passed in 1850. It said that all escaped slaves must be returned to the South.

Gadsden Purchase page 118
The Gadsden Purchase was land that the United States bought from Mexico.

general page 47
A general is an important army leader.

genes page 299
Genes are found in the cells of all living things. They are made up of DNA.

geographers page 17
Geographers are people who study different areas and people on Earth.

G.I. Bill of Rights page 251
The G.I. Bill of Rights is a law that helps veterans get loans.

global warming page 298
Global warming is the warming of Earth's air. It is made worse by air pollution.

goal page 140
A goal is something a person wants and tries to get.

gold rush page 125
A gold rush is a time when many people move into an area in order to find gold.

goods page 87
Goods are things people buy.

governor page 21
A governor is a government leader for a state, town, or area.

grains page 158
Grains are cereal plants that have small, hard seeds. Wheat and corn are grains.

grape growers page 269
Grape growers are farm owners who grow grapes.

grape pickers page 269
Grape pickers are farm workers who pick grapes.

Great Depression page 222
The Great Depression was the depression in the 1930s when many people lost their jobs and had little money.

Great Irish Famine page 176
In the 1840s there was not enough food in Ireland. Many people were starving. This time became known as the Great Irish Famine.

Great Spirit page 84
Many Native Americans believe in the Great Spirit, their most important god. They believe the Great Spirit made them and placed them on the land.

gun control page 297
Gun control is control over the sale of guns.

Harlem Renaissance page 216
The Harlem Renaissance occurred during the 1920s. During that time many African American artists, musicians, and writers created new works in Harlem. Harlem is a neighborhood in New York City.

hasten page 82
To hasten means to hurry.

health insurance page 311
Health insurance helps people pay for doctors and hospitals when they are sick.

hijacked page 303
Hijacked means to have taken over a truck, an airplane, or another kind of transportation by force.

Holocaust page 230
The killing of about six million Jews during World War II was called the Holocaust.

Homestead Act page 153
The Homestead Act was a law that gave settlers free land on the Great Plains.

House of Representatives page 66
The House of Representatives is one of the two houses, or parts, of Congress. It has 435 members.

human/environment interaction
  page 126
The geography theme of human/environment interaction tells how people can change an area. It also tells how people live in an area.

icebox page 162
An icebox is a box or room that is filled with ice to keep food cold.

illegal aliens page 284
Illegal aliens are people who enter a country without permission.

immigrants page 156
Immigrants are people who move to another country.

imperialism page 161
Imperialism is the idea that one country should rule other countries or colonies.

imports page 289
Imports are goods brought in from another country for sale or use.

in debt page 27
A person who is in debt owes money to other people.

independent page 46
Independent means free. An independent country rules itself.

Industrial Revolution page 87
The Industrial Revolution was a change from making goods by hand to making goods by machine.

industry page 201
An industry is all of a type of business.

insist page 82
To insist means to demand.

inspected page 199
Inspected means looked at carefully.

interest page 215
Interest is money paid for paying for something on credit.

Internet page 298
The Internet is a huge system that allows millions of computers to send information to one another.

invaded page 237
Invaded means entered a country by using force.

invented page 87
Invented means thought up or made for the first time.

invention page 167
An invention is something that is made for the first time.

Iraq War page 306
The Iraq War was the war fought between the United States and Iraq in 2003.

isolation page 214
Isolation is the act of being set apart from others. After World War I, the United States wanted to be isolated from other countries and their problems.

jazz page 215
Jazz is a kind of music that became popular in the 1920s. It was started by African Americans.

justice page 259
Justice means fairness. Justice is also another word for judge.

justices page 67
Justices are judges. There are nine justices in the Supreme Court.

labor unions page 189
Labor unions are organizations of workers who work together to get paid more money and to improve their jobs.

lame page 50
Lame means hurt. If a person's feet or legs are lame, it is hard for that person to walk.

launched page 259
Launched means started.

lead page 196
Lead is a very soft gray metal that is found in the earth.

lead poisoning page 196
Lead poisoning is a sickness that happens when people have too much lead in their bodies.

Liberty Bonds page 210
Americans bought Liberty Bonds to help the government pay for World War I.

location page 62
The geography theme of location tells where a place is found.

locomotives page 90
Locomotives are engines used to pull trains.

Louisiana Purchase page 76
The Louisiana Purchase was the sale of a large piece of land west of the Mississippi River. The United States bought it from France in 1803.

Loyalists page 47
Loyalists were Americans who did not want the 13 colonies to become independent. Loyalists helped Great Britain during the American Revolution.

mainland page 264
A mainland is the largest part of a country or continent.

manage page 58
To manage means to control and take care of something.

Manifest Destiny page 116
Manifest Destiny was the idea that the United States should rule land from the Atlantic Ocean to the Pacific Ocean.

march page 257
A march is a group of people walking together for something they believe in. They walk to win support from government leaders and other people.

mass production page 88
In mass production, people or machines make many goods that are exactly alike.

Mayflower Compact page 21
The Mayflower Compact was the Pilgrims' plan for ruling themselves in America.

medical page 310
Medical care includes the doctors and hospitals people need when they are sick.

Medicare page 310
Medicare is a government service for an older person that helps pay for medical care.

memorial page 276
A memorial is a building or object that is made to help people honor and remember others who have died.

mental illness page 103
People with mental illness have a disease or condition that changes the way they think.

Mexican Cession page 118
The Mexican Cession was land that the United States got as a result of the Mexican War.

migrant farm workers page 268
Migrant farm workers are workers who move from one farm to another in order to have work.

millionaire page 184
A person who has more than a million dollars is a millionaire.

miners page 126
Miners are people who dig in the earth to find gold or other metals or stones.

minister page 255
A minister is a leader in a church.

miserable page 84
To be miserable is to be unhappy.

missiles page 247
Missiles are rockets with bombs in them.

missions page 16
Missions are places where people teach others how to become Christians.

movement page 97
The geography theme of movement tells how people, goods, and ideas move from one place to another.

muckrakers page 200
Muckrakers were people in the early 1900s who wrote about problems in the United States.

nation page 40
A nation is a large group of people living together in one country.

NATO page 245
NATO is the North Atlantic Treaty Organization. The armies of NATO nations will fight for one another during a war.

natural resources page 201
Natural resources are things we get from the earth. Water, metals, trees, animals, and oil are natural resources.

naval base page 231
A naval base is a place near the sea where a navy keeps many ships, weapons, airplanes, and sailors.

navy page 81
The navy is a nation's warships and all the people who work on the warships.

neutral page 209
A neutral nation does not fight or help other nations during a war.

New Deal page 224
The New Deal was Franklin D. Roosevelt's plan for ending the Great Depression.

newspaper page 308
A newspaper reports the news that happens each day.

New World page 11
People in Europe called North America and South America the New World because they had not known about these continents.

Nobel Peace Prize page 258
The Nobel Peace Prize is a prize that is given to a person whose work helps people live together in peace.

North American Free Trade Agreement (NAFTA) page 284
NAFTA is a plan to help trade between the United States, Canada, and Mexico.

North Atlantic Treaty Organization (NATO) page 245
An organization formed to prevent the Soviet Union from attacking Western Europe.

occupied page 197
Occupied means lived in.

oil refineries page 184
Oil refineries are factories that clean oil after it is taken out of the earth.

optimistic page 313
Optimistic means to be hopeful.

ore page 183
An ore is rock with metal such as iron in it. It is found in the earth.

Oregon Trail page 122
The Oregon Trail was the trail that wagons followed through the West to Oregon.

organization page 245
An organization is a group of people or a group of nations that work together.

outline page 301
An outline is a written plan that puts information in order.

oxen page 122
An ox is an animal like a cow. Oxen is the word used for more than one ox.

Parliament page 41
The people who write laws for Great Britain are called Parliament. They work in the Parliament Building.

pass page 125
A pass is a trail through mountains.

passengers page 303
Passengers are the people who ride on planes, trains, or cars.

Patriot Act of 2001 page 304
The Patriot Act of 2001 is a law that helps the government fight against terrorism.

peace treaty page 22
A peace treaty is an agreement not to fight.

peril page 114
To peril means to put in danger.

permission page 284
Permission is the act of allowing a person to do something.

Persian Gulf War page 291
The Persian Gulf War was the war fought between the United Nations and Iraq in 1991.

pesticides page 270
Pesticides are chemicals that are sprayed on crops so insects will not eat the crops.

place page 17
The geography theme of place tells what makes an area different from other areas in the world.

plantations page 130
Plantations are very large farms where crops such as cotton and sugar cane are grown.

PNTR page 293
PNTR stands for Permanent Normal Trade Relations. When the United States gives PNTR to a nation, it agrees to keep tariffs on traded goods low.

polio page 251
Polio is a sickness that can cause leg muscles to become so weak that a person cannot walk. People can die from polio.

political cartoons page 232
Political cartoons are pictures that show an artist's opinion about an event or a person.

pollution page 283
Pollution is chemicals and wastes in air, in water, or on land. Factories and cars cause air pollution.

popular page 215
To be popular means to be liked by many people.

port page 42
A port is a place by an ocean or river where ships are loaded and unloaded.

priests page 16
Priests are people who lead religious services and teach about the Catholic religion.

primary sources page 28
Primary sources are the words and objects of people who have lived at different times. Some primary sources are journals, letters, and tools.

printer page 53
A printer is a person who prints books and newspapers.

printing shop page 53
A printing shop is a place with machines for printing books and newspapers.

progressives page 199
Progressives are people who work for reform.

promptly page 114
Promptly means soon.

property page 119
All the land and other things a person owns are his or her property.

prosperous page 313
Prosperous means to be comfortable because there is enough money.

protest page 257
A protest is something that people do to show they are against something.

protesters page 275
Protesters are people who march, give speeches, or do other things to show they are against something.

provisions page 114
Provisions are food and other supplies.

published page 53
Published means prepared a book or newspaper so it could be sold.

Pure Food and Drug Act page 201
The Pure Food and Drug Act is a law that says all food and all medicine must be safe for people to use.

pursue page 313
Pursue means to chase.

quarreling page 130
Quarreling means arguing or not agreeing about something.

race page 84
A race is a group of people sharing the same beginnings from long ago. They usually have similar eyes and skin color.

rationed page 236
When goods are rationed, people are allowed to buy only certain amounts.

rebuild page 141
To rebuild means to build something again.

Reconstruction page 148
The years after the Civil War were called Reconstruction. During Reconstruction the southern states became part of the United States again.

recovered page 50
Recovered means got better.

recycling page 297
Recycling is a way to turn old plastic, metal, paper, and glass into new products.

reenter page 259
To reenter means to enter again.

reform page 101
Reform is a change to make something, such as a school or government, better.

region page 134
The geography theme of region tells how places in an area are alike.

rejoined page 148
Rejoined means joined again, or became part of again. After the Civil War, the southern states rejoined the United States.

relations page 293
Relations is how two nations deal with each other. The nations might trade, work together, or fight.

relief page 114
Relief is help from others.

religions page 4
Religions are the ways people believe in and pray to a god or to many gods.

religious page 26
Religious means having to do with religion.

reporter page 179
A reporter learns about important news and then writes about it in a newspaper.

representatives page 66
People who make laws in the House of Representatives are called representatives.

republic page 113
A republic is a country where people vote for their leaders. These leaders make laws for the people and lead the government.

reservations page 155
Reservations are lands that American Indians were given to live on.

respect page 258
To show respect for others means to honor and care about them.

retire page 310
When people retire they stop working.

rovers page 263
Rovers are machines that travel to other planets. They take photographs that are sent back to Earth for scientists to study.

salaries page 150
Salaries are money people earn at jobs.

satellite page 261
A satellite is something that circles Earth. Some satellites are used to send information around the world.

secured page 82
Something that has been secured has been made safe.

segregation page 150
Segregation is the act of setting apart. Forcing African Americans and white people to go to separate schools is segregation.

Senate page 66
The Senate is one of the two houses, or parts, of Congress. It has 100 members.

senators page 66
People who make laws in the Senate are senators.

settlement house page 195
A settlement house is a place in a poor neighborhood where people can get help or take classes.

settlers page 25
Settlers are people who go to live in a new place.

shares of stock page 222
A person who owns shares of stock owns a small part of a business.

shortcut page 31
A shortcut is a shorter way to go to a place.

skyscraper page 168
A skyscraper is a very tall building with many floors.

slavery page 16
Slavery is the owning of people, or slaves. Slaves are forced to work without pay.

snowshoes page 33
Snowshoes are wooden frames that a person can attach to shoes to help him or her walk on deep snow.

Social Security page 310
Social Security is money that people who retire get from the government each month.

sod page 157
Sod is grass-covered land.

space race page 261
The space race was a race between the United States and the Soviet Union to see which nation could send people to the moon first.

space shuttle page 262
A space shuttle is a spaceship that can be used many times.

space station page 263
A space station is a place in outer space where astronauts can live and work.

Spanish-American War page 164
The Spanish-American War was the war that the United States fought against Spain in 1898.

spices page 9
Spices are added to food to improve the way it tastes and smells.

spike page 156
A spike is a very large heavy nail.

spread of communism page 245
The spread of communism happens when nations begin to have Communist governments.

Stamp Act page 41
The Stamp Act said that Americans in the British colonies had to pay a tax on things made from paper.

steamboat page 89
A steamboat is a boat that is powered by a steam engine.

steam engine page 89
A steam engine is a machine that uses steam to create power for other machines.

steel page 184
Steel is a strong metal made from iron.

steel mills page 184
Steel mills are large factories that use iron to make steel.

stock page 222
A person who buys stock becomes part owner of a business.

stock market page 223
The stock market is the place where stocks are bought and sold.

strike page 189
A strike is when workers stop working in order to force their employers to make changes.

submarines page 210
Submarines are ships that can travel underwater.

suburbs page 251
Suburbs are areas near large cities. Many people live in suburbs and work in the nearby cities.

sugar cane page 130
People get sugar from the tall plant called sugar cane.

sunk page 210
A ship that has gone underwater has sunk.

Supreme Court page 67
The Supreme Court is the highest court in the United States. It decides whether laws agree with the Constitution.

surrendered page 59
An army that surrendered in a war stopped fighting and agreed that it lost.

swastika page 232
A swastika was the symbol of Adolf Hitler's Germany.

tariffs page 96
Tariffs are taxes on goods from other countries.

tax page 41
Tax is money that a person must pay to the government.

Teamsters page 270
The Teamsters is a labor union that has helped farm workers.

technology page 298
Technology is the use of science to do work or make things.

terrorism page 302
Terrorism is the use of force to kill and frighten people in order to get them to obey.

Texas Revolution page 113
The Texas Revolution was the war that Texans fought in order to win their independence from Mexico.

themes page 17
Themes are main ideas. The five themes of geography help geographers learn about areas and people on Earth.

tobacco page 26
Tobacco is a plant. The leaves of this plant are smoked in pipes, cigars, and cigarettes.

Trail of Tears page 96
When the Cherokee were forced to move west to Indian Territory, they called their trip the Trail of Tears.

transform page 313
Transform means to change.

troops page 50
Troops are soldiers in an army.

unguarded border page 282
A nation has an unguarded border when there are no soldiers guarding the line that separates it from its neighbor.

Union page 133
The Union is the United States.

unite page 84
To unite is to join together.

United Farm Workers page 269
The union that César Chávez started for migrant farm workers is called the United Farm Workers.

United Nations page 245
The United Nations is an organization that tries to help nations solve their problems without fighting.

vaccine page 251
A vaccine is a kind of medicine that stops people from getting a disease.

veterans page 250
Veterans are people who have been in the United States Army, Navy, Air Force, or Marines.

victory page 114
A victory is a win.

wagon train page 122
Covered wagons that traveled together on a trail formed a wagon train.

weapons page 154
Weapons are objects used to attack or protect something. Guns are weapons.

weapons of mass destruction page 305
Weapons of mass destruction are weapons that can kill thousands of people at a time.

wildlife page 264
Wildlife is wild animals, birds, and plants.

working conditions page 188
Working conditions describe what a person's job is like. Working conditions include pay, hours, and safety.

Index

Abolitionists, 103, 104, 132
Acid rain, 283, 286–287, 297
Adams, John, 41
Addams, Jane, 195, 197, 202
Afghanistan, 304
Africa, 16, 230, 235, 293
African(s), 14, 16, 26, 177, 293
African American(s), 48, 61, 77, 83, 102, 103, 110, 125, 134, 140, 148–150, 151, 154, 156, 177, 195–196, 202, 215, 216, 217, 252, 255–258, 259, 296
Airmail, 218–219
Airplanes, 169, 210, 214, 216, 218–219, 225, 228, 229, 231, 235, 246, 262, 274
Alabama, 94, 150, 255, 256, 257
Alamo, 112, 113, 114
Alaska, 4, 161–162
Aldrin, Edwin, 262
Allies, 208–211, 229–231, 236–238
Al Qaeda, 304
Amendment(s), 68, 149, 195, 214
American Federation of Labor (AFL), 190
American Indian(s), 4. *See also* Native American(s).
American Revolution, 43, 46–49, 50, 55, 59–60, 62, 65, 74, 93
Americans with Disabilities Act, 296
Anthony, Susan B., 194–195
Apollo 11, 262
Appeasement, 229
Arab(s), 291
Arizona, 118, 268
Armistead, James, 48
Armstrong, Neil, 262
Asia, 4, 9, 10, 31, 162, 217, 230, 235, 237, 238, 247, 273, 274, 309
Asian Americans, 110, 296
Asians, 296
Assembly line, 170
Astronauts, 262, 263, 265
Atlantic Ocean, 9, 10, 14, 27, 42, 62, 74, 75, 90, 116, 118, 119, 161, 180, 209, 211, 216, 283

Atomic bomb, 238, 252
Austin, Moses, 110
Austin, Stephen F., 110, 111, 113
Austria, 229
Austria-Hungary, 209
Axis countries, 229–231, 235–238

Baby boom, 250, 251, 310
Bahamas, 11
Baltimore, Maryland, 83
Banneker, Benjamin, 61
Barrett, Janie Porter, 195–196
Barton, Clara, 140
Battle of New Orleans, 83, 94
Battle of the Alamo, 112, 113, 114
Battle of Trenton, 59
Beckwourth, James, 125
Beckwourth Pass, 125
Bell, Alexander Graham, 167–168
Berlin, 246, 290
Berlin Wall, 246, 290
Big business, 183–185, 200
Bill of Rights, 68
Birmingham, Alabama, 257
Bonaparte, Napoleon, 75, 76, 80
Bosnia and Herzegovina, 292
Boston, Massachusetts, 42, 43, 53
Boston Tea Party, 42
Boycott, 256–257, 259, 269
Branches of government, 67
Brazil, 285
British, 40, 41, 42, 43, 46, 47, 48, 55, 58, 59, 60, 65, 80, 81, 82, 83, 87, 88, 93, 230–231
Brown v. *Board of Education of Topeka, Kansas*, 252
Bush, George W., 302, 304–305, 311–312

California, 16, 117, 118, 124–125, 126, 127, 153, 154, 156, 162, 177, 216, 218, 236, 268, 269, 298
Campbell, Ben Nighthorse, 296
Canada, 31, 34, 40, 81, 82, 123, 124, 132, 157, 161, 236, 245, 282–283, 284–285, 287
Canals, 90, 126

Canaveral National Seashore, 264
Cape Canaveral, 264, 265
Cape Kennedy, 261–262, 264
Capitol, 66, 67
Caribbean, 34
Carnegie, Andrew, 184, 185
Carnegie Steel Company, 184
Cars, 167, 169–170, 216, 256, 283, 286, 287, 298
Cartier, Jacques, 31
Catholic(s), 16, 27, 32, 33, 111, 217
Central Pacific Railroad, 156
Central Powers, 209–211
Challenger, 262
Chávez, César, 268–270
Cherokee, 94–95, 96, 97–98
    alphabet and language, 94–95
Chesapeake Bay, 62
Chicago, Illinois, 177, 195
Child labor, 178, 188–189, 190, 191, 194, 197, 199
Chile, 285
China, 9, 125, 177, 247, 274, 293
Chinese, 156, 177, 180, 247
Churchill, Winston, 230, 231
Church of England, 20, 26, 27
Civil rights, 257–258, 259
Civil Rights Act of 1964, 258, 296
Civil War, 138–141, 148, 150, 154, 156, 161, 177, 183, 188, 255
Clark, William, 76–77
Clean Air Act, 283
Clinton, Bill, 285, 291
Cold War, 244–247, 252, 261, 274, 290, 291
Collins, Eileen, 263
Collins, Michael, 262
Colonies, 21, 25, 31–34, 110, 161, 228
    English in America, 25–27, 34, 40, 41, 42, 46, 47, 49, 54, 55, 58, 59, 60, 65
Colorado, 118, 154
Columbia, 262
Columbus, Christopher, 9–11, 14
Communism, 217, 244–247, 252, 274, 275
Communist(s), 217, 244–247, 252, 273, 274, 275, 276, 290

Confederate(s), 138–141
Confederate States of America, 133, 135, 138–141
Congress, United States, 66, 67, 95, 96, 117, 124, 125, 132, 150, 153, 163, 185, 201, 210, 217, 225, 251, 258, 283, 296, 297, 311
Connecticut, 103
Conservation, 201–202
Constitution
    Confederate States, 133
    Texas, 113
    United States, 55, 60, 65–68, 131, 149, 214, 252, 256, 257, 297, 327–354
Constitutional Convention, 60, 65
Coronado, Francisco, 15
Cotton gin, 88
Credit, 215
Creek, 93, 94
Cuba, 163–164, 247
Cubans, 164
Czechoslovakia, 229

Davis, Jefferson, 133
D-Day, 237
Declaration of Independence
    American, 46–47, 55, 74, 322–326
    Texas, 112, 113, 114
De Gálvez, Bernardo, 48
Democracy, 244, 245, 246, 282, 290
Denmark, 179
Department of Homeland Security, 305
De Soto, Hernando, 15
De Zavala, Lorenzo, 113
Dickenson, Suzanna, 112, 113
Dillon, Sidney, 156
Discrimination, 202
Dix, Dorothea, 103
Douglass, Frederick, 103, 104
Du Bois, W.E.B., 202
Dust Bowl, 224, 225
Dutch, 20, 26, 27

East, 5, 155, 156
East Berlin, 246
Eastern Europe, 245, 290

East Germany, 246, 290
Edison, Thomas, 168
Education, 102. *See also* Schools.
  for girls, 102
Egypt, 291
Eisenhower, Dwight D., 236–237, 250
Electric light bulb, 168, 170
Elevator, 169
Emancipation Proclamation, 140
England, 20, 26, 27, 34, 40, 189
English, 20, 21, 25–27, 31, 33, 34, 40, 282
  language, 178, 179, 195, 196, 282
Equal rights, 149, 150, 202, 257, 259,
  296–297
Erie Canal, 90
Estevanico, 14
Europe, 9, 11, 15, 16, 21, 27, 34, 54, 75, 83, 96,
  110, 125, 176, 178, 208, 209, 211, 214, 217,
  222, 228–231, 232, 235, 236, 237, 245, 290,
  291, 292, 293, 296

Factories, early, 87, 88, 89, 90
Farm workers, 268–270
Fifteenth Amendment, 149
Fiorina, Carleton, 297
First Lady, 61, 82
Florida, 15, 16, 74, 94, 96, 262, 264
Ford, Henry, 169–170
Ford Motor Company, 169, 170, 216
Fort McHenry, 83
Fort Sumter, 138
Fourteenth Amendment, 149
France, 31, 32, 34, 40, 47, 55, 58, 75, 80, 81, 208,
  210, 211, 228–230, 236, 237, 246
Franklin, Benjamin, 53–55
Freedom of religion, 20, 25, 26, 27, 31, 33, 49,
  68, 176, 178, 244
Freedom of speech, 244
Freedom of the press, 68
Freedom of the seas, 80–81
French, 31–34, 41, 47, 55, 61, 75, 76, 80, 81, 230,
  282
  language, 282
French and Indian War, 34, 40, 41, 58

Fugitive Slave Act, 132
Fulton, Robert, 89

Gadsden Purchase, 118
Gallaudet, Thomas, 103
Garrison, William Lloyd, 103
Geography themes, 17, 62–63, 97–98, 126–127,
  134–135, 157–158, 180, 218–219, 264–265,
  286–287
George III, King, 40, 42, 43, 46
Georgia, 27, 94, 97, 255
German(s), 197, 210, 211, 228–231, 237
  language, 210
German Americans, 110, 210
Germany, 48, 176, 208, 209, 210, 211, 228–231,
  232, 237, 244, 246, 290
G.I. Bill of Rights, 251
Giuliani, Rudolph, 303
Global warming, 298
Gold, 10, 14, 15, 16, 25, 31, 119, 124, 125,
  126–127, 154, 156, 162, 177
Gold rush
  Alaska, 162
  California, 124–125, 126–127, 154, 177
Gompers, Samuel, 189–190
Gore, Al, 302
Grant, Ulysses S., 140, 141
Great Britain, 40, 41, 42, 43, 46, 47, 49, 55, 58, 60,
  65, 66, 80, 81, 82, 83, 87, 88, 123, 124, 176,
  183, 208, 210, 228–231, 236, 246
Great Depression, 222–225, 228, 235, 250, 251,
  268
Great Irish Famine, 176
Great Lakes, 283
Great Plains, 5, 122, 153–158, 224
Greece, 178
Guam, 164, 237, 238
Gulf of Mexico, 32, 75
Gun control, 297

Hamilton, Alice, 196
Hampton Institute, 151
Harlem, 216
Harlem Renaissance, 216

Harrison, William Henry, 84
Hawaii, 162–163, 231, 236
Health insurance, 311
Hennepin, Father, 32
Henry Street Settlement House, 196
Hine, Lewis, 191
Hiroshima, 238
Hispanic American(s), 263, 269, 296
Hitler, Adolf, 228–231, 232, 237
Holland, 20, 21, 27
Holocaust, 230
Homestead Act, 153–154, 156, 157
Hoover, Herbert, 224
House of Representatives, 66
Houston, Sam, 113
Hudson River, 89, 90
Huerta, Dolores, 269, 270
Hughes, Langston, 216
Hull House, 195, 197
Hussein, Saddam, 291, 305–306
Hutchinson, Anne, 26

Idaho, 124, 154
Illegal aliens, 284
Illinois, 177, 195, 197, 199
Immigrant(s), 156, 167, 176–179, 180, 184, 188,
    189, 191, 194, 195, 197, 200, 217, 296
Imperialism, 161, 208
Independence, Missouri, 122
India, 9, 10, 11
Indian(s), 11. See also American Indians and
    Native Americans.
Indian River, 264
Indian Territory, 95–96, 97–98
Industrial Revolution, 87–90
International Space Station, 263
Internet, 298–299
Inventions, 167–170
Iowa, 153, 157
Iraq, 291, 305–306
Iraq War, 306
Ireland, 156, 176
Irish, 176–177, 191
Isabella, Queen, 10

Isolation, 214
Israel, 291–292
Italian(s), 180, 197, 237
Italy, 9, 178, 229–231, 237

Jackson, Andrew, 83, 93–96
Jamestown, Virginia, 25–26, 28
Japan, 177, 229–231, 236, 237–238, 245
Japanese, 231, 238, 245
Japanese Americans, 236
Jazz, 215
Jefferson, Thomas, 46, 55, 74, 75, 76, 77
Jewish, 178, 180, 189, 230, 291
Jewish American(s), 49, 110
Jews, 178, 197, 217, 230
John F. Kennedy Space Center, 264–265
Johnson, Lyndon B., 274–275
Jones, Mary, 191
Jordan, 291

Kelley, Florence, 199–200, 202
Kennedy, Edward, 311
Kennedy, John F., 247, 261, 274
Kennedy Space Center, 264–265
Kerry, John F., 312
Key, Francis Scott, 83
King, Martin Luther, Jr., 255–258, 269
Kitty Hawk, North Carolina, 169
Korea, 247
Korean War, 247, 250
Kosciusko, Thaddeus, 48
Kosovo, 293
Ku Klux Klan, 217
Kuwait, 291, 305

Labor unions, 188–191, 200, 269–270
Laden, Osama bin, 304
Lake Erie, 90
La Salle, René Robert Sieur de, 32
Latin America, 285
Latin Americans, 296
Lee, Robert E., 139–140, 141
L'Enfant, Pierre, 61
Lewis, Meriwether, 76–77
Liliuokalani, Queen, 163

Lincoln, Abraham, 132–133, 138, 139, 140, 141
Lin, Maya, 276
Lindbergh, Charles, 216
Locomotives, 90
Locust Street Social Settlement House, 195
Louis, King, 31, 32
Louisiana, 32, 34, 48, 75, 76
Louisiana Purchase, 75–76
Lowell, Francis Cabot, 89
Loyalists, 47
Lyon, Mary, 102

MacArthur, Douglas, 237
Madison, Dolley, 82
Madison, James, 81, 82
Maine, 163–164
Manhattan, New York, 180
Manifest Destiny, 116, 117, 124
Mann, Horace, 102
March on Washington, 257–258
Marshall, James, 124
Marshall, Thurgood, 252
Maryland, 27, 61, 62, 63, 83
Massachusetts, 21, 26, 42, 43, 53, 89, 102
Massasoit, 22
Mass production, 88–89
Matzeliger, Jan, 168
Mayflower, 21
Mayflower Compact, 21
McCarthy, Joseph, 252
Meat industry, 201
Medicare, 310
Merritt Island, 264–265
Mexican(s), 110, 111, 112, 113, 116, 117, 118,
    119, 177, 284, 285
Mexican American(s), 119, 156, 268
Mexican Cession, 118
Mexican War, 117, 119, 130, 131, 177
Mexico, 14, 15, 110, 111, 112, 113, 116, 117, 118,
    157, 177, 268, 282, 283–284, 285
Mexico City, Mexico, 117, 284
Middle East, 291–292
Midwest, 5
Migrant farm workers, 268–270

Miners, 126–127, 154, 177, 191, 200
Minnesota, 184
Missions, 16, 17, 112
Mississippi River, 15, 32, 34, 74, 75, 76, 81, 84, 95
Missouri, 122, 157
Montgomery, Alabama, 255–257, 259
Morgan, Garrett, 170
Mount Holyoke Female Seminary, 102
Mount Vernon, 59, 60, 61
Muckrakers, 200, 201

NAACP, 202, 252
NAFTA, 284–285
Nagasaki, 238
National Association for the Advancement of
    Colored People (NAACP), 202, 252
Native American(s), 4–6, 9, 11, 14, 15, 16, 17, 22,
    26, 27, 32, 33, 34, 42, 75, 76, 77, 81, 82, 83, 84,
    93, 94, 95–96, 97–98, 125, 154–155, 162, 176,
    296. *See also* American Indian(s) *and*
    Indian(s).
NATO, 245, 291, 292, 293
Natural resources, 201–202, 297, 299
Navarro, José Antonio, 112–113
Neutral countries, 209, 229
Nevada, 118, 154, 218
New Deal, 224–225
New France, 31–34
New Jersey, 59
New Mexico, 16, 17, 117, 118
New Orleans, Louisiana, 32, 34, 75, 76, 83,
    94, 134
    Battle of, 83, 94
New World, 11
New York, 27, 59, 89, 90, 104, 180, 196, 216, 218
New York City, New York, 59, 61, 90, 178, 179,
    180, 196, 216, 218, 219
Nimitz, Chester W., 237–238
Niña, 10
Nineteenth Amendment, 214
Nixon, Richard, 275
No Child Left Behind, 311
North, 103, 130, 131, 132, 133, 134, 135, 138,
    139, 140, 141, 148, 149, 150, 177

North America, 34
North American Free Trade Agreement (NAFTA), 284–285
North Atlantic Treaty Organization (NATO), 245, 291, 292, 293
North Carolina, 93, 169
Northeast, 287
Northern Pacific Railroad, 156
North Korea, 247, 274
North Vietnam, 273–276
Northwest, 5, 125

Oberlin College, 102
Ochoa, Ellen, 263
Oglethorpe, James, 27
Ohio, 102
Oil, 162, 184–185, 200–201, 218, 284, 286, 291, 297, 298
Oklahoma, 95, 98
Oregon, 122–124, 125, 153
Oregon Country, 122–124
Oregon Trail, 122–123, 124, 125
Orlando, Florida, 264
Osceola, 96
Otis, Elisha Graves, 169

Pacific Ocean, 77, 116, 118, 119, 161, 162, 164, 237, 238
Palestinians, 291–292
Paris, France, 211, 216, 230, 237
Parks, Rosa, 256, 259
Parliament, 41, 42, 46, 55, 65, 66
Patriot Act of 2001, 304
Peace treaty, 22, 49, 60, 83, 118, 211, 291
Pearl Harbor, Hawaii, 231, 236
Penn, William, 27
Pennsylvania, 27, 47, 50, 54, 59, 184, 200, 303
Pentagon, 303
Permanent Normal Trade Relations (PNTR), 293
Persian Gulf War, 291, 305
Philadelphia, Pennsylvania, 47, 54, 55, 60, 65, 218
Philippines, 164, 237, 238

Pilgrims, 20–22, 25
Pinta, 10
Pitcher, Molly, 48
Plantations, 130–131, 134, 140, 148, 163
Plymouth, Massachusetts, 21, 22
PNTR, 293
Poland, 48, 49, 178, 229, 232, 245
Polio vaccine, 251
Polish, 197
Polk, James K., 117, 118, 124
Pollution, 283, 286, 287, 297, 298
Potomac River, 62
President, Constitution and the, 67
Prison reform, 103
Progressives, 199–202
Protest(s), 257, 275
Providence, Rhode Island, 26
Pueblo Indians, 17
Puerto Rico, 163, 164
Pure Food and Drug Act, 201
Puritans, 26

Quakers, 27
Quebec, 282

Radio, 215, 218, 258
Railroads, 90, 118, 119, 134, 139, 155–156, 177, 179, 183, 184, 185, 218, 246
Reconstruction, 148–150
Recycling, 297, 299
Reform, 101–104, 199–202
Reno, Nevada, 218
Representatives, 66, 149, 150, 153
Republic of Texas, 113, 116
Reservations, 155
Rhode Island, 26
Richmond, Virginia, 140, 151
Riis, Jacob, 179, 200
Rio Grande, 117, 118
Roche, Josephine, 178
Rockefeller, John D., 184–185, 200
Rocky Mountains, 77, 122, 153, 156, 157
Rodriguez, Arturo, 270
Roosevelt, Franklin D., 224–225, 231

Roosevelt, Theodore, 200, 201–202
Russia, 161, 162, 178, 208, 209, 217, 290, 293
Russian, 197
Ruth, Babe, 215

Sabin, Albert, 251
Sacagawea, 77
St. Lawrence River, 31, 32
St. Lawrence Seaway, 283
St. Louis, Missouri, 32, 34
Salk, Jonas, 251
Salomon, Haym, 49
Sampson, Deborah, 48
San Francisco, California, 218
Sangre de Cristo Mountains, 17
San Jacinto River, 113
San Miguel Mission, 17
Santa Anna, Antonio López de, 112, 113, 114, 116
Santa Fe, 16, 17
Santa María, 10
Satellites, 261, 263, 264
Schools, 26, 54, 101–103, 132, 149, 150, 151, 179, 188, 196, 202, 210, 225, 252, 256, 258, 268, 270
    for African Americans, 149, 150, 151, 196
    for girls, 102, 196
Scotland, 167, 184
Scott, Coretta, 255
Segregation, 150, 252, 255–258, 259
Seminole, 96
Senate, 66, 252
Senators, 66, 149, 150, 153, 252, 296
Seneca Falls, New York, 104
Sequoyah, 94–95
Serbia, 209, 293
Serra, Father Junipero, 16
Settlement houses, 195, 196, 197
Shawnee, 84
Shoe-making machine, 168
Shoshone, 77
Sinclair, Upton, 201
Skyscrapers, 168–169

Slater, Samuel, 88
Slave(s), 16, 26, 33, 77, 83, 103, 111, 130–132, 134, 135, 140, 148, 149, 150, 177
Slavery, 16, 61, 101, 103, 130–133, 135, 139, 140, 148, 149, 151, 177
Smith, Margaret Chase, 252
Social Security, 310
Sod houses, 157
South, 93, 103, 130, 131, 132, 133, 134–135, 138, 139, 140, 141, 148, 150, 177, 202, 215, 255
South America, 14
South Carolina, 93, 96, 138
Southeast, 15, 95, 96, 97
Southeast Asia, 273, 274
Southern Pacific Railroad, 156
South Korea, 247
South Vietnam, 273–276
South Vietnamese, 274, 276
Southwest, 5, 14, 15, 16, 17, 118, 119, 177
Soviet Union, 217, 230, 237, 244–245, 246, 247, 252, 261, 274, 290
Space race, 261
Space shuttle, 262, 263
Spain, 10, 11, 14, 15, 16, 34, 75, 94, 110, 163, 164, 306
Spanish, 14, 15–16, 17, 31, 33, 48, 164
    language, 111, 283–284
Spanish-American War, 164
Squanto, 22
Stamp Act, 41, 55
Standard Oil Company, 184, 200–201
Standing Bear, Luther, 6
Stanton, Elizabeth Cady, 104, 194–195
"Star-Spangled Banner, The", 83
Statue of Liberty, 180
Steamboat, 89
Steam engine, 89, 90
Steel, 183–184, 185
Stephens, Allen W., 236
Steuben, Friedrich von, 48
Stock market crash, 223
Strike, 189, 190, 191, 200, 269

Suburbs, 251
Supreme Court, 67, 200, 201, 252, 256, 257
Sutter Creek, California, 127
Swastika, 88

Tahlequah, Oklahoma, 98
Taliban, 304
Tarbell, Ida, 200
Tariffs, 96, 285, 293
Taxes, 41, 42, 55, 96, 284
Teamsters, 270
Tea tax, 42
Technology, 298–299
Tecumseh, 81–84
Telephones, 167–168, 170, 299
Television, 218, 251, 258, 275, 287
Texan(s), 111, 112, 113, 114, 116
Texas, 16, 110–113, 116, 117, 118
Texas Declaration of Independence, 112, 113, 114
Texas Revolution, 112–113
Thanksgiving, 22
Thirteenth Amendment, 149
Trade, 284–285, 293
Traffic light, 170
Trail of Tears, 96, 97–98
Travis, William Barrett, 114
Trenton, New Jersey, 59
Truman, Harry S, 238, 250
Tubman, Harriet, 132
Tuskegee Institute, 150

Union, 133, 138–141
Union Pacific Railroad, 156
Unions. See Labor unions.
United Farm Workers, 269–270
United Nations, 245, 247, 291, 305
Utah, 118, 156

Valley Forge, Pennsylvania, 50
Viet Cong, 273, 274, 275, 276
Vietnam, 273–276

Vietnam War, 273–276
Virginia, 25, 34, 58, 59, 60, 61, 62, 63, 139, 141, 151, 195
Voting rights
    for African Americans, 149, 150, 202, 255, 258
    for women, 104, 149, 194–195, 214

Wald, Lillian, 196
Waldo, Albigence, 50
Wampanoag, 22
War of 1812, 80–83, 93
Washington, 124
Washington, Booker T., 150, 151
Washington, D.C., 61, 62–63, 67, 82, 218, 257–258, 276, 303
Washington, George, 34, 47, 50, 58–61, 62, 63, 82
Washington, Martha, 59, 60, 61
West, 74, 77, 96, 125, 131, 133, 154, 155, 156, 177
West Berlin, 246
West Coast, 236
Western Europe, 245, 291
West Germany, 246, 290
White House, 67, 82
Whitman, Narcissa, 123
Whitney, Eli, 88–89
Willard, Emma, 102
Williams, Roger, 26
Wilson, Woodrow, 210, 211
Women's rights, 101, 104, 119, 149, 194–195, 214
World Trade Center, 303
World War I, 208–211, 214, 215, 217, 228
World War II, 225, 228–231, 232, 235–238, 244, 245, 246, 247, 250, 251, 290
Wright, Orville, 169
Wright, Wilbur, 169

York, 77
Yorktown, Virginia, 60

Credits